The
ROUND CHURCH TOWERS
of
ENGLAND

STEPHEN HART
B.Arch. A.R.I.B.A.

With Photographs by the Author

LUCAS BOOKS
www.lucasbooks.co.uk

The
ROUND CHURCH TOWERS
of
ENGLAND

STEPHEN HART
B.Arch. A.R.I.B.A.

© Copyright 2003

Text and Photographs Copyright Stephen Hart

First Published by
LUCAS BOOKS 2003

ISBN 1-903797-32-7

British Library Cataloguing in Publication Data
A catalogue record for this book is available from the British Library

Printed in the UK by Print Wright Ltd, Ipswich

Contents

Acknowledgements

I would like to express my thanks to all the incumbents and churchwardens or custodians who allowed me access to the towers and often gave me assistance with ladders.

My thanks are also due to Cambridge University Press for permission to include extracts from *Anglo-Saxon Architecture, Vols I & II,* 1965 and *Vol. III,* 1978 by H.M. and J. Taylor and to Boydell & Brewer Ltd. for permission to include quotations from *Suffolk Churches* 1937, by H.Munro Cautley, revised 1975. I am also grateful to The Churches Conservation Trust (www.visitchurches.org.uk) for allowing me to reproduce Isaac Johnson's 1818 drawing from its guidebook to All Saints' Church, South Elmham, Suffolk, one of the churches is in its care.

Stephen Hart   2003

Introduction

Until the last quarter of the twentieth century, there was a general consensus that most of the English round church towers were Norman, with a few Saxon and later ones. Two competing theories then emerged. One suggested that few, if any, round towers could be shown to be pre-Conquest and that there were almost as many post-Norman towers as earlier ones; the other claimed that apart from a few Norman and later ones, virtually all the others were Saxon. This dichotomy of opinion suggested that the topic remained open to further examination and was a stimulus for a study that led to the writing of this book.

Following consideration of general aspects of the subject, the book's later chapters (chapter 9 onwards) look at groupings of round towers that are linked by common characteristics. These groupings are not intended as scientific classifications but are simply a convenient means of making distinctions between towers of different styles or appearance – many would, in fact, qualify for inclusion in more than one of the designations. Because of the large number of round towers, it would not be practicable in a book of this size to include detailed analyses of them all, and so just a few examples representative of each of the groupings have been described; these have been selected not only for their own particular interest, but to illustrate different ways in which their evidence may reveal sequences of construction or clues to their age. Again, because of space limitations, the main focus has been on the archaeology of the towers rather than on the whole church, except where the church's development has had a bearing on the tower.

During preparation of the book, all the English round towered churches were visited, many of them more than once, and it soon became apparent that often a proper appraisal of the towers could not be made without ascending to their upper stages where, unseen from the ground, there was evidence vital to reasoned attributions that had previously been overlooked or not taken into account. While my conclusions and attributions may differ from those of earlier commentators, this is not to underrate the value of their contribution to knowledge of round-towered churches, but arises largely from due evaluation of evidence hitherto neglected.

In the text, black and white illustrations are referred to with Arabic figures in brackets, and coloured ones by Roman figures in brackets.

Gayton Thorpe Church.
One of R. Ladbrooke's prints of Norfolk Churches,
drawn in the 1820s

CHAPTER 1

ROUND TOWER CHARACTERISTICS

In England, the circular west tower is essentially an architectural feature of minor churches in East Anglia. Including visible remnants of fallen towers and a few in semi-ruinous condition, there are 181 in England (see Appx. A), all of which are in East Anglia except for 3 in Sussex and 2 in Berkshire. Norfolk has the most – 126, compared with 42 in Suffolk, 6 in Essex and 2 in Cambridgeshire. Eight were built in the nineteenth and early twentieth centuries (see Appx. B) and so there are 173 of medieval origin dating from the eleventh century or perhaps earlier, to the fourteenth. Nine of these have suffered major post-Reformation restorations (see Appx. C), eight are truncated remnants or partially collapsed but still attached to churches fit for use (see Appx. D), and six are ruinous (see Appx. E). Excluding those from the total, 150 medieval round church towers remain standing in England, and apart from a few in East Anglia built of carstone or of ferricrete (ferruginous conglomerate, or puddingstone, as it is often called), all are built of flint.

Except for a single detached one at Bramfield (1), all the round towers are, or were, western towers joined to their churches; some were built at the same time as the nave, others are later additions, and often it is possible to tell from the way in which the junction between tower and nave is made whether they were contemporary or whether the tower was later. The Bramfield tower is the only one that was built as a freestanding structure, but there are four others now standing alone that were originally attached to churches. At Little Snoring (16) the original tower was retained when, little more than a century after being built, its church was demolished and rebuilt immediately to the north, and at Wolterton and Ringstead, ruined towers are the only above-ground traces of churches that were probably demolished during the eighteenth century following amalgamation of their parishes with neighbouring ones. At St Benedict's, Norwich, the tower survived when the church was destroyed by bombing during the 1939-45 war.

1. Bramfield round tower. The only one that was built detached from its church.

Judged simply on their architectural appearance, there are two kinds of round tower – those that are circular to the top and those with an octagonal belfry on a circular lower stage. The wholly circular ones are not necessarily of a single build and may show evidence of having been partially rebuilt or of having been raised. Conversely, although it has been widely believed that all octagonal belfry stages are later additions, there is a wealth of evidence to show that some of them were an original part of the tower. But, of course, there are many others where octagonal belfry stages have clearly been added to towers that were previously wholly circular.

The most common external wall facing for towers of all ages is as-found flint rubble and nodules taken from the fields, from gravel deposits or direct from its parent chalk in quarries and mines; walls often also include cobbly erratics of other rocks that abound in the glacial tills and boulder clays overlying much of the region, and this kind of flintwork containing a high proportion of brown non-flint cobble erratics, on average usually a little larger than flint cobbles is typical of the walls of many inland Suffolk churches as seen for instance in the towers at Little Bradley and Rickinghall Inferior. Near the coast, the flintwork of some towers like Witton and West Somerton consists largely of rounded water-worn cobbles brought from the beaches, while the circular stages of later medieval towers such as Potter Heigham or Edingthorpe sometimes contain knapped flints of a quality quite distinct from the roughly-cleft or fortuitously-broken flints found in earlier walls; at Surlingham and Tuttington (79) a higher percentage of the facing is of cleft or knapped flints. Occasional medieval bricks appear amongst the flints in the walls of many towers and are often particularly noticeable at putlog holes. Ferricrete, a coarse dark brown stone containing flint clasts and other gravelly fragments, occurs in the walls of a few round towers, for example in the circular stage of the tower at West Dereham or in the lower courses of Wickmere tower. Carstone, a ferrugenous sandstone of similar colour but without the fragments, is less common except in West Norfolk where it can be seen at Bexwell (I) and in the ruined tower at Appleton.

2. Typical flint fillet in the re-entrant angle between the curved wall of a tower and the nave west wall.

On about a quarter of the round towers, at the points where their curved walls meet the straight face of the nave west wall, the acute re-entrant angles so-formed are closed off with a filling of the same material as the tower walls, forming narrow vertical fillets (2). Sometimes flat, sometimes concave, but more usually of quadrant shape, these fillets typically have a girth of nine to fifteen inches and extend from ground level to about nave eaves level or a little higher. They are not specific either to added towers or to those contemporary with their naves, nor are they features of a particular architectural style, having been used with towers of the eleventh to the fourteenth centuries. It is confusing that these fillets have been described as quadrant pilasters, firstly, because they are not all quadrant-shaped, and secondly, because they are not pilasters in the proper architectural sense; in fact, they serve or express no structural function and seem to be a purely aesthetic expedient to ameliorate a visually awkward junction between curved and flat walls. Also, since 'quadrant pilasters' have been dubiously claimed to represent a parallel with Anglo-Saxon stone lesenes (pilaster-strips), this description has tended to give round-tower fillets a Saxon connotation – unwarranted because they occur on later towers.

Three towers, those at Colney, Witton and St Julian, Norwich, have a curious feature at the junction of the tower and nave walls that is distinctly different from a tower fillet (3). A vertical, shallow flint projection, like a pilaster, about a foot or more wide and protruding three or four inches, is located on the curved face of the tower wall, hard up against the nave wall, but unlike a fillet, it does not close the angle between the walls; again, it appears to have no structural purpose and its aesthetic contribution in this odd position is minimal.

The body of the tower below the belfry usually contains small slit windows, also known as "loops", to light the upper stages, and their external dressings may be flint (51), ferricrete (4), limestone (56), or medieval brick (82). The dressed stone windows are found with round, pointed or straight heads; the round-headed ones usually have a single lintel stone with a semi-circular 'arch' cut in its lower edge. The heads of windows with brick dressings may be simply two bricks propped against each other or they may have an arch of bricks laid as voussoirs, often with a fan-like array of bricks above as a relieving arch. Some towers entirely lack these windows, e.g. Poringland, many have only

3. Flat pilaster-like projection on the round tower wall where it joins the nave west wall at Colney. The north-west nave quoins (on the left) are flints augmented by a few alien stones.

4. Ferricrete nave quoins and ferricrete in the nave and tower walls at Bessingham. The four well-defined stages in the tower walls may each represent the extent of one year's building.

one or two and others have more; Norton Subcourse has, or had (some are now blocked), as many as ten.

Few early towers seem originally to have had ground-floor windows, but some of the post-Norman ones have west lancets and many others have had two-light Decorated or Perpendicular west windows inserted later, which, of course, have usually eliminated any evidence of earlier windows. Beeston St Lawrence (II) and Hassingham (XVIII) though, provide examples of where insertion of a later west window has not entirely destroyed evidence of an earlier one, and an altered one at Southease might be original.

String courses are common architectural features of round towers and are usually a plain stone weathering below the belfry as at Eccles or Threxton. On most towers with octagonal stages, they occur at the junction between circle and octagon but a few octagonal belfry junctions are made by a simple cambered merging of the circular flintwork to the octagonal shape without any form of string course. (See Chapter 19)

The average internal diameter of the towers is about ten feet or thereabouts though there is considerable variation. The smallest (Fishley) is 6'9", and although the biggest (Wortham) has a diameter of 20 feet, there are less than ten that are larger than 13 feet internally.

5. Experimental replica round tower built at the Eco-Centre, waffham.

Round tower wall thicknesses vary from 2'6" (West Lexham) to more than five feet (Thorpe Abbotts, Syleham) but most lie between 3'3" and 4'3". Owing to lack of documentary evidence, the precise methods used by early builders to construct these thick circular flint walls are unknown. This uncertainty is the subject of ongoing discussion, and while there is a measure of agreement on the probable principle of construction – i.e. building up of a few courses, or the equivalent in uncoursed work, of the outer and inner facing flints followed by filling of the core between – there is debate as to whether or not the facing work was built against shuttering.

The argument for the use of shuttering is that, without it, the facing flints in slow-setting lime mortar would not be sufficiently stable to withstand the pressure from the core material filled behind them. It is thought that the shuttering used would have been curved panels of wickerwork supported behind shored posts positioned close to the wall at suitable intervals in the manner suggested by the discovery at Hadstock church in Essex of post-holes close to the wall on both sides of it, with sloping post-holes in line with these further away[1]. In

2001, a full-scale replica of the lower part of a round tower (5) was built in the grounds of the EcoCentre at Swaffham to test this threory in practice, but the predominance of wicker-marked mortar in the finished walls, the irregularity of the flints that were visible and the cavities around them produced an effect quite unlike the wall surfaces of any existing round towers. In order to account for the lack of instances where mortar impressions of wickerwork or board shuttering can be seen today, it has been proposed that after the removal of the shuttering, the excess exuded mortar would have been cleaned off to expose the flints, or floated over to give a rendered finish.

In defence of the contention that round towers were built without the use of shuttering, it can be argued that stability of the facing work during construction without external support would not have been a problem provided that the facing flints were set in a stiff mortar and a prudent height for each 'lift' of work was observed, dependent on the size and type of facing flints used. In walls of the thickness of round tower walls, the degree of outward thrust from a relatively shallow 'lift' of carefully placed filling in stiff mortar need not cause displacement of the facing flints. The main grounds though, for the belief that vertical shuttering was not used when building round tower walls, is that no convincing examples have been found that show mortar impressions of shuttering boards or wickerwork like those on the Swaffham replica or as seen in the splayed reveals of the blocked circular windows at Hales. Where, occasionally, as in parts of the tower walls internally at East Lexham and Wissett, certain mortared areas might be thought to look as though they could have been built against shuttering, no shuttering impressions are visible in them; they are probably just areas where excess mortar exuded from the joints was smoothed off with a float.

It is quite clear that in many cases in towers internally, the walls were not built against shuttering because the excess mortar exuded as the flints were laid is still in place. An important consideration against the use of shuttering on external wall faces is the difficulty of building flintwork with a satisfactory appearance when the face of the work under construction is not visible behind the shuttering. The kind of relief work seen on the towers at Thorpe-next-Haddiscoe, Tasburgh, and Thorington or the decorative flintwork on Syleham or Cockley Cley towers could hardly have been built against shuttering, nor would galleting have been possible.

It seems therefore that shuttering of round tower walls may have been done where a rendered finish had been intended but it was by no means a universal practice, and the practical constraints that it would have imposed on the builders suggest that it is unlikely that it was used to any extent where facing flints were intended to be exposed.

Closely linked to whether or not shuttering was used in round tower wall construction is the question of their external finish – were they rendered or were they left with the flints exposed? There is no reason to doubt that some early towers were rendered and it may be that the walls of some of them were built against shuttering. Several still retain remnants of surface rendering, though it is not always possible to tell whether it is an original coating or a later medieval finish. At Fishley or Barmer, for example, remnants of rendering on the towers may be original, but where, as at Brampton or Hardley, the rendering is completely different in colour or texture from the flintwork mortar, then it is clearly later than the structure, and uncertainty remains as to the original state of the walls.

In contrast to the rendered towers there are many that bear no trace of an applied coating, and even though they may have been repointed to some extent, it is often possible to identify the original mortar in which their flints were set. Where attention has been paid to good appearance by skilful selection and coursing of the flints as at Haddiscoe or Gissing for instance, it seems probable that the flintwork had been intended to be seen. This is even more obvious in later towers where knapped flints were used, either partially as at Keswick or entirely as at Wolterton (6).

6. Knapped flint facing to the ruined round tower at Wolterton.

The original use of the ground-floor stage of the tower is uncertain, but the very tall arches between tower and nave in many churches suggest that it may have had some liturgical purpose. On the other hand, there are also many low tower arches and both kinds occur in early and later towers. Some, but not all, of the low ones were originally west doorways into towerless churches on to which a round tower was subsequently built, as at Pentlow. In some cases the tower may have served as a porch because there are a few which, like Forncett St Peter and St Benedict's, Norwich have west doorways. Sustead church is unique in having the only round tower with no access to the nave, the only entry to the tower being by an external door in its south wall; this suggests that the tower was built on to a previously towerless church simply as a bell tower. Aylmerton too, has a tower south door and there is reason to believe that, like Sustead, it may also originally have been built without a tower arch; the same may be argued for Gresham which also once had a tower south door, now blocked but still visible inside the tower as a pointed-arched recess. (see Chapter 21)

Inside most of the towers, the ground-floor stage is usually plastered but in the upper levels the walls are almost always unplastered, and so where they are not too disfigured by later repairs or depredations, it is often possible to get a fair idea of the character of the original internal flintwork. From examination of many towers, one thing seems certain: whatever the upper parts of round towers below the belfry were used for, it seems that there was little concern for aesthetic refinement. Some walls may be thinly skim-plastered or the joints roughly flushed but often they are just as left by the builders centuries ago, with the surplus mortar that was exuded from the jointing when the flints were laid still in place. Small window embrasures are often crudely constructed with a mixture of materials in their jambs and roughly-shaped arches, sometimes of flint, sometimes of medieval bricks, whose shape often bears scant relationship to the window's external arch shape. Board marks of the shuttering on which they were formed often show on the soffit (31) and sometimes there is a set-back on the reveals at springing level which would have provided a seating for the shuttering boards.

Several suggestions have been made regarding the purposes for which the upper floors of the towers were used – a priest's room, a village treasury, or simply a ringing chamber are some of the ideas advanced. No doubt the purpose changed over the centuries and many towers have evidence of changes in the levels of the floors. From earliest times and into to the fourteenth century, access to the first floor was by means of a narrow opening in the nave west wall above the tower arch. In contrast to the typical splayed jambs of windows, these upper doors have straight reveals; they can still be seen in the nave in several churches, but in others the opening has been blocked and plastered over and is only visible from within the tower. Most would have been formed when the tower was built, whether contemporary with the nave or added later, but at some churches that were originally towerless, former nave west windows were converted into upper doors, as at Rushall and East Walton. There is evidence of upper doors in about a third of all round towers; the others therefore probably had a trapdoor and ladder in the tower. The upper doors must also have been reached by some form of stair or ladder in the nave, but as it would undoubtedly have been an inconvenience when seating was introduced into churches, this method of access would then probably have been discontinued. Later, some towers were provided with permanent internal stairs, either incorporated during construction or as added turrets.

There seems little doubt that the primary purpose of round church towers was for the hanging of bells, in principle no different from the function of a square tower. There are a few very short round towers with no belfry openings in their walls, such as Barmer and Howe (IX) , but the likelihood is that they were originally taller with belfry stages, now lost through deterioration or disaster. With the exception of later inserted ground-floor windows, windows in round towers were generally small and narrow with splayed reveals internally; belfry openings, on the other hand, were larger and usually, but not always, parallel-sided. The form and size of the upper openings in the towers at Wortham and Kilverstone for example clearly identify them as belfry openings rather than as look-out windows, and as there is no reason to suppose that they and other comparable early ones are not contemporary with the tower's lower part, the logical conclusion is that the towers were built as bell towers.

In support of fragile early dates that have been attributed to certain towers – Wramplingham and Eccles for instance – tower windows below the existing top stage have been claimed to be former belfry windows of lower towers, originally without their present belfries. In both those cases, though, the openings are too small for that purpose and the ones at Eccles are far too low; nor are there any reliable precedents for belfry openings of those patterns. At Hasketon, Mettingham, Mutford and South Elmham All Saints, windows said to have been former belfry openings occur in the chamber to which the upper door gives access, and since that is hardly likely to have been the bellchamber, those windows would not have been belfry openings.

---

[1] Rodwell W. *Anglo-Saxon Church Building: Design and Construction in* Butler L A S and Morris R K (Eds). Council for British Archaeology Research Report No. 60, 1986.

CHAPTER 2

ROUND TOWER ORIGINS

There are competing theories about the origins of the circular towers. Were those in East Anglia built for defence against Viking marauders, being originally freestanding, and later having had churches built on to them, or were they originally western entrance porches to churches, later heightened to provide a belfry? How many are Anglo-Saxon and how many were built after the Norman Conquest? Was the round tower an indigenous concept or was it inspired by continental influences? Was the circular shape an aesthetic choice or was it the functional and economic outcome of a lack of freestone for the quoins of a square tower and the cost of obtaining it? Were the octagonal belfries on many of the towers added later or were they an original part of the tower? Different views have prevailed since round towers were first studied and diverse opinions on these questions continue to be expressed today.

There is no certainty about the date when the first English round church towers were built. On an interpretation of King Aethelstan's law of 937 AD as a requirement that a bell tower be erected on the land of every Thegn, it has been suggested that this was the reason for the erection of the earliest round towers. Superficially this may seem an attractive theory, but there is no proof that any surviving round towers are as old as the first half of the tenth century, and the theory has other weaknesses. It has been established that no round towers were built independently before their churches, and a flint tower would have taken three or four years to build. If the law's purpose had been to provide a means of instant warning or summons to the local populace, compliance could more promptly and effectively have been achieved with a tower constructed with wood. Contrary to Aethelstan's law being regarded as an injunction to erect a bell tower, it has also been interpreted as imposing a condition that a landowner aspiring to the status of Thegn, should show possession of a certain area of land and other property that included a chapel and bell tower. In any event, a circular flint structure would not necessarily have been implied. The association of chapel and bell tower in this context suggests that the latter's use may have been related to church liturgy.

As an alternative to the idea that a bell tower, whatever its shape or construction, stood as a symbol of thegnly status, round towers might be considered as having a similar raison d'etre as the original lower stages of early Saxon square towers that incorporate a west door, like the one at Brixworth, for example. That kind of western adjunct to a church, perhaps almost as high as the nave roof level, probably served as a tall west entrance porch to the church, only later being heightened to become a bell tower. A west porch, though, does not seem to have been the purpose of early round towers because, of the low ones without a contemporary belfry that have evidence of a west door, probably only the one at Howe is attributable as pre-Conquest.

Writing in 1829[1] after visiting over fifty round towers accompanied by Norfolk architect, J.C.Buckler, John Gage considered most of those he saw to be Norman but with many of 'the pointed style'; he considered only one, Tasburgh, to be earlier than the twelfth century, though not earlier than Norman. His paper is illustrated with several of Buckler's drawings.

In 1910, George Allen of London published *County Churches, Norfolk* (2 vols.) by

Charles Cox, followed in 1912 by *County Churches, Suffolk* (2 vols.) by Hugh Bryant. Having visited two-thirds of the Norfolk round towers as well as all those in Suffolk and Essex, Cox believed that a fair number were of the ninth, tenth or early eleventh centuries, that the majority were Norman and that only a few – a dozen at the outside – were of later date. He attributes not more than about twenty of the Norfolk round towers as Saxon, and most as Norman. Bryant holds that a large number of the circular towers are of Norman date and a few Saxon, but that some were erected or rebuilt with old materials as late as the beginning of the fourteenth century. He dates about half of the Suffolk round towers, calling only two Saxon. These books by Cox and Bryant were small pocket books, and because of the vast field they covered, necessarily contained only brief descriptions of each church, with no evidence or argument given for the attributions.

The defence-tower theory is championed by H.Munro Cautley[2]. He asserts: *"That many towers now attached to churches were built for defensive purposes admits of no doubt whatever. I have little doubt that many of the round towers of Suffolk and Norfolk are of the period of the Danish invasions and were built for defence." "If shorn of later additions, many exhibit common features which point to a defensive origin. These have no windows near the ground, and all lower storey windows have narrow openings and are few in number. None have western doorways, but all have on the eastern face a narrow arched opening cut through the wall. The cill of this is never less than 10 ft from the ground and in some cases much more. This is suspiciously like the entrances to the Pictish forts of the Iron Age, e.g. Dun Bornaigil, Sutherlandshire. There a similar entrance is so narrow that only one assailant could enter at a time and with so little freedom of his limbs that a single defender could effectively deal in turn with a large body of assailants. I suggest therefore, that these towers, whether they were built detached near the place of worship or even if they were built attached and at the western end of a church built of wood, originally had but the one entrance approached by a ladder and that they were built primarily for defence."*

Later, when times had become more settled, so the theory goes, a church would have been built to the east of the tower, the east face of the new nave west wall being aligned about six or seven inches in advance of the tower's curved east wall, and an arch cut through it and provided with stone dressings on the nave side.

As a result of careful study of the different ways in which the junctions between round towers and church naves have been made (see Chapter 6), Cautley's conclusion that churches were added to earlier towers has now been discredited. Some were built at the same time as their churches and many others can clearly be seen to be later additions, but none can be shown to have been built before their churches except in a few cases where a new or rebuilt church replaced an earlier one in later medieval or Victorian times. Other weaknesses of the theory are the small internal size if their purpose was for defence or refuge: many are under ten feet in diameter and would only have been able to accomodate a few people, and, contrary to Cautley's statement, some of the early towers, e.g. Howe and Aslacton, did have ground-level entrances on the west, which, though now blocked, show internally. And, one has to ask, why should the high-level entrances have always been in the tower's east wall?

When considering Cautley's theory, it is important to realize that logically it would only apply to those towers that were standing during the times of the Danish raids, and based on his own datings, this might amount to only a little over a quarter of the total number. But the theory seemed to take root and developed into a popular belief that round towers in general were originally defence or watch towers, to the extent that some church guides perpetuate the myth even for towers attributed by Cautley as twelfth-century!

Any discussion as to whether particular towers may have been built before or after the Conquest must inevitably be linked to consideration of the distinctions between Anglo-Saxon and Norman architecture, and one looks therefore to the work of such authorities on these periods as G. Baldwin Brown[3], Sir Alfred Clapham[4], H.M. & J.Taylor[5] and E.Fernie[6].

Baldwin Brown, Clapham and the Taylors all identified features – some technological, some stylistic – that they considered could be regarded as characteristic of Anglo-Saxon workmanship but recognized that any of them might also have been used after the Conquest. These features are individually considered in Chapter 5.

Baldwin Brown alludes to *"some specially Saxon features that make their appearance sporadically in work that must have been done, if not by Norman hands, yet at Norman bidding and on Norman design"*, and, as examples, he instances *"the double-splayed windows, a distinctly non-Norman feature, in what must be Norman work on the west side of the cloisters at Norwich"*, and *"a narrow external opening, the rounded head of which is cut out of a single stone often pronounced Saxon whereas there is an equal or greater likelihood that it is Norman"*. He thought a few towers were almost certainly Saxon, mentioning Bessingham, Colney, East Lexham, Great Ryburgh, Howe, Herringfleet and St Julian, Norwich but referred to the difficulty of reaching decisions as to the comparative dates of round towers in the absence of cut-stone details.

Sir Alfred Clapham saw the revolutionary effect of the Norman Conquest as even greater in the realms of art and learning than in the civil and political status of the country, saying *"The new Norman hierarchy, which, with few exceptions, dispossessed the native ecclesiastics within a few years of the Conquest brought with it an established order both of church-governance and architecture which, almost without effort, overthrew the loosely-knit organization and somewhat haphazard architecture of the Anglo-Saxon church."* *"Hardly ever before or since has a national culture been so easily, so rapidly, or so completely submerged as was the Anglo-Saxon in the last thirty years of the eleventh century. Here and there the old traditions lingered on but by the time that the last entry of the Anglo-Saxon Chronicle was penned the last trace of Saxon art or architecture had disappeared."* *"The new Norman prelates, drawn largely from the then flourishing monasteries of Normandy, were impatient of the lax practices and somewhat inchoate architecture of the Saxon church, and hastened to reform both the one and the other to the Norman model, and…the reconstruction of the majority of the English cathedrals was undertaken within a few years"*.

Clapham believed that there were a few round towers that could be assigned to the late pre-Conquest period, while a number more belonged to the immediately succeeding age, with the circular form continuing through the thirteenth century into the fourteenth. His contention that after the Conquest all traces of Saxon art or architecture were completely submerged to the Norman model rests uneasily with his attribution of a number of round towers as Norman. Whatever may have been the origin of the East Anglian round tower, it was not a Norman importation, and so its continuation after the Conquest represented acceptance by the new hierarchy of an important element of the indigenous architecture; there are probably more minor churches in East Anglia which have round Norman west towers than square ones. Clapham's perception of the subordination of Anglo-Saxon architecture may be true for the cathedrals, many of which were begun in the last thirty years of the eleventh century, but Saxon practice, workmanship and particularly the circular tower shape seem to have persisted in minor churches for many years after the Conquest.

In their definitive work on Anglo-Saxon Architecture, the Taylors review those architectural features they considered to be characteristic of Anglo-Saxon style and follow this with a comprehensive catalogue of more than 400 churches in this country in which such features were found and these are described in detail in support of their Saxon attributions for the particular church or part of it. Of the 49 round-towered churches in their inventory, Anglo-Saxon attributions for ten of them derive from nave features; hence, 39 round towers are regarded by the Taylors as having features which they considered to be indications of Anglo-Saxon workmanship.

Those features which the Taylors considered could be regarded as characteristic of Anglo-Saxon workmanship had been identified by them on the basis of historical or archaeological evidence related to particular churches and did not rely on a comparison with other churches with similar features; such evidence they called 'primary evidence'. By contrast, 'secondary dating' of a church as Anglo-Saxon relied on its possessing features which had been established on primary evidence in other churches as being characteristic of the Anglo-Saxon period. The Taylors warn that, to avoid risk of circular argument, if a feature is to be reliably regarded as characteristic of a particular period, it should appear in several churches that are primarily dated and there should be a demonstrable absence of it from any neighbouring period. They point out that, since we have no evidence to prove that Anglo-Saxon styles of building were given up immediately and wholly throughout the country after the Conquest, a building's possession of characteristic Saxon features does not necessarily prove that it was erected before the Conquest. The persistence of Saxon features for many years after the Conquest is demonstrated by the style of the belfry openings, the tall and narrow tower arch and the fillets of the round tower of Haddiscoe church which, on the evidence of its considerable use of Caen stone and the Norman billet mouldings round the belfry openings, is now accepted as unlikely to have been built earlier than the late eleventh or early twelfth century.

As features of minor churches relevant to the period of the Conquest, the East Anglian round towers are thought by Eric Fernie to date from the first half of the eleventh century but with the majority belonging to the late eleventh, twelfth and the first part of the thirteenth centuries and barely half a dozen attributable with any conviction to before the Conquest. He affirms that the type does not occur in Normandy at any date, and while recognizing that it could be an indigenous development in an area lacking good building stone, argues that this doesn't explain why it was not adopted in other such areas, or the similarities between the East Anglian examples and the round towers of North-West Germany. He concludes that the Conquest had no significance for the round tower as it seemed to have been introduced well before the 1060s, reaching the zenith of its popularity in the twelfth century. He considers that, though restricted to minor churches, the round tower could hardly be seen as a survival or a product of the backwaters of architectural development, as is amply demonstrated, for example, by the assurance of design and craftsmanship of Little Saxham tower (X).

In Nikolaus Pevsner's Suffolk and Norfolk volumes[7], published in 1961 and 62 respectively, he suggested that the majority of the round towers were Norman but that there were good arguments in favour of an Anglo-Saxon dating for about twenty or so. In the revised Norfolk editions of 1998 and 99, his successor, Bill Wilson, dates about a dozen medieval ones as post-Norman.

None of these writers traced the history of the round tower through the three-and-a-half or more centuries of its development; their observations on the type were made in the context of Anglo-Saxon architecture generally, with perhaps, particular attention given to the so-called Saxo-Norman overlap – the second half of the eleventh century and early twelfth – when features of Saxon style persisted into the post-Conquest period. Nor in the books devoted to Anglo-Saxon architecture, is there discussion of the absence from early East Anglian flint churches of many recognized features of the style as expressed in stone in the corpus of Saxon buildings elsewhere in the country, with the consequent difficulty this imposes on the making of attributions for flint buildings.

The first work devoted exclusively to round towers was a book by the Rev. Claude Messent, published in 1958[8]. This was a record of all the English examples, each illustrated by a line sketch and little more than captions for descriptions; his designations of date for Norfolk towers generally echoed those of Cox but with rather more attributed as Saxon or Saxo-Norman; for Suffolk churches he attributed about three-quarters as Norman and about a quarter as earlier. His favourite comment seems to have been *"There is nothing to show that the tower is earlier than the Norman period"* and there is no indication that he even considered the possibility that any, apart from the Bardfield Saling tower, might be post-Norman.

Perhaps the first detailed research on East Anglian round towers was the study undertaken by Stephen Heywood for an M.A. dissertation in 1976/7[9]. He advances the proposition that the circular tower form may be of continental origin. This supposition rests largely on the fact that there are about thirty round church towers in regions of North Germany, Poland and South Sweden bordering the Baltic Sea. Most of these have been dated to the twelfth century but the earliest, at Heeslingen in Germany, now demolished, may have been built in the late tenth or early eleventh century. He sees the round towers of East Anglia as a cultural legacy of trading links between the East Anglian ports and these continental Baltic regions, and holds that the circular shape was adopted, not for functional reasons, but as an aesthetic choice. Arguing against the functional explanation, he suggests that the difficulties of laying out, shuttering and constructing a round tower are greater than for a square one, and that, since there are in East Anglia a few circular structures that have been built with materials that are more generally associated with conventional buildings with right-angled corners, the functionalist theory does not stand to reason. These arguments are unconvincing for several reasons; firstly, accurate setting-out of a circular building is far simpler than for a rectangular one – all that is required is a stake driven into the ground at the geometric centre of the tower and a length of string equal to its radius; secondly, as discussed earlier, the balance of probability based on the external and internal evidence of the towers themselves is that shuttering was not used for the construction of the walls of most round towers; and thirdly, there are only a few East Anglian round towers faced with materials other than flint. One example, though, is West Dereham which is built of ferricrete; this stone has a very coarse texture and although used extensively at this church and for early quoins elsewhere, its use in a circular structure does not negate the functional rationale for the circular tower shape, nor likewise does the use of ashlar in a different context on the round radiating chapels at Norwich Cathedral. With the mighty circular bastions of the Roman ramparts at Burgh Castle as archetypes, there is no need to look to the continent for building precedents of this shape, and since the East Anglian round towers outnumber their North European parallels by about six to one and a dating for the earliest of them has not been firmly estabished, it is possible that the English ones may have been the inspiration for the continental examples, rather than vice versa.

Working from the premise that all parts of a building are contemporary with each other unless there is evidence to the contrary, Heywood also reviews those architectural features that have been considered as Saxon, instancing cases where they appear in the same structures as Norman features. Although not making detailed appraisals and attributions, he lists all the East Anglian round-towered churches, noting instances in them of Norman and pre-Norman features. His schedules make a radical departure from previously established canons by showing nearly half of them as having towers that he considered to be post-Norman. As no individual grounds for these attributions are given, they are presumably based on the presence of post-Norman features in the towers, following the principle quoted above.

In a later paper[10], Heywood suggests that, despite the survival in them of techniques and decoration normally considered Anglo-Saxon, by far the greater number of round towers belong to the late eleventh and the first half of the twelfth centuries. More recently[11], he has proposed that the source for the round west tower could have been the radiating chapels of the eastern arms of the Abbey of Bury St Edmunds and Norwich Cathedral, begun respectively in 1081 and 1096, but against this, the possibility of Northern Europe as the source should be weighed.

A completely contrary theory has been advanced by a local antiquary, W.J.Goode, in a book he published in 1982[12], later revised and retitled in 1994[13]. After general explanations of his ideas, he provides individual descriptions and attributions of date for all the round-towered churches and towers, accompanied by their principal measurements. Essentially, his interpretations differ from all previous assessments of these towers in that, apart from about a score of post-Conquest ones and a few of uncertain date, he considers them all to be Saxon. This conclusion relies substantially on the belief that techniques and features generally regarded as characteristic of Saxon workmanship were never used after the Conquest, that a specific wall thickness can be used as a demarcation between the Saxon and Norman periods and that any dressed stonework, medieval brick or post-Conquest stylistic features in round towers should be seen as later insertions or alterations. He regarded virtually all octagonal upper stages as additions to or modifications of earlier circular towers, assuming the height of the circular stage in most cases to be the original height of a Saxon tower.

The foregoing reviews show that until the advent of Heywood's and Goode's theories within a decade of each other, there seemed to be a fairly wide consensus that most of the round towers were Norman, with possibly a score or so Saxon and a few of the thirteenth century or later. It seems almost certain though, that the earlier writers probably did not ascend the towers as they give no internal details of the upper parts, and so they would have been unaware of important evidence.

The lack of local sources of suitable freestones for the quoins of square towers is widely accepted as a functional explanation for the adoption in East Anglia of the circular shape for church towers and for the high concentration of round towers in the region. Without the materials for building the square corners of a tall masonry structure in the conventional manner, and because of the expense and difficulty of obtaining them, it would have been logical to build towers of a shape which did not require corners. It therefore seems that constructional and economic factors were pivotal to the advent of the round tower in East Anglia. It is true that quoins of flint or ferricrete were built before freestones had become more widely introduced after the Conquest, as can be seen for instance at the western corners of the early church naves at Colney (3), augmented there with a few alien stones, and Bessingham (4) respectively, but East Anglia has only three square western towers with flint corners that may be earlier than the twelfth century – Hethel, Warham St Mary and Little Bardfield. (Beeston Regis tower which also has flint quoins, is probably thirteenth-century, and Heigham later still.) Clearly, for tall flint structures of the height of towers, the square shape with flint corners was not popular with early builders and round towers outnumbered square ones, including those of the eleventh and twelfth centuries with stone quoins.

While there are, of course, a number of early pre-Conquest square western towers in other parts of the country, round west towers certainly seem to pre-date square ones in East Anglia, a fact which tends to favour an indigenous origin. Whether the circular tower shape was a practical or an aesthetic choice, and whether or not it was inspired by continental precedents, it is inescapable that it was a logical solution to the technological challenge of building towers in a region lacking suitable stone for quoins. It will probably never be known for certain whether the East Anglian round tower was a local phenomenon or an imported cult. Perhaps this is not important – what is significant is that, irrespective of the origin of the concept, it quickly became adopted and spread throughout the region, being recognised as an appropriate form for its function and one that in an area without freestone could be built without the need of stone for corners. Natural conservatism ensured that it continued to be built concurrently with square towers long after freestone was widely imported into the area, suggesting that what may have originated as the solution to a functional problem, persisted as an economic aesthetic choice.

[1] Gage J. *Archaeologia, Vol.XXIII*. Society of Antiquaries, London, 1831.

[2] Cautley M. *Suffolk Churches*, Boydell, Ipswich, 1937, 4th revision 1975. *Norfolk Churches*, Adlard, Ipswich, 1949.

[3] Baldwin Brown G. *The Arts in Early England, Vol.II, Anglo-Saxon Architecture*. John Murray 1925.

[4] Clapham A. *English Romanesque Architecture, Vol.I Before the Conquest*, 1930, *Vol.II After the Conquest*, 1934, Oxford.

[5] Taylor H.M. and Taylor J. *Anglo-Saxon Architecture, Vols. I & II*, 1965, *Vol.III*, 1978, Cambridge University Press.

[6] Fernie E. *Architecture of the Anglo-Saxons*, Batsford, 1983.

[7] Pevsner N. and others *The Buildings of England, Suffolk*. 1961, *North-East Norfolk and Norwich*. 1962, and *North-West and South Norfolk*. 1962, Penguin.

[8] Messent C. *The Round Towers to English Parish Churches*. Fletcher, Norwich. 1958.

[9] Heywood S R. *Minor Church Building in East Anglia during the Eleventh and Early Twelfth Centuries*. University of East Anglia. 1977.

[10] Heywood S R. *The Round Towers of East Anglia*. Chapter XII in *Minsters and Parish Churches. The Local Church in Transition 950-1200* Ed. J Blair. Oxford University Committee for Archaeology, Monograph no 17, 1988.

[11] Heywood S R. *The Round towered churches of Norfolk and northern Europe*. Norfolk Churches Trust Annual Report, 1999/2000

[12] Goode W J. *East Anglian Round Towers and their Churches*. Friends of the Round Tower Churches Society, 1982.

[13] Goode W J. *Round Tower Churches of South-East England*, Round Tower Churches Society, 1994.

CHAPTER 3

TECHNOLOGY AND STYLE

The characteristics of minor churches that provide their archaeological evidence and create their architectural style are of two distinct kinds – technological and stylistic. The former represent technical solutions to functional or constructional problems, whereas the latter are those aspects of a building which contribute to its visual effect such as the shapes, architectural detailing and compositional arrangement of its elements, and its purely decorative features. This is not to say that a building's technology is not also part of its aesthetic impact.

It is only through appreciation of the difference between a building's constructional technology and its stylistic elements, particularly as they apply to round towers, that we can more fully understand the interplay of influences that is recognized as the Saxo-Norman overlap in East Anglia.

Despite the claims by Sir Alfred Clapham[1] that Anglo-Saxon architecture was rapidly supplanted by the Norman style, and despite all the arguments about the new hierarchy suppressing Saxon art and architecture and using their own style to impose their authority and prestige, one crucial and undeniable fact seems to have been entirely overlooked: that the Normans readily adopted a major indigenous artefact of Saxon technology, **the round tower itself.**

Whatever may have been the origin of the round tower, it was not an import from Normandy. The building of round towers after the Conquest represented, therefore, the perpetuation in England by the Normans of a Saxon technology, and it seems unlikely that, having adopted it, but being unfamiliar with its shape and materials, they would, at a stroke, have departed from all its established constructional methods. As the Taylors point out[2] *"We have no evidence to prove that Anglo-Saxon styles of building were given up immediately and wholly throughout the country after the Conquest. In default of evidence to the contrary it is reasonable to believe that some of the surviving buildings in the styles characteristic of the later Anglo-Saxon periods were erected by Anglo-Saxon workmen in the manner to which they were accustomed, but after the Norman Conquest. For the later architectural styles, from the Norman period onward, the recorded history of surviving buildings provides clear evidence that there are considerable local variations in the dates at which the changes took place from one style to the next, and we have no reason to doubt that there were similar delays in certain parts of the country in the introduction of Norman methods."* And so, just because a round tower contains features of Saxon technology, that does not necessarily mean that it is of pre-Conquest date.

In the context of minor flint churches generally and round towers of the eleventh and twelfth centuries in particular, aspects of technology include the thickness of walls, flintwork techniques, construction and materials of openings, window types and methods of forming arches, quoining methods and materials, and the construction of twin belfry-openings.

After the Conquest, although under Norman patronage, minor churches would probably still have been built by local labour following traditional methods. Wall thicknesses and other features associated with pre-Conquest flint technology such as double-splayed window openings, triangular-headed arches, windows and doors formed without dressed stone, and the practice of setting back arches at their springing points to accommodate the shuttering on which they were built, would therefore probably have continued unchanged for some time in the post-Conquest period, in the same way as happened with the stylistic features of, for example, the belfry openings, fillets and tall tower arch at Haddiscoe.

Appropriate thicknesses for the walls of Saxon round towers would probably originally have evolved empirically through an acquired understanding of working with flint, taking account of such technical factors as the properties of the material and the mortar, the proposed height of the tower, the nature of the ground on which it was to be built, and whether it was to be built concurrently with a church's nave and bonded to it, or as a later addition.

The walling flintwork of eleventh- and twelfth-century towers shows little technological change. As described in the next chapter, the material was as-found flint, laid uncoursed or coursed, both methods being found in Saxon and Norman towers; differences in material as between rubble field flints, cobbles and erratics depended on location rather than technique. Late in the thirteenth or early in the fourteenth centuries, incorporation of medieval bricks or knapped flints in the fabric of some towers, uniquely with galleting on the later tower at Wolterton, represented a minor, essentially aesthetic,

7. Saxon through-stone type of double belfry opening, with stripwork on the face of the jambs and over the triangular heads of the lights, all built in ferricrete, at Bessingham.

8. Norman stone details in the Saxon-style through-stone type of double belfry opening on Haddiscoe tower.

development in the technology of facing flintwork, but the traditional methods continued to be used in many of the later towers.

After the Conquest the introduction of limestone ashlar as dressings for window and door openings, quoins and belfries was an important Norman technological innovation. As it became more widely available, details of Norman style in stone were introduced, but the underlying Saxon constructional technology was slow to change. The same is true for the circular tower itself; its persistence into the post-Conquest period is demonstrated by the fact that there are probably more round Norman west towers in East Anglia than square ones. Their small windows with stone dressings externally and sometimes internally, were invariably single-splayed, continuing another technology inherited from earlier times – Saxon loops were not always double-splayed.

The Normans also introduced a different method of construction of twin belfry openings. In Saxon belfry openings of this kind like those at Beachamwell (46) or Bessingham (7) and elsewhere, two separate arches, with either round or triangular heads, pass through the full thickness of the wall, centrally supported on a through-stone carried on a pillar in the middle of the wall or exceptionally on a spine wall as at Roughton (42). Although the Normans followed Saxon technology and style in the belfries at Haddiscoe (8) and Herringfleet, albeit incorporating stone dressings and elements of their own stylistic detail, their normal constructional method was to dispense with the through-stone and to span the full width of the two lights with a single arch, with a pair of sub-arches and their supporting column beneath it. The sub-arches were barely thicker than the capital of the column and were usually placed at the outer face of the wall with the principal arch behind, as at Gissing, Snailwell, Merton, Kilverstone (9), Titchwell and Thorpe-next-Haddiscoe. On the belfries of Gayton Thorpe (78), Thorington and Little Saxham (X) though, the sub-arches are recessed, forming inner orders, with the principal arches extending through the full wall thickness and showing at the wall face; externally they are faced in stone but at Thorington the lower part of the jambs are of flint. Internally, in this kind of Norman belfry opening, the voussoirs of the principal arch were either dressed stone as at Kilverstone, or flints as at Gayton Thorpe; at Thorpe-next-Haddiscoe, the principal arches, also of flint, are set back on the reveals which have flint jambs, and at Merton (58), not only are the jambs and heads of the principal arches internally formed with flints, but also those of the double openings at the external wall face, though the repaired arches may originally have been stone. These flint practices demonstrate the continuation of earlier technology in Norman construction.

9. Norman-style double belfry, on Kilverstone tower.

At Merton, and at East Lexham where double openings (43 - 45) also follow the Norman mode, the external flint dressings of the belfry openings might be considered a reason for attributing these towers as Saxon, but more significant perhaps than the material of the exterior finish of the openings is the basic technology of their design, i.e. an arch spanning the full width of the opening, in contrast to two separate small arches. As Taylor says[3] *"the distinction between the two types of window does not depend on details of the masonry but on a fundamental principle of design"*.

Although, as is demonstrated in the Haddiscoe and Herringfleet belfries, the Saxon principle was sometimes followed in the post-Conquest period, it seems improbable that the Norman technology would have appeared in minor churches before the Conquest. The conclusion therefore must be that, irrespective of details of the masonry, a belfry with double openings beneath a semi-circular arch spanning the two lights of the opening is likely to have been built after the Conquest, and consequently unless it can be shown to have been a later addition to the tower in which it occurs, that tower must be of Norman date. It is perhaps significant that none of the belfries with rere-arches spanning the full width of the two lights have triangular heads to their sub-arches.

The technology of quoining, though not of course directly relevant to the construction of round towers, may nevertheless be significant for their dating because the methods and materials used for the nave quoins may provide indications of the nave's date, and where it can be established that the nave and tower are contemporary, the date of the tower also.

Before the Norman Conquest, quoins were built with the materials at hand; flints, erratics, carstone, ferricrete and re-cycled Roman bricks and stones were used individually or in combinations, and although quoins of these materials may be thought to imply work built before the Conquest, often, no doubt, rightly so, this was not always the case. Cost and the difficulties of transport from the sources of the earliest limestones used – Barnack near Stamford and Caen in Normandy – would have meant that their

10. Random-sized erratics used for the south-west nave quoins at Ilketshall St Margaret.

11. Megalithic ferricrete quoins at the north-west nave corner of Great Ryburgh church. Bricks in a buttress built up against them show their size.

introduction after the Conquest would not have been universal or immediate, and consequently established quoining methods and local materials would be likely to have persisted in some minor churches, particularly in poorer communities and those not easily accessible by water. Roman material, for example, is found in Norman churches as at High Easter and flint quoins, whole or cut on two faces, were used in work even as late as the thirteenth-century tower at Beeston Regis, the fourteenth-century nave and aisle at Rackheath, the fifteenth-century nave extension at Warham St Mary and on the tower and nave quoins at Heigham. On the other hand, the rudimentary workmanship of, for example, the erratics in the south-west nave quoins of Ilketshall St Margaret (10) or the large irregular blocks of ferricrete laid on end and randomly sized at Great Ryburgh (11) make such a contrast with the precision of typical Norman quoins of neatly-squared uniform stones as to suggest earlier work, and so perhaps a pre-Conquest date. But, should artless workmanship necessarily be equated with greater antiquity than more refined work, or might it just be the result of the cost and difficulty of obtaining stone for dressings?

Because of the lack of indigenous limestone, long-and-short quoins, widely considered a hallmark of Saxon technology, made a late appearance in East Anglia, perhaps not before the Saxo-Norman period of the late eleventh century. St John's, Timberhill, Norwich, said to have been founded between the Conquest and the compiling of Doomsday Book in 1086 provides an example, and at Great Dunham church they occur on nave and tower in proximity with contemporary Norman stone details, double-splayed flint windows and Saxon belfry technology. The clearest example on a round-towered church is the north-west nave quoin at Beachamwell (12), perhaps also of the late eleventh century.

In the round tower context, stylistic features, as opposed to technological ones, include the shapes of arches, windows and other openings, the architectural detailing of belfries, belfry openings and their dispositions, window tracery patterns, stone mouldings, blank arcading, pilaster-strips (lesenes), fillets between nave and tower, and the arrangement of tower windows.

By comparison with areas where workable stone was available, there are in round towers and in minor flint churches generally throughout East Anglia, only a few stylistic features that could be regarded as having a Saxon provenance. They can be summarized as follows: sequences of circular windows in such towers as Forncett St Peter and Burnham Norton, recessed blank arcading as on Tasburgh tower, the

12. Long-and-Short quoins of Barnack stone on the north-west nave corner at Beachamwell church.

13. Typical Saxon stone stripwork, or lesenes, on the square tower of Earls Barton church, Northants.

pilaster-strips around Kirby Cane and Thorpe-next-Haddiscoe towers and the wider single ones adjacent to the nave west wall on Colney, Witton and Norwich St Julian towers, fillets on some round towers, architectural detail of twin belfry openings as at Haddiscoe or Herringfleet, tall and narrow tower arches, and perforated stone slabs in tower windows as at Cranwich. Features of Saxon style in square flint towers are flint stripwork at Guestwick, the arrangement of alternating round-headed and circular windows (blocked) at Warham St Mary, and the disposition of the windows at Little Bardfield.

This dearth of Saxon stylistic architectural detail is understandable in a region devoid of suitable stone in which it could be expressed and poses the question of how under those circumstances a strong decorative or stylistic, as opposed to a technological architectural tradition could have become established. Minor flint churches and their round towers have nothing to compare with the characteristic Anglo-Saxon details as seen externally on say, Earls Barton (13) and Barnack towers, or internally on Wittering's chancel arch. One wonders from where the inspiration came for the few examples that do exist in East Anglia, such as the stripwork motif around the belfry openings at Bessingham (7) or the Norman belfries in Saxon style at Haddiscoe and Herringfleet. Were these perhaps echoes of a strong local decorative timber tradition? Stripwork, triangular-headed openings and the typical angular-headed panel patterns of the stone towers mentioned can easily be understood as decorative interpretations in stone of timber constructional details, and the use of a through-stone as a double-cantilevered slab in belfry openings, though quite unsuited to the nature of stone, is clearly an echo of a form of construction that would have been eminently appropriate in timber. Whatever views one may hold regarding the date of the earliest flint churches in East Anglia and stone ones elsewhere in England, there must have been a tradition of wooden churches; within this tradition, a decorative vocabulary derived from timber practice would, no doubt, have evolved which may have been the inspiration for some of the stylistic details of Saxon buildings and could account for their occurrence in stoneless East Anglia.

[1] Clapham A Op. Cit. Vol.II.
[2] Taylor & Taylor Op. Cit. Vol.I, pg.2.
[3] Taylor H.M. Op. Cit. Vol.III, pg.873

CHAPTER 4

THE ARCHITECTURAL DEVELOPMENT OF ROUND TOWERS

The walls of earlier towers were built with rubble flints of all sizes, randomly laid or roughly coursed, with wide mortar joints between the irregular pieces and they often contained quite large lumps of flint, carstone, ferricrete or erratics, especially in their lower parts as at Roughton (41), where some courses are laid in herringbone fashion. In later eleventh-century work the flints tend to be of more regular sizes as in the walls of Colney tower. Not easily distinguishable from this style of workmanship, rubble flints of compatible shapes and sizes are characteristic of Norman walls, which, while sometimes built randomly, are more typically laid coursed as in Haddiscoe tower or in the lower, Norman parts of the towers at Rickinghall Inferior and Rushmere. Shallow relief features in flint provided simple wall surface decoration on a few towers in the eleventh and twelfth centuries (see chapter 10), and on some towers, e.g. Hengrave, Kilverstone and East Walton, the flintwork shows marked stratification where, at vertical spacings of about a foot, the flints are brought to horizontal levels: at East Walton (14), forty-two distinct layers can be counted between the ground and belfry cill level. These layers perhaps represent the amount of flintwork laid at one time between the intervals allowed for the slow-hardening lime mortar to attain adequate strength to support succeeding work. Stratification seems to have been a practice of the late twelfth and early thirteenth centuries.

14. Flintwork stratification on East Walton tower.

In the early towers, the jambs and arches of openings were formed with flints as at Forncett St Peter or with carstone or ferricrete as at Bessingham and Beeston St Lawrence, but after the Conquest, limestone from Caen and Barnack was imported into East Anglia and was used more and more for the dressings of tower openings. Early tower arches, like the one at Bedingham were formed entirely without dressed stonework, but soon, chamfered stone imposts came to be used at the arch springings and then stone dressings to the jambs and arches, sometimes on the nave side only and sometimes also within the tower. But not always: plastered openings of round-headed tower arches, and later, pointed ones, were still formed without dressed stone.

Belfry openings of the earliest round towers were probably single-light with triangular or semi-circular arched heads and unsplayed reveals. They were formed with flints as at Cranwich and Great Hautbois (III) or with ferricrete as in the probable original belfry below the present one at Beeston St Lawrence (II). The early twin-light type in which a pair of small semi-circular or triangular arches passes through the full wall thickness, centrally supported by a through-stone carried on a single column, was probably introduced in the eleventh century. It has come to be regarded as a hallmark of Anglo-Saxon workmanship and style, but continued, nevertheless, to be built after the Conquest; the belfries at Haddiscoe and Herringfleet, formed with Caen stone and exhibiting billet mouldings, are Norman examples and could perhaps be regarded as the round tower equivalents of the so-called Lincolnshire towers with this type of belfry opening that are currently the subject of debate as to whether they are pre-or post-Conquest.

The usual belfry arrangement was four openings at the cardinal points, but the early tower at East Lexham has only three, facing east, south-west and north-west. The original Norman belfries at Holton St Peter (77) and Bexwell (I) have sequences of eight and ten single-light openings respectively spaced round the towers, and in the original Norman belfry at Blundeston (70) below the present one, small stone-framed sound-holes alternate with six belfry openings, now mostly blocked with brick. The Norman version of the double belfry opening described earlier continued through the twelfth century reaching the zenith of its development at Little Saxham tower where stone belfry openings of three orders (X) combine with blank arcading to produce the finest of all the Norman round tower belfries. Belfry openings in post-Norman towers were occasionally sited at the four diagonal orientations instead of the usual cardinal positions, as at West Lexham and in the later upper stages of Brooke and Kirby Cane towers, and, because of the disposition of the tower buttresses at Ramsholt, the arrangement of three recurs there.

Stone string courses were introduced below the belfry on a few early Norman towers; Haddiscoe has two others at lower levels dividing the tower into stages (IV). Only four other standing medieval round towers, Beyton, Bardfield Saling, Rockland St Peter and Great Shefford, and two of the modern ones, Higham and Welford, have string courses lower down in their circular stages. Most string courses are plain stone weatherings, but those below the Norman belfries of Gayton Thorpe (78) and Little Saxham (X) have carved decoration all the way round, and at Old Catton and Kirby Bedon they are brick. The use of a string course below the belfry continued on later towers, though not on all; it became the norm, however, where an octagonal belfry was added to an earlier tower.

The basic design of round towers with a

15. Round-headed belfry openings with Y-tracery in Syderstone tower.

circular belfry changed little through the twelfth and thirteenth centuries and into the fourteenth. The transition from Norman round-headed openings and tower arches to the pointed styles of the Early English period is seen in the thirteenth-century tower of Norton Subcourse which has ten small stone-framed lancets at various levels, most pointed, but some round-headed (The belfry has been rebuilt and according to Ladbrooke's drawing of 1823, formerly had lancet openings). The tower at Syderstone, said to be a replacement for a former Norman crossing tower that collapsed in circa 1200 (though the church shows no positive evidence of one), has two-light, round-headed belfry openings, which though of Y-pattern, have a shaft with moulded capital instead of a central mullion in the east and west openings (15). At Sedgeford, where the tower and nave may be contemporary (see Chapter 18), the pointed Y-traceried belfry openings also have a shafted centre member.

Whether as a result of structural deterioration of the previous belfries or to satisfy a desire to comply with current architectural taste, there seems to have been in the late thirteenth century and the fourteenth a trend of altering, adding or rebuilding belfries in

the lancet style. In some towers, it appears that former belfry openings have simply been altered, and that may have occurred at Hardley where the earlier tower has stone lancet belfry openings, or in the eleventh-century tower at Colney unless a small difference in the flintwork of the upper stage above the double-splayed windows there signifies that the belfry stage with its lancet openings has been entirely rebuilt.

At Blundeston (70) and Fishley (XII) new lancet belfries, both incorporating much brick, were built on top of the existing Norman ones and the original blocked belfry openings beneath can be clearly seen; at Hales (67), though the Norman belfry openings below the added lancet belfry are not obvious externally because of skilful insertion within them of lancets, they show clearly inside (69).

In other towers, the evidence of the walls shows that an original belfry must have been demolished before a new one was added; apparently this happened at Tasburgh where, above the round-headed blank arcading that encircles the tower,

16. Detached tower at Little Snoring, with dormer openings in its conical tiled roof.

complementary recesses in the flintwork suggest that an upper tier has been truncated for the lancet belfry (51).

In several cases where a belfry with lancet openings has replaced an earlier one, the lancet belfry itself has been surmounted by a yet later one built on top of it. Where this has occurred the lancet openings have usually been skilfully blocked leaving only slight indications in the external flintwork, but usually the evidence inside the tower is clearer, as for example at Rickinghall Inferior or Rushmere where the blocked lancets are unmistakable.

The original belfries of certain towers seem to have disappeared without being replaced. Short towers at Moulton, Barmer and Howe have no recognisable belfries; Little Snoring (16) and Welborne both have dormer belfry openings in their conical tiled roofs, and the presence of brick in the top five or six feet of their tower wall flintwork suggests that these windowless upper sections are later work, taking the place of former belfries. At St Michael's, Lewes, evidence on the flat east face of the tower of a former higher nave roof probably indicates that this tower was also originally taller than now, and the present two small circular windows near the top, which are located at a lower level than the apparent former nave roof apex, certainly seem inadequate as original belfry openings.

Concurrently with the trend of adding or rebuilding lancet belfries on existing towers, entire wholly-circular towers with lancet belfry openings were built in the late thirteenth and the fourteenth centuries - Bartlow, Bawburgh (17), Needham before its octagonal belfry was added, Stockton, Onehouse, Frostenden, Weybread, Syleham and Bradwell to name a few. In others such as Threxton or Eccles and several more, the two-light pattern of belfry openings with Y-tracery was introduced, and this style was also adopted for the added circular belfries at Beeston St Lawrence and Rushmere, mentioned above.

In several towers built at about this time, ground-floor west windows were introduced as lancets and, a little later, as two-light types. Uncusped lancets in this position in the towers at Aylmerton, Croxton and Stuston (18) among others seem to be original features of the towers' construction, the one at Stuston having a medieval brick relieving arch

17. Lancet belfry openings framed with medieval bricks in Bawburgh tower.

18. Lancet west window in Stuston tower with a rough relieving arch of medieval brick above.

above it. Cusped lancets are found at Needham, Thorpe Abbotts and Syleham, and there is no reason to suppose that the early two-light west windows with Y-tracery at Threxton and Hasketon, the pattern repeated in their respectively circular and octagonal belfries, are not contemporary with the post-Norman fabric of their towers. Later fourteenth-century towers followed with later styles of Decorated two-light west windows as seen, for example at Horsey or Potter Heigham. Concurrently, two-light Decorated or Perpendicular west windows were inserted into many older towers.

Knapped flints exposing a flat cut face, as opposed to roughly cleft or broken pieces first appeared in round tower walls early in the fourteenth century, and, in mixtures with as-found flints as in the towers at Burgh Castle, Horsey or Potter Heigham they represent another small but aesthetically important step in round tower development. Subsequently, they were used in greater concentrations in a few towers like Tuttington (79) or Keswick, and later at Wolterton (6) the entire facing is of knapped flints. In rare decorative usages, two horizontal bands of knapped flints about a foot high at about 12 and 24 feet above the ground can still be seen in the standing remnant of the rubble flint wall of the early fourteenth-century tower at Cockley Cley (73) that collapsed in 1991, and on the fourteenth-century belfry stage of Syleham tower alternating squares of knapped and rubble flints encircle the belfry base and surround the belfry windows (19).

19. Alternating squares of knapped and rubble flints around the belfry base and openings on Syleham tower.

After the departure of the Romans, brickmaking in England ceased for about 900 years and it was not revived in East Anglia, it is now generally believed, until the thirteenth century, and the earliest use in round towers of locally-made bricks, as opposed to re-use of Roman material, appears to have been during the second half of the century. Thereafter, in addition to their frequent use in added belfries of the thirteenth and fourteenth centuries, medieval bricks appear in the earliest parts of more than a score of round towers, at random in the fabric where they were used mainly as headers to improve the bond between the facing of a wall and its core, in the framing and bridging of putlog holes and in the arches and jambs of windows and upper doors internally. One of the earliest uses of medieval bricks in a round tower is probably the belfry stage of Burgh Castle church tower where they also frame lancet belfry windows; in later walls of Old Catton and Lound towers, they are used more prolifically, creating a check pattern.

An early west window with external brick dressings occurs in Hassingham tower where remnants of its jambs can be seen below the present window (81). West Somerton tower also has an early brick window (82), and its internal embrasure and the jambs and arch of the upper door are formed with medieval bricks. At Ashby (20), they are used to weather the tower's circular plinth, as quoins for the octagonal belfry, as dressings of the belfry openings, and internally for the upper door. But by no means all round towers of the late thirteenth century and the fourteenth have medieval brick features; those without bricks include Syderstone, East Walton or Tuttington.

Hassingham, West Somerton and Ashby were the pioneers of a major innovation in the

architectural development of round towers that occurred in the later thirteenth and early fourteenth century – an octagonal belfry built from the outset on a circular base stage. However, because of a generally-held belief in the antiquity of round towers, and the fact that no octagonal belfry stages have Norman or earlier features, it has long been widely supposed that all octagonal belfries on round towers were additions to Saxon or Norman structures, and no serious consideration seems to have been given to the possibility that they could be the same date as the circular stages, even though in about three-quarters of all round towers with octagonal tops there is no trace of former belfry openings in the circular stages, inside or out.

Four possible reasons could account for the absence of belfry openings in the circular stage of this kind of round tower. Firstly, any belfry openings that there might have been in the circular stage have been blocked so skilfully that no trace is detectable in the flintwork, outside or in; secondly, a later belfry stage has been added to a lower original tower; thirdly, an original belfry stage has been demolished to be replaced by the octagonal

20. Ashby tower has a tall octagon on a low circular base stage. Medieval brick is used at the angles and for the belfry openings.

one, and lastly, the circular stage and the octagonal belfry were built together.

The first alternative is highly improbable because, although such skilful blocking as to make former openings virtually undetectable is not unusual externally, such a degree of care would hardly be taken internally, and assuredly some evidence of former openings such as their interior arches, would remain; there would have been no reason for their removal, thus weakening the structure, and indeed, where former belfry openings have been skilfully blocked externally as at Barsham or Rickinghall Inferior, they still clearly show within. The second alternative is equally unlikely because it implies that an assumed lower original tower to which a later belfry was added was originally built without any belfry openings, and so, in effect, we are left with the last two alternatives as realistically probable.

The possibility that a tower's octagonal belfry replaces an earlier one, applies to towers where there is evidence in the circular stage of work earlier than the octagon, such as a round-headed tower arch. More than a dozen such towers, like Bedingham, Breckles or Quidenham for example, retain no evidence of a belfry of comparable early date and so in those cases it seems certain that their octagonal belfries must be replacements of earlier ones. It shouldn't however be overlooked that although upper doors or round-headed tower arches may seem to imply an early tower, there is always a possibility that the whole tower could be a replacement of an earlier fallen one and therefore later than the tower arch and upper door.

Lastly, if the circular stage has no evidence which can be reliably dated as earlier than the octagon but contains features which could be contemporary with it such as a pointed tower arch, a lancet window or medieval brick in the fabric or putlog holes, then clearly these point to the circular stage and belfry having been built together, unless those features can be proved to have been later alterations or insertions. Hassingham, West Somerton and Ashby are examples of towers in this category.

Of the fifty-five round towers with a medieval octagonal belfry stage, the octagon is probably contemporary with the circular base in nearly half of them, and many of those have a wealth of evidence to support that probability. Such evidence includes continuity of the internal circular shape into the octagon as at Thorpe Abbotts or Ilketshall St Andrew; similarity of flintwork in the two stages, externally and internally, as at Sedgeford; the presence of medieval brick features in the circular stage that are only likely to have been incorporated in a wall when it was built, such as the framings and bridgings of putlog holes, brick arches through the full wall thickness, relieving arches whose later insertion would create a weakness greater than any additional strength they might contribute, and, not least, individual medieval bricks within a flint wall which can often be confidently recognised as integral components of the original fabric rather than repair insertions.

21. The tower of St Benedict's church, Norwich which escaped destruction when the church was bombed during the 1939-45 war.

A little later perhaps, than the fully octagonal thirteenth-century towers at Toft Monks and Buckenham, some towers such as Ashby (20), Topcroft (35) or Rollesby were built with an octagonal superstructure twice the height of the circular base or more; some had circular and octagonal stages of about the same height as at Horsey and Ilketshall St Andrew, while the octagons of others like Hassingham and West Somerton were shorter than the circular stages. The earlier octagonal belfries contemporary with circular lower stages, like those at Hassingham (XVIII) and West Somerton, and possibly Acle and Mautby have single lancet belfry openings with stone dressings and dressed stone angles to the octagon. At Ashby and Topcroft, probably a little later, the dressings of the lancets and the octagon's angles are formed with medieval brick. Soon after, others with two-light belfry openings followed, such as Ilketshall St Andrew, Thorpe Abbotts, Rushall and several more, some with stone dressings, some with medieval brick.

The tower of St Benedict's, Norwich is of unique interest in being the only round

22. The tower of Needham church with later stair turret and octagonal belfry.

23. The upper part of the circular stage of Bedingham tower appears to have been rebuilt when the octagonal belfry was added. The lower part is probably Saxon.

tower with brick flushwork (21); it is also one of only two, with Potter Heigham, in which a circular stage of mixed flint rubble has a contemporary octagonal belfry faced with knapped flints. The post-Norman credentials of the circular stage are firmly established by its pointed west door, the medieval brick putlog holes, and the open and blocked lancet windows framed and arched in medieval brick, notwithstanding that the south-facing one has been renovated after the wartime bomb damage. As the circular stage has no evidence of earlier belfry openings, there is no reason to suppose that the octagon is a later build even though it is faced with knapped flints by contrast with the rubble flintwork of the circular stage. The belfry windows in the cardinal faces, though much repaired, appear originally to have been framed in medieval bricks similar to those in the lower stage, and similar bricks are used in Y-tracery brick flushwork in the diagonal facets and in the continuous hoodmould over the windows and the flushwork replicas. The proximity of dates suggested by the brickwork and the style of both stages seems to rule out the possibility that the octagonal belfry replaces an earlier one.

The popularity of the architectural arrangement of an octagonal belfry on a circular lower stage found further expression in those round towers that had octagonal belfries added to them in the fourteenth and fifteenth centuries. In some of them, the octagon was built directly onto the original belfry as at Beachamwell, Bexwell or Needham (22), but in others like South Pickenham, Quidenham or Bedingham (23) a former belfry must have been demolished before the octagon was added since nothing of it remains – indeed, at Bedingham the upper part of the circular stage also seems to have been rebuilt.

Virtually all the added octagonal belfries had two-light belfry openings; Raveningham,

Heckingham, and Acle and Mautby if they were not contemporary with the circular stage, are probably the only added ones with lancets.

An architectural variation on the octagon theme was provided by the multi-stage octagon and this was introduced on a few towers – in original and added belfries. Examples of the former include Ilketshall St Andrew (89), Rollesby, Topcroft (35) and Thorpe Abbotts (XVII), whereas Woodton has a two-stage octagon added to an earlier circular tower.

In a few of the later round towers of the fourteenth century, a newel stair was built as an integral part of the tower's original construction like those at Shimpling (87), Rockland St Peter (88), and Bardfield Saling. Subsequently, in the fifteenth and sixteenth centuries permanent staircases of brick and flint were built onto some towers as external turrets as at Needham (22), Stody and Long Stratton, or formed internally either in the tower as at Yaxham or in the nave as at Witton. Turrets partially built on squinches are seen at Matlaske and Wickmere, the former spanning the re-entrant angle between nave and tower on the south side, and the latter crossing the north-west corner of the nave internally.

In some towers, a spiral stair appears to have been formed entirely within the tower's wall thickness. In the Norman tower at Wissett the stair is clearly a later insertion because the apex of the Tudor arch of the stair entry in the south reveal of the tower arch cuts into the tower arch impost. The bottom step is 2'8" above the floor and the rubble steps with thick oak treads are very steep and narrow. The tower fillet in the south re-entrant angle between nave and tower forms the outer wall of the stair and a small window in the fillet shows that the wall at that point is only four inches thick. At Lound, the whole section of tower wall enclosing the stair appears to have been rebuilt, partly encroaching within the tower space, and upwards from about 17 feet above ground level, the tower walls inside and out contain just about as much brick as flint, suggesting comprehensive rebuilding in the sixteenth century or later with re-set or restored fourteenth-century belfry openings. At Haddiscoe, the north arcade's west respond and the tower wall were simply broken through to provide stair access from the north aisle.

Faced with fine quality galleted knapped flint, and with a brick and flint west window arch, a brick-framed upper window, and much brick in the fabric, the Wolterton tower (6) must be one of the last of the medieval round towers, and may be as late as the fifteenth century. It marks the end of a continuous period of four centuries or more during which round church towers of flint had been built in East Anglia.

After medieval times, many towers suffered neglect and deterioration. Several, like those and their churches at Appleton, Burgh St Mary and Kirby Bedon St Mary fell into ruin and there are records of many others that have entirely disappeared. Stumps of fallen towers still remain attached to their churches at Dilham, Feltwell, Hardwick, Ingworth, Morton on the Hill and St Julian, Norwich (a wartime air-raid casuality), and at Denton, following collapse of the round tower in the late eighteenth century, a square one of brick was grafted onto a surviving curved section of wall still attached to the nave; later, in the nineteenth century this received a flint top. Others to have undergone major restorations comprising mainly new upper stages, included Clippesby, Freethorpe, Roydon, Gresham, Brome, South Elmham All Saints, Lamarsh and South Ockenden. Then there are those that were completely rebuilt in the nineteenth and early twentieth centuries:

Ashmanhaugh, Weeting, Belton and Spexhall were made fully circular but at Sidestrand, where the whole church was rebuilt further inland with materials from the original cliff-top church now lost to the sea, the tower has a two-stage octagonal top. Similarly, at Welford (96) the wholly rebuilt church incorporates much of the original ashlar stone, particularly in the tower's octagonal belfry and stone spire. A new tower at Brandiston, retaining the original fillets where it joins the church, also has an octagonal top though without windows – the belfry openings are at a lower level. At Higham an entirely new church designed by Sir George Gilbert Scott in Geometric style was built in 1861; its round tower (24) has lancet belfry openings with blind arcading between and is crowned with a conical shingled spire.

24. The circular tower of the nineteenth-century church at Higham.

CHAPTER 5

ROUND TOWER DATING

Methods of dating medieval churches have traditionally depended on the recognition of particular architectural features as being representative of particular periods, which through association with datable evidence such as, for example, personalities, consecrations or bequests, have established a broadly consensual basis for dating.

These methods alone, though, have serious limitations: firstly, they overlook the possibility that a feature may have been inserted into an earlier fabric or reset in a later fabric or altered at a later date, and secondly they take no account of the fact that many features, some more than others, continued in use for a long time after they first appeared. Thus, even where a feature can be established as contemporary with the fabric in which it occurs, dating by this method can only provide the earliest date from which a particular feature was current – it cannot establish a date beyond which the feature was not used. Nevertheless, conventionally, the method of dating round towers and their churches for which there is no documentary evidence has been based on the assumption that those with features characteristic of Saxon building methods could be considered as pre-Conquest whereas those without such evidence were probably Norman; some, even, with post-Norman features and

25. Triangular-headed blocked opening in the east face of the Norman square tower at Flitcham.

no Norman evidence, have been attributed as Norman in the belief that few round towers were built after the end of the Norman period.

In the context of the Saxo-Norman Overlap there is, as has been shown in chapter 3, a strong likelihood that features of pre-Conquest technology persisted well into the post-Conquest period, and many features that have been considered as characteristic of Saxon workmanship can be shown to have also been used in post-Conquest work, thus calling into question their reliability as proof of Saxon date. As the Taylors say, *"if a feature is to be reliably regarded as characteristic of a particular period. . . . .there should be a demonstrable absence of the feature from churches of any neighbouring period"*.

Relying only on a fallible assumption that they were never used after the Conquest, features characteristic of Saxon techniques have nevertheless been claimed as proof of a pre-Conquest date for all buildings in which they occur. However, the following occurrences in undisputed post-Conquest work of such features demonstrate their continuation despite the changes in political and ecclesiastical hierarchies.

Twin belfry openings with centre column and through-stone. Examples in the round towers of Haddiscoe (8) and Herringfleet are confirmed as Norman by Caen stone and billet mouldings.

Triangular-headed openings. A blocked opening in the east face of the Norman crossing tower of Flitcham church has a triangular head formed with flints (25) as are its jambs. Upper doors giving access to the upper stages of some round towers that may be Norman such as Gayton Thorpe have triangular heads, and small windows with heads formed with propped stones or bricks are not uncommon in post-Norman towers as at Sedgeford or Bylaugh.

Double-splayed windows. Although circular flint windows of this type at Forncett St Peter (26) may be pre-Conquest, those in the west wall of Norwich Cathedral Cloisters and in the round tower at Gissing can be convincingly shown to be Norman; likewise the large double-splayed round-headed window in Gayton Thorpe round tower. Castle Rising, built about 70 years after the Conquest, has double-splayed rubble windows in the wall between chapel and ante-chapel (27).

Tower fillets. In addition to those of the towers at Haddiscoe and Herringfleet, Norman examples elsewhere include Seething, Rushmere and Holton among others, and post-Norman examples include Frostenden, Wramplingham and Lound.

Flint jambs and arches to external openings. Norman flint dressings are seen in the belfry openings in Wortham (59) and Thorington towers, and post-Norman instances in tower windows at Runhall and Morningthorpe and in the jambs of the tower south door at Aylmerton.

Flint jambs and arches to internal openings. The rere-arches of the Norman belfry openings at Gayton Thorpe and Thorpe next Haddiscoe are formed with flints, and there are countless internal tower windows with flint jambs and arches in other Norman and later towers.

26. Double-splayed circular flint window in the tower of Forncett St Peter church.

27. Norman double-splayed rubble window in a wall at Castle Rising

Arches set back from the jamb line at their springing. Norman arch springings of this kind include the flint rear arches of the belfry openings at Thorpe next Haddiscoe and the stone voussoirs of Heckingham tower arch (37).

Flint and ferricrete quoins. Quoins are relevant to round tower dating insofar as the tower may be contemporary with a nave that has quoins of these materials. Flint quoins occur on the Norman middle stage of Guestwick tower and post-Norman examples include the angles of the octagonal belfry at Croxton (V), the nave and aisle quoins at Rackheath and the south-west corner of the fifteenth-century nave extension at Warham St Mary. The window dressings and the large, irregular quoins on the angles of the octagonal tower of Edgefield's abandoned church show a fourteenth-century use of ferricrete (VI).

How then, can one differentiate between pre-Conquest towers and later ones that incorporate features characteristic of Saxon workmanship? One effective method is through the identification in the tower's fabric of materials which are known to have been unavailable before certain times.

A major difference between Saxon and Norman construction in East Anglia lies in the use of limestone for quoins and dressings. East Anglia has no indigenous material comparable to the famous oolitic freestones of the limestone belt further to the west, and although stone from the Barnack quarries near Stamford may occasionally have reached some western parts of the region before the Conquest, the likelihood is that most, if not all, round towers that contain limestone in the original fabric as dressings to openings, in putlog holes or as random pieces amongst the flintwork will be post-Conquest. After the Conquest, Barnack stone was supplemented by the importation of Caen stone from Normandy and its earliest use in East Anglia seems to have been in Norwich Cathedral, started in 1096; it is therefore likely that towers containing Caen stone will not be earlier than the twelfth century unless any such stone in them can be shown to have been inserted. Caen stone is easily distinguished from Barnack: Barnack has a fairly coarse shelly texture whereas Caen is finer grained without shells and is a creamier grey than Barnack.

Unless, therefore, it can be established beyond reasonable doubt or deduced by logical reasoning that features of dressed limestone are later insertions into a tower, it follows that, as integral parts of the structure, they confer a post-Conquest date to the tower. Hence, towers with stone-faced loops, stone plinths and string courses, stone tower arches or stone in belfries that are contemporary with the circular stage are likely to be post-Conquest.

In the east wall of some round towers, above the present nave roof, the profile of an earlier nave roof may be indicated by the sloping stones of projecting weathercourses built into the tower wall; their purpose was to facilitate a neat weathering at the junction of the nave roof, and at Rockland St Peter, where the nave roof is thatched, an example can be seen still fulfilling that function (88). Not to be confused with the copings of the nave west wall gable, weathercourses of this kind are independent of the nave wall. Unlike coping stones, they do not rest on a wall; their stability is dependent on being firmly tailed into the structure, and that implies integral construction with it. Because of the practical difficulties of cutting a diagonal channel of adequate depth into existing curved flintwork and positioning and holding implanted stonework on the slope in slow-setting mortar, it is unlikely that a weathercourse of this kind would be a later insertion, and so it would probably only have been used during a tower's original construction, whether the tower was contemporary with the nave or a later addition.

To support a contention that towers that have this feature may be pre-Conquest and built before stone had become available, it has nevertheless been proposed that stone weathercourses could be post-Conquest insertions. This though is unlikely, not only because of the difficulties of insertion described, but also the fact that satisfactory weathering of a later nave roof to an existing tower wall could have been achieved far more simply with a lead flashing or mortar fillets, as was frequently done. There are countless instances in the medieval period where later roofs of chancels, porches or chapels have been abutted to existing straight flint walls without insertions of weathercourses; they only appear to have been incorporated into 'new' walls, as in the nave east wall at Aylmerton, rebuilt when the nave was enlarged in about 1400. A stone weathercourse in the curved wall of a round tower is unlikely therefore to have been a later insertion, and as an integral part of the structure, it provides evidence that the tower must have been built after ashlar stone had become more widely available, and consequently be of post-Conquest date.

Instances in Norman towers include Holton (77) and Rickinghall Inferior (64), but several occur in towers that can be established on other evidence as post-Norman; the most unusual one is at Edingthorpe where the weathercourse is medieval brick (90). At Frostenden and Stuston tiled nave roofs follow the line of the weathercourses but appreciably below them, as though replacing thicker roofs of thatch; at Ramsholt, different tower fabric above and below the weathercourse is a clear indication of it having been built as part of the tower structure; at Brampton and Norton Subcourse, where the naves were widened southwards in the fourteenth century, the north limb of the weathercourse was extended upwards in the tower wall to suit the higher roofs, and, where inserted at the former, or set in the lower part of the rebuilt belfry at the latter, the extended lengths show as work of a quality different from the lower original length.

In addition to its applications as dressed stone, pieces of limestone, as distinct from erratics, also appear in the wall fabric of several towers, sometimes as random fragments not much larger than the flints, sometimes as broken pieces of moulded stone and sometimes showing the pink colouring of stone that has been subjected to fire. Where the mortar in which these non-conforming pieces of stone are set is continuous with and identical to that of the surrounding flintwork, they are clearly original fabric components and not later repair insertions, and so they are evidence for dating the wall as post-Conquest. Stones of these kinds whose mortar setting clearly shows them to be part of the original fabric are to be found for example in the tower and nave west wall at Merton and in the tower at Lound.

Since the mortar of repair work will always show some variation in colour, texture or composition from the original walling mortar, the mortar in which a wall's flintwork is built can often provide forceful evidence as to whether particular features, stonework or brickwork were original elements of the wall or later insertions. One fascinating case is the circular stage of Heckingham tower where short lengths of Norman billet moulding have been used as putlog hole bridgings (92) and the mortar in which they are set can be clearly seen to be the same as and continuous with the surrounding walling mortar. At

Rushmere, the jointing mortar of the Norman stone quoins at the western corners of the nave has weathered back to such an extent that there can be no doubt that it is the original mortar in which these quoins were set. It can be seen to be continuous with the mortar in which the flints of the nave west wall, the tower fillets and the tower wall are set, thus establishing that all these parts of the church were built together. The stone quoin can therefore date the church, the fillet and the lower part of the tower as Norman since they can all be seen to be original fabric.

Where a nave has been widened or aisles added, former quoins in the west wall or evidence of their removal can sometimes provide indications of the date of the wall in which they were set. Original quoins of flint remain in situ where the nave has been widened on both sides at Titchwell, and flint and stone quoins in the west wall at Hardley show that the nave there has been widened on the north side. Flint quoins are retained in the nave west walls of Bedingham and Burnham Norton among others, where the west walls of later aisles have simply been butted against them, and similarly at Wickmere (28) or Roughton the conglomerate quoins of the nave are still in place at the aisle wall junctions. Although quoins of these types may be pre-Conquest, they are not, as has been shown above, de facto proof of it, but where original Norman features of a tower can be established as being later than a wall containing these quoin types, as at Titchwell for example (see Chapter 12), the probability is that they are pre-Conquest.

28. Original ferricrete nave quoins retained at the junction of the later south aisle at Wickmere.

In contrast to the many cases where flint or ferricrete quoins remain in situ at a junction with later work, there are, with the possible exception of the three squared carstone quoins at the north-west corner of the original nave at Gayton Thorpe, no instances in round towered churches of nave widenings or aisle additions in which dressed stone quoins have been retained at the original nave corners; there are however several cases where the junction between a later wall and the original nave west wall has been made by roughly bonding the later flintwork to the old, e.g. the nave widening at Blundeston or the north aisle addition at Haddiscoe. This implies that where the original quoins had been dressed stone, they were removed before the later walls were added, perhaps to be reused in the later work, but where they had been flint, conglomerate or other inferior material not worth salvaging, they were left in situ. It can therefore be deduced that, where at these positions there are no remnants of former nave quoins, the probability is that they had been dressed stone, and that consequently the nave is likely to be post-Conquest. The north-west corner of Merton church (29) provides a particularly striking example: here, a later buttress in the same plane as the nave west wall has been built, and it is quite obvious from the difference between its flintwork and mortar and that of the nave wall that the buttress fabric extends into the nave west wall to the extent of the space formerly occupied by

stone nave quoins. Similarly at Fishley, the distance between the tower and the line where the later north aisle wall bonds with the nave west wall is less than that between the tower and the south-west nave corner of Caen stone quoins, showing that the north-west nave quoins were removed. The length of the aisle east wall confirms the original north-west corner position

Another case of robbing of quoin stones is apparent at Seething (60) where the nave was widened by rebuilding both side walls a few feet further out than the original alignments (See Chapter 11). No quoins remain at the former south-west and north-west nave corners, and since there would have been no reason to remove them had they been of flint or other inferior material, they were likely to have been dressed stone, thus suggesting a post-Conquest date for the original nave.

29. Merton. Flintwork of an added buttress bonded into the nave west wall where former north-west quoins have been removed. The line of the nave north wall is defined by the right-hand end of the buttress plinth.

Conversely also, where an aisle has been demolished as opposed to added, the nave west wall may be able to show whether the aisle had been an original part of the church or a later addition to the nave. At Syderstone, for example, where it is obvious from the blocked Norman south arcade that a Norman aisle has been demolished, the south-west corner of the nave is of flints (30); but these are not flint quoins, they are the facing flints of normal walling that with the help of a few inserted pieces have been trimmed to make a vertical angle at the point where the aisle west wall was removed. This is confirmed by the south face of this corner; it is not a former external surface but a patched-up cross-section of the original aisle west wall, still showing the built-in faces of stonework of the western arch of the arcade. It follows therefore that the west walls of the nave and the aisle were of a single build, proving that the church is the same date as the Norman arcade.

Just as the use of ashlared limestone for quoins and dressings can be a means of differentiating between pre- and post-Conquest towers, so can the use of medieval brick distinguish post-Norman towers from Norman ones. As regards dating, the introduction of medieval bricks in the later thirteenth century and the early fourteenth was of great significance because their presence as part of the original fabric of a tower must inevitably bestow on it a post-Norman date. Their use for framing and bridging putlog holes, a requirement only necessary during the original construction of a wall, and the way they are laid in window arches demonstrate convincingly that they were not later insertions or repairs but were part of the original structure of the towers in which they occur; thus they positively date those towers as no earlier than when such bricks came into use. As would be expected in the second half of the thirteenth century and after, all such towers have pointed tower arches, corroborating a post-Norman attribution, and conversely, of all the towers with round-headed tower arches none have medieval bricks in their fabric except Ramsholt which can be shown to have been built after the Norman tower arch in the nave wall (see Chapter 14). Other dating evidence which tower arches can provide is discussed in the next two chapters.

There are about thirty round towers in which medieval bricks occur in the original parts of the tower in applications in which it is improbable that they could have been later insertions. In none of these is there any evidence of Norman or earlier work.

30. The south-west nave corner at Syderstone church where the west wall of a demolished aisle was originally integral with the nave west wall.

Since knapped flints, as opposed to those with irregular broken faces, do not appear in flint walls much before the end of the thirteenth century, their inclusion in a tower's facing material can be regarded as an indication of a fourteenth-century or later date. In the circular-stage fabric of the towers at Edingthorpe and Potter Heigham knapped flints of a quality not found before the early fourteenth century are mixed with flint rubble or cobbles and comprise perhaps up to a quarter of the facing material, their extent being much greater and their distribution more composed than can be accounted for as repairs. At Surlingham and Tuttington (79), they make up more than half of the total, and at Cockley Cley they were used decoratively in two bands encircling the tower (73). The highest standard of workmanship, though, is found on the semi-ruined tower at Wolterton (6) where the circular stage and the octagonal belfry both have a facing entirely of knapped flints with galleting in characteristically fifteenth-century style.

Diagnostic features of pre- and post-Conquest belfry windows were discussed in Chapter 3; smaller windows in round towers can also provide information for dating. A tower window with external dressings of stone or medieval brick could be an original feature of the tower's construction or it could have been inserted in the wall at a later date; alternatively, its dressings may be just a later enhancement of a previously flint window. Perhaps because of the number of towers that have small windows with pointed heads of stone or medieval brick, the idea became prevalent that their facings must be later enhancements. If most round towers were Norman, it was argued, then most windows with pointed, square, or brick heads must have been modified or inserted later, and likewise, in towers thought to be Saxon, the same would apply to round-headed stone windows. With careful examination though, it is often possible to establish whether a window was built integrally with the wall or broken through later, and whether the external dressings are original or inserted; this provides valuable evidence for dating the tower.

31. Board-marks of the shuttering on which the splayed internal arches of loops at Barsham tower were built can be seen to be in contact with the back of the exterior facing stonework.

32. Medieval bricks in the internal arch soffit of one of the original lancet belfry openings below the present octagonal belfry in Needham tower.

Apart from very narrow unsplayed slit openings crudely spanned with large flints, small tower window openings that were formed as the wall was being built are usually splayed internally and spanned with an arch. The inside jambs may be formed with flints or flint and brick and sometimes incorporate dressed stones; arches are flint or brick, and rubble flint voussoirs at the inside wall face may often give the impression of being laid non-radially because of the irregularity of the material. For the same reason, the shapes of the interior arches can be quite irregular and may differ from the exterior head shape.

The soffit material of flint arches is usually the mortar in which the arch flints were set and may show the board-marks of the centering on which the arch was built. Where the board-marks on the arch soffit are contiguous or nearly so with the backs of the external stone voussoirs, as in the small tower windows at Thorington and Barsham (31) for example, that establishes beyond any doubt that the external stonework was built with the opening and not inserted later, confirming a post-Conquest date, and if the arch is round-headed and of Caen stone, probably a twelfth-century one. In brick arches which extend through the wall, the arrangement of the bricks on the soffit is clear evidence that they also were also built on centering (32).

In order to construct arches of flint or brick on centering in walls which may be over four feet thick, it is necessary for the builder to be able to reach the centre of the wall to actually place the material; this fact alone is a good indication that a window with such an arch would have been an original part of the wall because that method of construction could not be employed in an existing wall of the thickness of the average tower wall without considerable disturbance to it inside and out. A hole through the existing wall, wider than the window's internal splay would have been required which would have had to be needled and propped to prevent collapse of the flintwork above; the hole would have had to be high enough to allow the builder to lean over the finished arch level inside and out in order to actually build the arch on the shuttering and to pin up from it to support the wall above. However skilfully the walls were subsequently made good externally, it is likely that some indication of insertion would remain, particularly above the arch internally, and so if the flintwork at the sides and above an arched window opening is undisturbed (47), that is a very positive indication that the window was built as an integral part of the wall.

Because of the capability of the masonry above a hole cut through an existing wall to act as a natural arch, it is possible to form small openings in existing flint walls without the necessity for a structural arch or lintel at the head, and window openings of this kind have been broken out through the walls of some round towers. In unplastered tower interiors they are easily distinguished from openings that were formed when the wall was built by the irregularity of their reveals and soffit and by the absence of any arch-voussoirs in their construction. Even when roughly rendered, the method of their formation is still usually apparent. On the belfry of Hengrave church tower, external patched flintwork surrounding two pointed windows at south-east and north-east shows that they have been inserted, and this is confirmed internally by comparing them with the round-headed north, west and south windows that were built with the wall: the differences in construction are unmistakable. A similar comparison can be made at Gayton Thorpe between the board-marked splays of the upper west window of the tower, built with the wall, and the rough irregular splays of the inserted lower window. The small west window in Welborne tower is another example of an inserted window; its crudely-shaped jambs and head and the lack of arch-voussoirs are characteristic features of an opening cut through an existing wall.

In the light of the practical constructional difficulties of building arched openings in existing thick walls and the fact that small openings without an arch or lintel can be comparatively easily formed, it is not unreasonable to conclude that where tower windows have arches of flint, brick or stone that were built on centering and there is no evidence of disturbance to the flintwork above them and each side, those windows would have been part of the wall's original construction, and consequently their characteristics would date the wall.

Comparative wall thicknesses have long been considered to be a means of differentiating pre- and post-Conquest walls, and although no systematic study has, it seems, been made to establish its validity, a widely-held notion has persisted that Norman parish church walls were thicker than Saxon ones. Now, as an extension of this idea, it has been further claimed that specific wall thicknesses and nave widths can be used to separate pre- and post-Conquest flint round towers and churches.

The conventional wisdom, recognized with reservations by Baldwin Brown and the Taylors, that generally speaking, Norman walls were thicker than Saxon probably derives largely from wall thickness comparisons of Saxon and Norman churches built of stone. But in relation to flint walls, no consideration appears to have been given to the possibility that the Normans, being unused to building with flint before their arrival in England and then being faced with this unfamiliar material, or Anglo-Saxon builders under Norman direction would not immediately have departed from well-tried indigenous methods of construction, and their flint walls would therefore have been built in the same way and generally to the same thicknesses as previously. In any event, local labour rather than Norman newcomers would be more likely to have been employed on minor churches, and traditional techniques would no doubt have prevailed for some time after the Conquest. Changes of technology, and this also applies to the introduction of dressed stone, would have been very gradual at this level.

It has been said that the Normans built thicker flint walls because their mortar was inferior; although Norman masons in control of major projects like Norwich Cathedral may have followed imported practices, elsewhere the mortar would probably still have been prepared by local artisans in the same way as previously with ingredients from the same local sources as before the Conquest. In any case, are there any grounds for the contention that Norman mortar was inferior to Saxon, or is this simply one of those unproved myths that has been repeated so often that it has entered the domain of fact? If Norman buildings have stood for 900 years, their mortar can't be much inferior to Saxon!

It has also been suggested that Norman walls had to be thicker than Saxon walls because, whereas the latter were built of solid flints right through, the Normans are said to have built solid inner and outer skins and filled between with small flints and rubble. Although some Norman stone walls (and for that matter later ones) may have been found to be ashlar-faced with rubble infill, is there any evidence that any Norman walls wholly of *flint* have been built in this way? As suggested above, is it not more likely that the Normans would have followed established practice rather than experiment in a medium with which they were unaccustomed?

In their comments on comparative thicknesses of Saxon and Norman walls, Baldwin Brown and the Taylors refer only to church walls and give no indications of wall thicknesses to be expected in Saxon and Norman church towers, stone or flint, round or square. Even were it to be established that flint walls of Norman churches are generally thicker than Saxon, it doesn't follow that this would necessarily apply to tower walls as, Saxon or Norman, they are generally appreciably thicker than church walls anyway. It is pertinent therefore to question whether there are any grounds for a basic assumption that

Norman round tower walls were thicker than Saxon ones.

An inherent weakness of the idea that a specific wall thickness can be a demarcation between Saxon and Norman towers, lies in the fact that no satisfactory method of validation of a particular measurement has been established and in any event, the thickness of a flint wall measured at different places can vary by inches. On what grounds can any particular measurement be defined as a minimum thickness for Norman walls? If it is accepted that Norman tower walls were built, say, four feet thick, how can it be said that some might not have been built one, two, or three inches thinner?

Of all the round towers whose circular stage is earlier than about 1200 AD, i.e. before the post-Norman period, the wall thicknesses of those that have been claimed as Saxon vary between 2'10" and 4'10", and as Norman tower walls can be shown to have a similar range of thicknesses, there seems to be no basis for establishing any particular thickness as a reputable threshold between Saxon and Norman. It is much more likely that tower walls of typical, average thicknesses could be Saxon, Norman or post-Norman.

There is no reason to suppose that the thickness of a round tower's walls is related to its building period; other practical factors, such as height or the bearing capacity of the ground are more likely to have been of greater relevance. The tower walls at Forncett St. Peter, for instance, widely accepted as Saxon, were probably made more than four feet thick because of the tower's original 58-foot height and those at Hasketon may have been made five feet thick because of its intended height of 60 feet (its features suggest it was of a single post-Norman build); the walls of the unattached tower at Bramfield were probably made 4'6" thick to compensate for the absence of stability normally provided by attachment to the church, and the thick walls of Syleham tower may have been necessitated by unreliable soil conditions of the low-lying ground where it is situated.

The theory that pre- and post-Conquest churches can be differentiated by their nave widths needs only a brief mention. A width of twenty feet has been defined as a dividing line between the two periods, it being claimed that all naves of less than this width were built before the Conquest. How the measurement was established remains unexplained, and the large number of round-towered church naves less than twenty feet wide that possess no reliable pre-Conquest evidence illustrates the fragility of the theory – a theory that apparently relies on an assumption that naves with walls less than three feet thick cannot be Norman.

It is improbable that the nave widths of small churches of the eleventh, twelfth and thirteenth centuries derived from the period in which they were built; it is more likely that they were dictated mainly by the width that could be conveniently spanned by available timber beams for the simple roofs that would have been used on these early small churches. As a general rule, this would not often have exceeded about twenty feet during those three centuries. The size of a particular church would presumably have been dependant on the size of the population it served and its length decided accordingly, the width being fairly standard as governed by the timbers.

The idea that specific measurements for wall thickness or nave width can be markers for separating different architectural periods is essentially unsafe since, by setting the measurements at particular values, it could be possible to manipulate attributions that depended on them.

CHAPTER 6

ROUND TOWERS – CONTEMPORARY WITH THE NAVE OR ADDED?

Since the only round towers that can be shown to pre-date their churches are the few where an earlier church has been replaced or rebuilt in later medieval times as at Aylmerton, Blundeston and Tuttington for example, or in the nineteenth century as at Keswick, there remains for the rest the question of whether they were built at the same time as their churches or whether they were later additions. This is important because a church's features may be relevant to the date of its tower.

Before examining ways of distinguishing contemporary towers from later ones, it is important to appreciate two facts which have a bearing on how the junction between a tower and a nave is made.

Firstly, the walls of a round tower are usually appreciably thicker than the nave walls. On average, tower walls are about 3'9" thick whereas nave walls might be about a foot less, with the west wall sometimes three or four inches thicker; a tower built against an earlier church and showing the flat nave wall within, will therefore inevitably have a thinner east wall above because the upper part is built on the thinner nave wall. The effect of this is that externally the tower east wall above the nave roof shows as a flattened curve giving the tower a D-shaped or distorted oval form, (e.g. Gayton Thorpe). Apparent ovality of the upper part of a tower is more an indication of how it joins the nave, rather than of archaic workmanship.

Secondly, when a parallel-sided or splayed archway is formed through the curved wall of a round tower, the wall thickness measured centrally at the apex of the arch which represents the actual combined thickness of the nave and tower walls, will be less than if measured at the reveals, and consequently the face of the arch at the apex in the tower will be in a different plane from the face of the archway jambs; this gives the face of the actual arch in the curving wall an odd distorted profile above its springing level and would make it more awkward to build. There are nevertheless many tower arches like that, some of them formed with dressed stone and some without. It appears though, that in order to avoid an arch with the kind of distortion described, the east wall of the ground stage of a few internally circular towers (e.g. Herringfleet) was deliberately built flat.

When seeking to establish whether a round tower was built with its church or added to an earlier one, there may be direct visual evidence, or evidence may become revealed during alterations or repairs, that a particular church once stood without a west tower: from within the upper part of the towers at West Dereham and Gayton Thorpe, the shape of the original nave west wall gable can be seen with the tower east wall superstructure built onto it; at Gayton Thorpe and Pentlow stonework of the tower archway, formerly a west entrance to the nave, is partially covered by the later tower walls; and at Thorpe-next-Haddiscoe and Welborne there is a window in the nave west wall.

Occasionally direct evidence may show or imply that a tower and nave are contemporary. At Quidenham, coursed flints of the nave west wall match exactly and align with those in the fillet and tower wall (33), showing beyond reasonable doubt that the nave and tower were built together, and at Herringfleet, a curved east wall upwards from first-floor level in the tower above a thicker, flat nave west wall on the ground floor would clearly not have been the gable of a former towerless nave, thus proving that church and tower must have been a single build. At Beachamwell, since the early belfry details could hardly be later than the long-and-short Barnack stone quoin on the north-west corner of the nave, the implication is that the nave and tower are contemporary.

33. Barnack stone quoins on the north-west corner of Quidenham church nave, with the flintwork of the nave west wall coursing with the flintwork of the fillet and tower. The knapped flint to the left of the quoins is a later facing of the nave north wall.

In the absence of such clear indications in most churches, it has been proposed that a flat east wall within the tower indicates that the tower has been built onto an existing church, and conversely that a curved east wall implies that church and tower were built together. However, these homespun formulae take no account of instances where the flatness or curvature of a tower's east wall is independent of whether the tower was built with the church or added later.

The idea that a flat east wall in a tower indicates that the tower was added to an existing church is based on the belief that the flat wall is the nave west wall of a formerly towerless church and there are many cases where this is confirmed by the absence of any bond between tower and church; sometimes a probe can be inserted between the two walls. But this cannot always be assumed without verifying by measurement that the wall thickness at the apex of the tower arch is the same as for the nave west wall outside the tower; even if it is, it is not proof that the flat wall within the tower is the west face of a formerly towerless nave because, as shown at Herringfleet, it may only be flat in the ground stage. Also, a flat east wall that is thicker at the tower arch than the nave west wall measured outside the tower, as at Rockland St Peter, clearly cannot be the face of an original nave wall.

Where a church was originally towerless, it is probable that the thickness of the nave side and west walls would not have been greatly different, although the west wall might be expected to be a little thicker because of its greater height. And so, where the nave west wall measured outside the tower is substantially thicker than the nave side walls, being the same thickness as the tower wall as at Gissing, Rushmere, Quidenham, Herringfleet and Little Saxham or thicker as at Hardley, it is most likely that tower and nave were built together because if the church had originally been towerless, there is no reason why the nave west wall should have been so much thicker than the side walls.

If a tower added to an existing nave had been required to have a reasonably good circular shape at upper level externally (as opposed to the oval or D-shape as described above), it would have been so positioned that the east wall thickness at the tower arch apex (including the existing nave west wall) would equate approximately to the tower walls proper and the flat face of the nave west wall would have disappeared behind the inner curvature of the material used to increase its thickness to that of the tower walls. The east and west walls of the tower would therefore be about the same thickness, but the curved east wall would be thicker than the nave west wall measured outside the tower (e.g. Thorpe Abbotts). Likewise, if a tower built with the nave was to appear circular above the nave roof, its east wall would be likely to have been made about the same thickness as the rest of the tower wall, whether internally curved as at Little Saxham, or flat at ground level as at Herringfleet, irrespective of the nave west wall thickness.

If a tower with a curved east wall internally has been added to a church, the thickness at the tower arch apex will obviously be at least a few inches more than the nave west wall's original thickness (indicated by its thickness measured outside the tower), the extra representing the minimum thickness of a curved layer of flints superimposed over the original west face of the nave wall.

Conversely, where the thickness of a curved east wall at the tower arch is the same as or less than that of the nave west wall measured outside the tower (e.g. Haddiscoe), church and tower must have been built together because otherwise, quite unnecessary and improbable structural disturbance to an existing nave west wall would have been necessary to accommodate within it the the tower's internal east curvature.

In most towers that have a flat east wall, the width of the flat part is greater than the width of the tower arch, but in a few towers the width of the flat part is, surprisingly, less than the tower arch width. In these cases, where the circular profile changes to flat, the flintwork coursing nevertheless continues uninterruptedly indicating that the circular and flat parts of the wall were of the same build. Quidenham is one such tower, and this detail corroborates the external evidence of contemporary construction of this nave and tower referred to above.

These considerations show that towers built with their churches and those that have been added can both have curved or flat east walls within. It cannot therefore be determined with any certainty purely on the flatness or curvature of a tower's east wall whether a tower was built with its church or added later. In order to make a reasoned judgement on this, it is necessary not only to establish the thickness of the nave west wall outside the tower as well as at the tower arch, but also to take account of the internal tower shape at upper level and the evidence provided by other features.

Foremost among this other evidence is the external flintwork; if tower and church had been built together, it is to be expected that the flintwork of both would be similar, as shown for example, by a comparison of the nave west wall and the tower at Little Saxham. A difference therefore, between a church's original fabric and the tower flintwork, as seen at Gresham (VII) for instance, is a strong indication that the tower is a different build and has therefore probably been added.

At certain churches, Ilketshall St Andrew and Old Catton for example, the opening between nave and tower can be seen to comprise two distinct and separate arches– one passing through the original nave west wall and the other built as part of the tower's

curved east wall. This shows that the tower is a separate entity and is thus clear proof that it was added to an earlier nave.

Where a tower arch is formed in medieval brick through a nave wall clearly built before medieval brick had become available, as at Fritton St Edmund or Aldham, those are obvious cases of the towers having been added. Similarly, where there is medieval brick in the tower fabric, as at Fritton and Aldham and in many others where the church walls can be shown to pre-date the bricks in the tower, the bricks establish those towers as added.

At Fritton, a segment of the tower's curved east wall projects into the nave above the tower arch; since this cantilever type of construction is most unlikely to have been used had the tower been contemporary with the early church, it is another indication of the tower being later. The same could be said of Burgh Castle church where part of the tower's east wall is corbelled over the nave west wall above the tower arch.

34. Chevron-moulded Norman stones reset in the head and jambs of the depressed-pointed tower arch at Runhall.

Recycled masonry in a tower arch can also be an indication of an added tower. Assuming that such masonry came from a redundant or altered feature of the church, it is obvious that any feature in which it is reset must be later than the structure from which it came. A few large stones, identifiable by their chevron mouldings as Norman, used randomly in the construction of the low, pointed tower arch at Runhall (34) clearly date it, and hence the tower, as later than the church. The upper door can also provide other valuable pointers. Where medieval brick has been used in its construction but the church has evidence of pre-thirteenth-century work, as at West Somerton, that is a clear

35. Unlike in most round towers, the east wall of Topcroft tower is built up against the nave west wall rather than on top of it.

indication that the tower has been added to an existing church.

In some upper doors, for instance at Edingthorpe, two distinct arches can be seen, one cut through the original nave wall and the other built as part of the wall of an added tower. By contrast, a clear opening with uniform reveals and arch through the full wall thickness (as far as can be seen) probably implies original construction rather than an opening broken through an existing wall, particularly where, as at Haddiscoe, the opening has stone dressings both sides.

Where a former window in the nave west wall has been converted into an upper door, this is obviously proof that the tower has been added to a previously towerless church. This is the situation at East Walton and Rushall where, within the tower at first-floor level, there is indisputable evidence that the openings were originally pointed windows; stone dressings have clearly been removed from around the arch and jambs, and at Rushall, the window reveals splayed towards the nave can also be seen. The size of the lower lancet window in East Walton tower corresponds so well with the size of the upper door as to suggest that its stone dressings could be those from the former nave west window.

The east walls of most towers, whether contemporary with the church or added later, are to a greater or lesser extent built as part of the nave west wall or onto it, but there are a few towers that seem to be virtually independent structures. When viewed from the side, they appear to be tangential to the nave west wall, and internally, the thickness of the wall measured at the apex of the tower arch is roughly equivalent to that of the nave and tower walls added together.

Wramplingham, Welborne and Broomfield – three towers built to this plan arrangement – all have evidence confirming the external impression they give of being additions to an existing church; all have generous fillets to fill the very acute-angled gap that occurs between a nave and tower built in this way, and the flintwork of the fillets can be clearly seen to be different from that in the nave walls. Although similarly positioned relative to the nave, the tower at Topcroft (35) is a little different in that its upper stages are octagonal; the flat east facet of the octagon is built against the flat west face of the nave gable, and where the low circular stage meets the nave west wall, instead of fillets, its outer circumference appears to have been widened to a horse-shoe shape to reduce the acute angle at the junction.

CHAPTER 7

TOWER ARCHES

On the assumption that a tower arch would have been formed when a tower was built, whether concurrently with the church or as a later addition, it is to be expected that, unless it had formerly been a west door to the church or the tower had been rebuilt, logically it should indicate the date of the tower. There are cases, though, of eleventh- or twelfth-century towers with pointed tower arches and post-Norman towers with round-headed ones. With little doubt, the former result from alterations, and these are discussed more fully below. A probable explanation of the latter is that the arch may originally have given access to an earlier tower that has been replaced by the present one – judging from the number of round towers that have collapsed during living or recorded memory, it is to be expected that a number of ancient ones are likely also to have been lost in earlier times, to be replaced by later medieval ones.

Several aspects of tower arch design have relevance to the dating of round towers and to whether they were contemporary with or added to the nave. These are now examined.

Splayed Tower Arches

Tower arches which on plan are splayed into the tower, whether low arches as at Runhall, Thorpe next Haddiscoe, East Walton or Tuttington, or relatively taller ones as at Eccles and Fritton, St Edmund, are good indications of arches formed at the time the tower was built whether as part of the original church or added later as it is unlikely that a splayed opening would formerly have been a western entrance to the church and there seems no logical reason why an opening that was originally parallel-sided should have been altered to this plan shape. Also, the reveals are clearly not those of a Saxon or Norman west entrance as early doorways went straight through the wall with parallel sides, Norman ones usually having a rebate on the inside for the actual door. It therefore follows that towers with splayed arches are likely to be post-Norman, a probability confirmed by the fact that none are semi-circular and virtually all have pointed heads. Exceptions at Thorpe next Haddiscoe and East Walton, where flat segmental arches are constructed with brick, have apparently been modified, though it is difficult to understand why.

Tall Tower Arches

Tower arches with semi-circular heads which are tall and narrow such as those at Bedingham, Forncett St Peter and Tasburgh (within the tower) are widely considered to be characteristic Saxon features, but it should be recognised that tall and narrow proportions are not exclusive to Saxon tower arches. Haddiscoe and Little Saxham, where the openings are framed with dressed stone, provide two post-Conquest examples, and later arches of comparable proportions but with pointed heads are found in post-Norman towers, such as Shimpling and Hasketon. Conversely, there are low tower arches or doorways of all periods.

The persistence of the tall tower arch through the Norman period and into the post-

Norman seems to indicate the continuance in some churches of a requirement for this feature while at the same time lower arches were acceptable in others. It can even be shown that some low arches were heightened, for instance, the present tall pointed arch at Holton St Peter (see chapter 15).

Tall arches allow better admission of light from a west window in the tower but as most early round towers had no west window or only a small one, this is unlikely to have been the reason for tall arches. The use of tall banner staves has been suggested as another reason and this idea is borne out by two semi-circular recesses in the walls, 14 inches wide x $7^{1}/_{2}$ inches deep, for the full height of the ground stage of Haddiscoe tower, whose purpose may have been the storage of the staves. Perhaps the churches with lower arches used shorter banner staves.

A tall tower arch is a fairly safe indication that it was never originally a west entrance, but was formed when the tower was built, whether contemporary with the nave or added later.

Low Tower Arches

It has often been assumed that if a tower arch is a low one, of the height and proportions of a doorway, then it must have been the original west door of a previously towerless church. However, there are circumstances, such as the splayed openings described above, where the characteristics of the opening indicate that it would not have been a west entrance but that it had been built as a low tower arch, either with the church or formed as one in the nave west wall later, when a tower was added to a towerless church.

Where the impost returns of a semi-circular tower arch are returned on the nave wall face and in the tower, this is a sure indication that it was formed as a tower arch because the projecting impost mouldings would make it impossible to hang a door within the opening or on the nave face. Little Bradley has a low arch of this kind in the nave west wall, but as the tower walls overlap the impost returns on the tower side of the wall, the tower is apparently a later one than the one for which the Norman tower arch was formed. (see Chapter 14)

If, therefore, an opening has not been altered, or the tower rebuilt to replace an earlier one as must have happened in other cases besides Little Bradley, this kind of low arch between nave and tower must be of the same date as the tower.

Where the impost mouldings are returned on the tower side only, a low arch could have been a west entrance to the church, with the door hung to the nave face.

Flint, Brick and Plastered Tower Arches

As freestone was not generally available in East Anglia before the late eleventh century, or medieval brick before the late thirteenth, Saxon tower arches would necessarily have been formed with flints, or sometimes ferricrete. That is not to say that arches were never built with these materials after the Conquest. That archways have been formed with flint jambs and heads as late as the fourteenth century is shown for example by doorways in Norwich city walls or the arcade at Heckingham church where pointed arches were cut through the former north wall and finished without stone dressings. The absence of dressed stone is not therefore an indication that flint tower arches are pre-

TOWER ARCHES

Conquest arches altered to pointed shape to comply with the current architectural style as has been suggested; rather, it tends to confirm that that is their original shape because if they had been altered for aesthetic reasons they would probably also have been given stone dressings. Many pointed tower arches with a plaster finish give access to towers with no pre-Gothic evidence and it is therefore entirely plausible that these arches are original and unaltered and contemporary with the tower; clearly, if a plaster finish to the arch had been intended from the outset, there would have been no point in using stone in its construction.

Several towers have windows with jambs and heads incorporating medieval brick which can be shown to have been built with the tower wall and not inserted later, and it is not unreasonable to expect that plastered tower arches which give access to these towers may be of similar construction. Medieval bricks in quantity in the tower arches at Fritton St Edmund and Edingthorpe can be clearly seen within the tower and in the tower arch reveals and nave west wall at Burlingham St Peter (VIII), and the way they are used shows that they must have been part of the original construction of these arches and not later restorations. Any tower arches formed with medieval bricks are unlikely to be earlier than the fourteenth century, and so unless there is any evidence to the contrary, towers to which they give access will be post-Norman.

Many round-headed tower arches have a plaster finish and since no stone dressings can be seen, it might be assumed that the edges of the opening are formed with flints, but this is not always so. At Beachamwell (36), where plaster has been stripped from the tower arch face and soffit, stone voussoirs that have been scored as a key for plaster are revealed, and likewise at Fritton St Catherine, recent stripping of a small area of plaster at the arch shows stonework underneath. Generally though, where the builders' intention had been simply to plaster the arch, presumably for economy as often seems the case, there would have been no need for stone dressings.

36. The tower arch at Beachamwell. Plaster has been stripped from the arch face and soffit, revealing stone construction, the stones being scored to form a key for the plaster

Cruck-shaped Arches.

It is important to appreciate the distinction between an ordinary pointed arch and a type described by H.M. & J.Taylor as a cruck-shaped arch. Their definitive example of this type seems to be the chancel arch at West Barsham church, the general shape of which can be roughly described as half a vertical ellipse; the arch curvature starts at floor level and the apex is radiused. The Taylors describe it thus[1]: "of most unusual shape, as though it had been built over the inverted hull of a boat or over a pair of crucks that were often used for framing the gable ends of medieval houses", and they infer a pre-Conquest date. The 1999 edition of Pevsner's Buildings of England, however, describes the West Barsham chancel arch as part of a restoration of 1935-8; this seems much more likely, since a span of 13'9" is very wide for a Saxon arch and there is no authenticated Saxon precedent for an arch of this shape. The Taylors describe in the same way the tower arches at Wickmere and Roughton and tentatively assign them to the Saxo-Norman Period "C", (1050-1100). There, the arch curvatures spring from lower than normal though above floor level and the apexes are rounded, but there is no certainty that they are original unaltered arches; in fact at Wickmere the opening is of the double type with a higher arch on the tower side.

Stephen Heywood[2] refers to four other examples – at Onehouse, Letheringsett, Guestwick and the city walls in Norwich. Though not rounded at the apex, the plain pointed arches of the arcade at Heckingham could also be described as cruck-chaped, being nearly 14 feet high with the arch curvature springing from about six feet above the floor.

In the belief that the type could have "Saxon implications", tower arches at Aylmerton, East Lexham, Needham, Rushall, Shimpling, Stody, Titchwell,, Fostenden, Holton and Syleham have also been called cruck-shaped. Of these, though, only the one at East Lexham has a rounded apex; Titchwell has an odd distorted profile and Rushall has a Tudor-style depressed head, but the others are ordinary plain plastered pointed arches. This list is longer than others because the scope of the Taylors' definition has been expanded to include arches regarded as having a "cruck-shaped head". That expression could, of course, apply to the head of almost any pointed arch and so seems to nullify the special meaning that the Taylors' original description "cruck-shaped" imparts. Their analogies of an inverted boat or the frame of a cruck house indicate that the term "cruck-shaped arch" applies to an archway with a low springing level, not just to the head of an ordinary pointed arch; nowhere do they describe an arch as having a cruck-shaped head.

Notwithstanding his tentative dating of the Wickmere and Roughton examples, H.M.Taylor apparently didn't regard cruck-shaped arches as a reliable indication of Saxon work because they are not included in his detailed summary of features characteristic of Anglo-Saxon style[3].

Several of the towers to which these arches give access have no pre-Conquest or Norman features and some can be convincingly shown to be post-Norman, and as the form has been proved to have been current in the early Gothic period, it is clear that this type of arch is neither a positive indication of pre-Conquest work nor a reliable diagnostic feature for dating.

Double Arches

In the double tower arch arrangement at Ilketshall St Andrew and Old Catton referred to in the last chapter, each of the two arch elements are pointed and those in the tower are taller than the ones in the nave wall, so that from inside the tower the west face of the nave wall can be seen above the apex of the 'nave' arch. Comparison of the wall thickness at the 'nave' arch with that of the nave west wall measured outside the tower, showing them to be about the same thickness, provides confirmation that the wall at the nave arch is indeed the original nave west wall. The double arch arrangement also occurs at Wramplingham but there, the two arches are the same height at the interface of the original nave west wall and the added tower's east wall. As a result, the west face of the nave wall does not show although its position is discernable from cracks in the plaster and the start of a splay of the opening towards the tower.

A rare, probably unique, variant of the double tower arch is a type seen at Pentlow where two separate arches are formed within the thickness of the nave west wall. A plain Norman arch of dressed stone with radial voussoirs appears to have been formed within an earlier doorway and then a later Norman arch with engaged shafts, scalloped capitals and moulded arch superimposed on the west face of the earlier one; these are clearly separate builds because there is a straight vertical joint at their interface, and their springing levels, architectural details and stone coursing do not coincide. Where the walls of the tower meet the nave west wall, they cover the mouldings of the later arch, clearly showing that the tower was a later addition still. The tower has Y-tracery belfry openings and in the absence of any Norman features, the conclusion must be that it is post-Norman as it seems most unlikely that there would have been three phases of Norman building.

Although not appertaining to tower arches, a type of double arch should be mentioned that is often used in nave doorways where a round-headed or pointed door opens inwards within the thickness of a wall. In those cases, in order to allow the door to be fully opened to 90°, the inner, or rere-arch of the opening has to be taller than the outer arch and the door, with the springing of the inner arch not lower than the crown of the door. Non-appreciation of this necessity has sometimes led to a mistaken interpretation of a taller round-headed rere-arch behind a Norman doorway as being a Saxon arch into which the Norman arch has been inserted.

Depressed Tower Arches

Depressed arch shapes can be considered as including four-centred pointed arches with a low pitch, three-centred arches, pointed segmental, segmental arches and so-called Tudor arches, and despite the fact that these are generally considered to be late Gothic styles, they are found in early fourteenth-century and even late thirteenth-century tower arches in round towers. To dispel any doubt that depressed arches were used from early Gothic times, one has only to notice the great numbers of rere-arches of these shapes behind pointed and even round-headed north and south nave doorways of all dates. They have also been used quite often as rere-arches within the tower behind normal two-centred arches facing the nave as can be seen at Runhall and Old Catton, or behind an earlier Norman arch at Ramsholt. Depressed arches of these kinds may go straight through the wall as at Rushall, but at Hemblington, behind the apparently stone head facing the nave, a series of five upward steppings of the same profile form a unique rere-arch. Except where there is clear evidence to the contrary as at Beeston St Lawrence for example, there seem no good reasons for believing that the towers in which these depressed arches occur are not contemporary with them and therefore that the towers are post-Norman.

Unaltered Arches

Tower arches that are unlikely to have been altered do not follow set patterns but are identified through having particular characteristics which suggest or show that the arch must in all probability have been built as now seen.

Simple plastered pointed arches generally, though there are exceptions, are more likely to be original than altered because if they had been earlier round-headed arches altered

for reasons of architectural fashion, it is most unlikely that a face-lift of that order would have been limited to just the alteration of the arch shape without the additional embellishment of stone dressings; such an alteration would have been an awkward and structurally risky undertaking for little aesthetic and no functional gain.

At Heckingham (37), the tower arch soffit is unplastered and the board-marks of the centering on which the round-headed arch was built can be seen to extend right to the back of the voussoir stones of the arch dressings; this proves that the stonework and the flint soffit of the arch were built on the same centering, and hence that the arch is unaltered because if the stonework had been inserted later, there would be discontinuity between the arch's board-marks and later inserted stonework. (Although the stonework proves that the arch is Norman, the present tower appears to be a post-Norman replacement of the original Norman tower because the circular stage contains putlog holes framed and bridged with sections of Norman stone billet mould, probably taken from

37. Heckingham tower arch, showing the shuttering board-marks contiguous with the backs of the dressed voussoir stones

the outer order of the north door arch when it was reset in the thinner north aisle wall.)

At Bartlow, the integration of the dressed stonework and flintwork of the tower arch within the tower is executed in such manner as would have been virtually impossible to achieve if the tower and tower arch had not been built at the same time or if an earlier tower arch had been altered. The tower arch is pointed and dates the whole tower as probably late in the Early English period, an attribution consistent with the lancet belfry openings.

The tower arch at Runhall (34) is datable as post-Norman by the Early English stone doorway on the nave side, within a depressed-pointed (Tudor-style) backing arch in whose jambs and head a few carved Norman stones are randomly incorporated. The grounds for belief that the arch was originally built like this rather than being an altered earlier arch are, firstly, that it is a structural arch extending through the full thickness of the wall between tower and nave whereas if its purpose had been simply to reduce the size of a former larger opening or to update an earlier arch to Gothic style, it would have been built as a relatively thin membrane rather than the full wall thickness, secondly, there is no evidence of an earlier, larger arch which the present arch might be supposed to have filled, and thirdly, the splayed reveals, as mentioned above, are indicative of original construction because there seems no plausible reason for alteration of an originally straight-sided opening. If, as the evidence suggests, the tower arch, dateable by the Norman stones in it, is an unaltered opening formed when the tower was added, then the tower will not be earlier, despite its flint-framed lancets that have been widely regarded as exclusively Saxon. It was probably built when the nave north door, presumably originally Norman, was converted to pointed shape and its billet hoodmould reset above the adjacent pointed window.

Altered Arches

The obvious cases of alteration are pointed arches in towers which are undisputedly pre-Gothic, such as Beeston St Lawrence, Wortham, Snailwell or Holton, and arches which clearly have Victorian or later stonework embellishment such as Thorington. Less immediately obvious cases include those where there is architectural evidence like the different stone of arch and jambs at Barmer or the remnants of stone impost returns of an earlier arch as in the tower at Woodton which now has a lower pointed arch.

Apart from cases of this kind which are not difficult to identify, there are four main types of modification which could have been made to existing earlier arches, as follows:
Case 1. *The angles at the reveals of the jambs and the voussoirs of the arch, originally of flint, could have been replaced with dressed stone.*

In simple round-headed tower arches, while jambs and heads formed with flints may suggest pre-Conquest work, dressed stone implies a post-Conquest date. It is however not usually possible to be certain whether such stonework is original or a later aesthetic enhancement unless the tower contains other positive Saxon or Norman evidence. In the absence of this or such evidence as is shown by the Heckingham tower arch mentioned above (37), it has to be accepted either that the arch stonework is original construction thus dating the tower as Norman, or, in support of a Saxon attribution for the tower, assumed that it is a Norman embellishment of a Saxon arch. In other words, a judgement has to be made based either on the visible evidence, or on an unsupported assumption that what is seen has been altered.

It has been suggested that dressed stone arches with set-back heads, that is those in which the diameter of the arch at the springing exceeds the width between the jambs of the opening, are in fact Saxon flint arches faced with Norman stonework. The basis of this theory is that the stonework follows the profile of a Saxon opening, allegedly identifiable as such by the setting back of the arch relative to the jambs, a practice claimed to be an exclusively Saxon device for the support of the arch centering during construction. Tower arches with this feature are found at Gisleham, Ingworth and South Elmham All Saints. The technique however is unreliable as a diagnostic feature for dating because there are several undisputed instances of Norman arches with "set back" heads that clearly were not altered Saxon arches, for example Heckingham tower arch mentioned above, the superimposed "outer" tower arch at Pentlow, internal belfry arches in the Norman square tower at South Lopham and the two arches at the west end of the basement in the keep of Castle Rising.

As well as the round-headed tower arches which have stone dressings, there are some with a plaster finish but which have dressed limestone imposts; the imposts are usually of a simple section with a single chamfer along the lower edge. It seems most improbable that the insertion of stone imposts only would have been regarded as a worthwhile later enhancement of an arch and therefore they are more likely to be part of the original construction; having in mind the general unavailability of dressed limestone before the Conquest, the implication is that these would probably be Norman. Also, it has been said that imposts formed from a single stone are Saxon, whereas Norman imposts are formed with several smaller stones. This again is unreliable since the undisputed Norman stonework of some tower arches, e.g. Risby, Quidenham and Feltwell includes single-stone imposts.

Case 2. *The shape of the arch head could have been altered, either with or without the use of dressed stone.*

In support of Saxon attributions for towers, many pointed tower arches have been professed as altered, but as this can rarely be proved, there must inevitably remain some doubt about an earlier date for the tower unless it has undisputed earlier features. There are over eighty round towers with pointed tower arches, and, while some have obviously been modified, it is difficult to accept without any supporting evidence the speculation that a large number of the others have been altered from earlier patterns; is this really credible, particularly as so many of these towers have other convincing post-Norman evidence and no earlier indications? It has been argued that successive generations constantly altered their churches to accord with prevailing architectural fashions, but did this really happen on such a scale in small village churches? Windows certainly were altered, particularly in the fourteenth and fifteenth centuries, but this was for the functional purpose of admitting more light or displaying stained glass. It is difficult to believe that so many tower arches were altered just for aesthetic reasons and it is more likely that this happened much less often than has been supposed. The primitive, round-headed tower arch without stone dressings at Bedingham church, for example, has remained unaltered when over the centuries the church and tower have clearly undergone several phases of costly enhancement.

It is not unreasonable therefore to assume that many, perhaps most, of the plain pointed tower arches are as originally constructed even though they may be built with flints; if so, in the absence of evidence to the contrary, they date the towers to which they give access as post-Norman.

Case 3. *A smaller arch could have been formed within an original wider or taller arch.*

These situations are relatively easy to identify. At Tasburgh from within the tower, insertion of a low pointed arch and the blocking of the original tall round-headed archway is unmistakable and similarly at Fritton, St Edmund, a modern nine-inch plastered brick arch is inserted within the original taller pointed arch which goes through the full wall thickness; at Ashby, the narrower ogee-headed doorway can be seen inside the tower to be formed within an earlier two-centered pointed arch, and at Wramplingham, the low pointed arch in the nave can be seen from inside the tower to be formed within an original

38. Ramsholt tower arch seen from within the tower.

round-headed opening in the nave west wall. Ramsholt has an arrangement that is less immediately obvious: a Norman stone arch at the nave wall face, only eight inches thick within a wall 3'7" thick measured at the arch apex, was apparently built within a presumed former wider tower arch, not now visible, of an earlier fallen tower. The Norman arch is now backed by a depressed pointed arch (38) formed integrally with the rebuilt east wall of the present Early English tower. At Sedgeford, it can be seen that the inner order of the tower arch is a later insertion into an original twice-chamfered pointed arch: its stonework does not course with the original, its imposts overlap the backing stonework and the radius to which its voussoirs are laid is not concentric with the original arch (85).

Case 4. *The opening may have been enlarged to the extent that nothing of the original arch remains.*

Possible cases of this kind are pointed tower arches of greater than average width and height. As well as straight-through openings as at Hasketon or Surlingham, some may have more elaborate plan profiles (e.g. double-splayed) in conjunction, often, with stone responds, multi-moulded imposts and moulded arches. Whether they are alterations or originals can only be decided in conjunction with appraisal of the tower. If the tower has undisputed pre-Gothic evidence, then such arches are clearly later but where a tower, such as West Somerton for example, shows convincing post-Norman evidence and lacks any earlier features, then the pointed arch and tower may well be contemporary. Large arches of this type at Potter Heigham, Swainsthorpe and Witton have the more elaborate plan forms and incorporate stonework; other post-Norman evidence at Potter Heigham (see chapter 16) suggests that the tower and tower arch are contemporary, but at Swainsthorpe the date of the circular stage is less certain. At Witton, pilaster-strips on the tower's circumference at the re-entrant angles between tower and nave suggest an earlier date for the tower though much of it has probably been rebuilt.

Off-centre Tower Arches

Although it is usually possible to see why some towers and tower arches are off-centre relative to the nave, it is less obvious why certain tower arches have been formed off-centre relative to the tower axis. As this arrangement seems ostensibly perverse, there must be particular reasons why it was adopted and the elucidation of these can help towards revealing the history of church and tower.

At Beeston St Lawrence, for instance, since the tower arch is central to the nave's original width (before its later widening southward), and yet off-centre southwards within the tower, the mystery is not so much why the arch is off-centre to the tower, but why the tower, apparently built at the same time as the original nave whose ferricrete quoins are still visible, was positioned off-centre to it; the south-west corner is about five feet from the tower and the north-west corner only about 3'6". The unusually low small blocked window below the present one in the tower west wall suggests that the ground floor chamber may originally have had a low ceiling level; if so, it must have had a low door to the nave. An off-centre position of the door in this chamber (though central to the nave), might have been regarded as being functionally more convenient to the original use of the room. This low doorway was probably converted to the present tall tower arch when the later belfry and contemporary west window were formed. There is no upper door; if there originally had been one, giving access to a much lower first floor than now, it would have disappeared when the arch was heightened.

Tower arches off-centre to their towers have also been noticed at Brampton, Cockley Cley, Shimpling and Topcroft, and these are considered with their churches in later chapters.

[1] Taylor & Taylor, Op. Cit. Vol.I, page 51

[2] Heywood, Op. Cit. U.E.A. 1977

[3] Taylor, Op. Cit. Vol.III, p 756 et seq.

CHAPTER 8

PUTLOG HOLES IN ROUND TOWERS

It is well understood that a church or tower cannot often be dated with certainty by the style of the features in its walls because windows and doorways may have been inserted at later times. In order, therefore, to establish the age of the original structure, it is necessary to try to date the walls themselves, and in flint walls useful clues can be provided by constructional features which by their nature, purpose or construction are self-evidently more likely to have been part of the original structure than they are to be later insertions or alterations. Putlog holes are features of this kind and can often tell us quite a lot about a tower's construction.

Putlog holes are the small gaps left in the face of a wall during construction as bearings for the ends of the horizontal scaffolding poles (putlogs) which support the scaffold boards at each working level (39). When each 'lift' of walling reached a height at which it became difficult to build, a higher working deck was formed in the scaffolding with one end of the putlogs resting on the top of the completed 'lift' of walling. As the next stage of work proceeded, the ends of the putlogs resting on the wall were boxed at the sides and bridged over, the purpose of this being to allow building to continue over the ends of the putlogs while still allowing for their easy withdrawal on completion. After withdrawal, the holes were usually filled with flint to match the wall and often the mortar used for the filling can be seen to be different from that in the wall.

The arrangement of putlog holes in a tower wall can often, but by no means always, be traced; they are usually about six feet apart horizontally and spaced roughly one above another at four- to five-foot intervals. They may be bridged with short thin wood planks, large flints, stone or bricks and the sides framed with flints, stone or bricks. Those bridged with wood are more often seen internally, e.g. at Eccles, but sometimes external wood bridgings have survived, as at Hengrave and Pentlow. Where of flint, they are difficult to spot because of lack of contrast with the general walling, but there are some striking examples in stone and medieval brick, e.g. at East Walton and Wramplingham respectively, where at the latter the internal putlog holes are also of brick.

From the above description of the purpose and formation of putlog holes, it will be apparent that boxing or framing round the ends of the putlogs and bridging over them is a practice only necessary during the actual building of a wall, and so putlog hole framings and

39. A typical putlog hole bridged and framed with medieval brick.

bridgings can confidently be regarded as the same age as the wall.

Nevertheless, in order to explain the presence of stone or brick putlog holes in towers claimed as pre-Conquest, it has been suggested that they were inserted later to facilitate frequent erection of scaffolding for renewing thatched roofs. This does not explain their use in internal putlog holes and it is open to question as to whether any holes would have been needed externally for scaffolding from which to undertake external repairs – such work might have been done from scaffolding independent of the walls or from ladders. In any event it is most unlikely that a complete pattern of framed holes all round a tower from top to bottom as seen on some towers would have been needed. If support from the walls for scaffolding had been required for repairs to the tower or its roof, holes would simply have been chopped into the wall where required or existing ones reopened; framing and bridging of the holes would have been quite unnecessary.

If the bricks or stone of the putlog holes had been inserted at a later date than the wall, it is likely that the mortar in which they were set would be different from that of the adjacent flintwork but close examination of putlog holes where the original wall surface appears not to have been compromised by later pointing shows uninterrupted continuity of their mortar setting with that of the surrounding walling. The compelling probability therefore is that stone or brick in the framing and bridging of putlog holes in a round tower's fabric are part of the original wall and not later insertions.

If it is accepted that limestone was not generally available in East Anglia before the Conquest, then it follows that towers having putlog holes lined with limestone must be post-Conquest, and likewise, since it is widely agreed that brickmaking in East Anglia, having ceased after the Roman period, was not revived until the thirteenth century, towers with medieval brick putlog hole linings must be post-Norman. At least twenty round towers have definite patterns of putlog holes lined with medieval bricks and in all these cases the probability of a post-Norman date is corroborated by pointed tower arches. Conversely, of towers which have round-headed tower arches, none have medieval brick putlog holes. It is surprising that these medieval bricks either have not been noticed or their significance for dating has been overlooked by many past historians, including Cautley and Pevsner.

What else can be learned from a tower's putlog holes? They can show that a tower never had belfry openings below the present belfry; they can provide evidence that the circular stage of some towers was built at different times; they can imply that an octagonal belfry is contemporary with the circular stage below, and they can contribute to the dating of the wall in which they appear.

Where there is an unbroken pattern of stone or brick putlog holes all round the tower up to the level of the belfry openings, this is a sure indication that there never were earlier belfry openings in the lower stage because, if there had been, the spacing of the putlog holes would have been interrupted. In the walls of the wholly round tower at East Walton, a regular pattern of putlog holes bridged with dressed stones shows that there never were earlier belfry openings below the present ones; this is confirmed by the absence of blocked openings internally. The present belfry is therefore likely to be contemporary with the lower stage, except in the unlikely event that it replaces, or has been altered from, an earlier one (which obviously couldn't have been earlier than the lower stage). The tower can therefore confidently be dated by the present Early English belfry openings, with confirmation from the two lancets in the west wall, the dressings of the lower one probably having been taken from a former pointed west nave window that was converted into an upper door, now altered and blocked, when the tower was added. At West Somerton, where the tower's uninterrupted medieval-brick-lined putlog holes date it as post-Norman, the same reasoning establishes that there never were belfry openings below the present ones and that unless the octagonal stage replaces an earlier post-Norman belfry which is unlikely, it must be contemporary with the circular part, a conclusion confirmed by the fabric similarity in both stages as well as other evidence.

40. Dummy lancet in a rough sort of flushwork of knapped and rubble flints, framed with medieval bricks, in the belfry stage of Weybread tower.

The tower at Aldham, circular to the top, is in three stages with windows of a similar brick-framed lancet pattern in all three including the belfry. The putlog holes tell us that the tower wall we see was built in three separate stages coinciding with the three window levels. Those in the lowest stage are lined with medieval bricks of the same kind as are used in the single ground-floor window and in the tower arch; this stage extends up to the level of the cills of the centre windows and could be fourteenth- or fifteenth-century. The middle stage, perhaps seventeenth- or eighteenth-century, can be seen to be a separate build from the lower because not only are the bricks lining the putlog holes and framing the windows thicker than those below, but the first row of putlog holes in this stage, at window-cill level, occurs only about eighteen inches above the topmost row of the lower stage. The top stage, probably nineteenth-century, is faced with different flintwork, using apparently later bricks again in putlog holes and belfry windows. The lower stage is about half the total height of the tower and the evidence described suggests that an original post-Norman medieval tower lost its upper parts which were subsequently rebuilt in matching styles in two later episodes.

Putlog holes can show whether an octagonal belfry is contemporary with a tower's circular stage or a later addition. At Thorpe Abbotts (XVII), where the circular stage is surmounted by two octagonal stages, all three have similar flintwork and putlog holes lined with medieval bricks; the first row in the octagon is about a foot above the stone string course between the circular stage and the octagon, and its height above the topmost row in the circular part is the same as the normal vertical interval between rows. This is an indication that construction was probably progressive at the level of the change of shape because, if the octagon had been a later addition, the first row of putlogs for staging from which to build it would be likely to have been immediately below the start of the 'new' work, not just above it. The same applies at Potter Heigham (XVI), although there the flintwork of the octagon is different from that in the circular stage. Likewise at Weybread (40), the first row of putlog holes in the belfry, which is circular there, is just above, rather than just below the string course that separates the two stages. Conversely, at Old Catton, where the upper half of the circular stage has flint putlog holes, they are of medieval brick just below the start of the octagon; this, and a difference in the flintwork of the top few courses of the circular stage suggesting that they have been rebuilt, indicate that the octagonal stage is likely to have been an addition, probably replacing an earlier belfry.

An instance of where putlog holes can reveal something of the history of a tower and help to date it is seen at Heckingham where putlog holes bridged with pieces of Norman billet moulding (92) date the wall in which they occur as probably contemporary with the construction of the north aisle (see Chapter 20).

Putlog holes can also help to date other features in the same wall. Since they are part of the original wall construction, it is obvious that other features cannot be earlier than them, and where, for instance, such features are formed with the same kind of brick as the putlog holes, as in the lancet windows in the circular stages of towers like Ilketshall St. Andrew, West Somerton or Wramplingham, it is arguably more likely that they are original and contemporary with the putlog holes than that they are later insertions.

Since a tower is unlikely to be earlier than its church unless the church has been rebuilt, putlog hole framings in the nave walls that provide evidence for dating the nave can also be a guide to the date of the tower. At St Mary's, Moulton, putlog holes in the nave west and side walls are framed and bridged with medieval bricks of unusually large size – 11" x 5½" x 2¾". Bricks of the same size for putlog holes in the round tower provide convincing evidence that nave and tower were built at the same time, and Y-tracery in the nave windows suggests an early fourteenth-century date. Even where unexceptional medieval bricks are used for putlog holes in nave walls, as in the west wall at Weybread, they provide confirmation of the tower's own evidence for a post-Norman date.

CHAPTER 9

ELEVENTH-CENTURY AND SAXO-NORMAN ROUND TOWERS

A theory that the earliest round towers were short, often barely higher than the ridge of the nave roof, seems to have been based largely on the assumption that where a round tower has a post-Conquest belfry, whether circular or octagonal, the height of the circular stage below the belfry defines the tower's original height, the belfry having been added later. More than half of all round towers have post-Conquest belfries, and the assumption that they are all additions has caused many of the lower stages of such towers to be attributed as pre-Conquest; the present low height of towers like Howe (IX) or the circular stage at Taverham has, no doubt, also contributed to the idea that early towers were all short. However, as most of the towers of this kind have no evidence of former belfry openings in their circular stages below the present belfry, the implication is that the circular stages alone had never stood as complete towers. It is more likely therefore, that their present belfries are either renewals of earlier ones or integral elements of the original structure, and that low towers now without belfries such as Howe or Barmer, have simply lost them, probably as a result of past deterioration and neglect. The height of low towers or the measurement to the base of a tower's belfry is not, therefore, a reliable indication of its original height.

Since double belfry openings having a central column and through-stone like those at Beachamwell (46) or Bessingham (7) are widely considered as being characteristic of later Saxon technique, towers with single, round-headed or triangular belfry openings such as Great Hautbois (III) or Beeston St Lawrence (before the addition of its later belfry) could arguably be regarded as earlier than the double-opening type. However, the original heights of those with single belfry openings are not consistently less than the ones with the double type whose original heights vary from about 35 to nearly 60 feet. It seems then, that irrespective of belfry type, early towers show no relationship between height and age.

In view of the fact that virtually all the features that are considered as characteristic of Saxon technique can be shown to have also been used in post-Conquest buildings (see chapter 5), it is impossible to be certain whether towers in which they appear are pre- or post-Conquest. Nevertheless, towers or the lower stages of towers that possess characteristic Saxon features and contain no dressed limestone or Norman features (except manifestly later alterations or insertions) can probably safely be accepted as pre-Conquest, particularly where the tower arch is tall and narrow and formed without dressed stone. Towers of full height with a belfry stage that conform with these criteria would include those at Cranwich whose pierced stone slab facings to upper windows may be later insertions, Great Hautbois and Haveringland with single-light belfry openings and Aslacton, Bessingham, Forncett St Peter, Norwich St Mary at Coslany and Roughton (41) with double-light openings; Holy Trinity, Bungay has claims to be included in this group although its present belfry openings are Perpendicular patterns. At Roughton though, the two-light belfry openings are not the usual type to be expected in a Saxon tower that comprise a double-cantilevered through-stone carried on a single column at the centre of the wall; instead, the intermediate support for the triangular heads of the twin openings is provided by a spine wall built with ferricrete, showing a crude, primitive capital at the wall face, and extending through the full thickness of the belfry wall (42).

41. Ferricrete and flint in the tower at Roughton. 42. Internal view of the spine wall between the twin triangular-headed lights of one of the double belfry openings of Roughton tower.

Several more towers of which a greater or lesser extent of their lower parts may be Saxon include Bedingham, Beeston St Lawrence, Bexwell, Brooke, Colney, Hales, Hardley, Howe, Intwood, Kirby Cane, Letheringsett, Norwich St Julian, Tasburgh, Taverham, Titchwell, Woodton and Ilketshall St Margaret. It is almost inevitable that amongst the later Saxon towers, there must have been some whose construction was halted at the time of the Norman invasion to be continued later in Norman style – Titchwell possibly, or Bexwell for instance.

East Lexham, an early tower that has been attributed as Saxon by most authorities, has not been included above on the grounds that its double belfry opening (43) seems to conform more to the Norman mode than to the Saxon (see Chapter 3). It ought strictly, therefore, to be considered as falling within the so-called Saxo-Norman Overlap – a period of indeterminate length lasting for perhaps two or three generations after the Conquest during which features of Saxon technology and style persisted alongside Norman techniques. 'Overlap' round towers can perhaps be considered as of two kinds –

43, 44, and 45 South-west, east, and north-west belfry openings in East Lexham tower.

those built by Saxon artisans after the Conquest according to indigenous practices but tentatively introducing some Norman innovations, and those essentially Norman towers that nevertheless still retained elements of pre-Conquest technology or incorporated Saxon features.

The lack of aesthetic discipline, its misshapen profile, its rough construction and its belfry stonework give the tower at East Lexham an ambience of primitive antiquity and it is not surprising therefore that it has been universally regarded as early Saxon; nevertheless, its three belfry openings, unusually positioned at east, south-west and north-west and all of different form, provide evidence to suggest that it could be an Overlap tower of the first kind mentioned above. The south-west opening (43) has two round-headed lights separated by a stout cylindrical column supporting a heavy Barnack stone abacus of pseudo-cushion shape – not a through-stone; the jambs of the opening are formed with flints and the arches of the lights, also of flint, are slightly recessed within an outer flint arch encompassing the two openings; the central column is near the outer face of the wall and the two small arches it supports are only the thickness of the column's diameter, while behind them, the full width of the double opening is spanned by a single round-headed arch of flints. The openings facing east (44) and north-west (45) have monolithic pierced Barnack stone slabs carved out of the solid set at, or slightly recessed from the wall face, each of a different two-light design, behind which a round-headed flint arch spans the full opening. The arrangement of a single backing arch at the three openings suggests proto-Norman technology; might this be an early attempt at Norman technique by local indigenous artisans under Norman direction? It is also significant that all the four corners of the church have Barnack stone quoins; the lower ones are laid in a sort of long-and-short manner, and rising from chamfered plinth stones, suggest original construction rather than later insertion.

Burnham Norton is another early tower in which Norman influence is apparent in the belfry openings. Here, single-light openings, framed and arched in flint, are recessed several inches from the wall face forming an inner order within a wider and taller embrasure of similar flint construction. Coexistent associations of other Saxon and Norman features are seen in 'Overlap' round towers elsewhere: at Herringfleet described below, dressed stonework in the tower windows and the stonework of the belfry openings, despite their Saxon style, imply a post-Conquest date, and at Wissett, Norman nave doorways, dressed stone nave quoins, a Norman tower arch and stone tower windows suggest that three double-splayed circular flint openings in the tower below the belfry must also be Norman unless it can be proved that all those Norman features are later embellishments of a Saxon church and tower.

It would, no doubt, have been in the larger buildings such as the earliest Norman monastic churches that features of a recognizably distinct Norman Romanesque style first made an impact in East Anglia; thereafter wider dissemination of these Norman details would have been only gradual and it would have been some time before they were incorporated into minor churches. As the earliest of the Norman monasteries in East Anglia was not founded before about 1090 AD, it is unlikely that any minor churches of the eleventh century and few of the early twelfth would have absorbed Norman technology or style; unless, therefore it were to be established that there was a complete cessation of minor church building for many years after the Conquest, these churches and their towers seem likely to have continued to follow largely unchanged building methods for at least two generations after the Conquest.

In defence of a contention that Saxon features were never used after the Conquest, it has been proposed that under the new regime no Saxon styles would have been permitted on any new churches, and in order to impose their prestige and authority, the Norman patrons would have demanded Norman styles; but it is at least questionable whether Norman patrons at local level would have had the understanding to concern themselves with the technology or aesthetics of building, and the very adoption of the round tower by the Normans and their use of elements of Saxon style, as for instance in the classic example of an Overlap tower at Haddiscoe, disproves the idea. It is clear that under the Normans, traditional indigenous building practices continued to have a significant role.

The extensive use of Caen stone in its string courses, windows inside and out, the belfry openings and in the tower arch dates the tower at Haddiscoe as not before the last decade of the eleventh century at the earliest, on the grounds that the first use of Caen stone in Norfolk was probably at Norwich Cathedral, and that was not started until thirty years after the Conquest. Triangular-headed through-stone belfry openings, half-round fillets between church and tower and a tall, narrow tower arch are all features considered to be characteristic of Saxon workmanship, and their use on Haddiscoe tower provides the clearest example of such features being continued well into the post-Conquest period. The use of billet moulding round the Saxon-style belfry openings introduces a Norman detail, confirming a post-Conquest date.

Beachamwell.

The tower is circular for about three-quarters of its height; near the top of the circular part there are four two-light, through-stone type belfry openings; those facing south and east have round heads arched in flattish flints and those to the north and west have triangular heads formed with paired sloping stones (46). The circular part has two slit windows, one in the form of a vertical slot cut through a single stone and the other without stonework; there is also a Perpendicular west window in the ground stage. The Perpendicular top stage is octagonal with two-light belfry openings in the cardinal faces and flushwork replicas in the diagonals.

46. Double belfry opening of through-stone type in Beachamwell tower.

The tower's inside diameter is 8'7" and its walls are 3'2" thick, the same thickness as the nave west wall measured outside the tower; its east wall is flat internally in the ground stage but curved above. The tower arch is six feet wide and 10'6" high to the crown, with a plain semi-circular arch without imposts; its reveals and the nave walls are plastered but the plaster has been stripped from the arch itself facing the nave and from the arch soffit, exposing radially-laid limestone voussoirs at both nave and tower faces, with rubble flint and some stone to the soffit between. The voussoir stones, though suitably shaped for their purpose, are not 'dressed' and were clearly not intended to be exposed because they are scored on face and soffit to form a key for plaster. Above the tower arch and off-centre to the north is the upper doorway, partly obscured by the nave roof timbers.

Nave and chancel are the same width. The north-west nave quoin of Barnack stone is in long-and-short work (12) and though the chancel quoins and east wall have been rebuilt on a stone-capped plinth, one upright stone and two or three flat ones in the south-east quoin suggest that these stones might also originally have been components of long-and-short work.

Chiefly on the evidence of the early belfry openings, the tower has been widely accepted as Anglo-Saxon, but despite the formidable weight of this virtually unanimous opinion, there are convincing grounds for dating the church and tower to the Saxo-Norman Overlap period. The basis for this attribution is simply that, if, as current opinion seems to agree, limestone was unavailable in the area before Norman times, its use in the tower and nave at Beachamwell rules out a pre-Conquest date. Here, it was used for the triangular heads, imposts and through-stones of the early belfry openings, the tower arch voussoirs, the long-and-short north-west quoin and the east quoins. Although recognised as a feature of Anglo-Saxon workmanship, long-and-short quoins persisted beyond the Conquest and were used, for example, at St John's, Timberhill, Norwich, founded between the Conquest and Domesday.

The six-foot width of the tower arch suggests that it was too wide to have been the west entrance to a formerly towerless church, and because of the absence of mouldings or imposts and the scoring of its voussoirs as a key for plaster, the archway stonework does not appear to be a later embellishment of a rubble arch. Since the tower arch and tower are obviously unlikely to be earlier than the nave, and if the nave is dated by the north-west quoin as Saxo-Norman, it follows that the tower and tower arch must either be the same date, or later if the tower was added. It is unlikely that the tower is an addition because the style of the original belfry openings is hardly likely to be later than the long-and-short nave quoins; in any event, the stonework of the tower arch tends to support a post-Conquest date for arch and tower.

Despite the flat east wall within the ground stage of the tower, often evidence of a tower having been added to an earlier nave, its curvature in the storeys above shows that this wall would not have been the west gable of a towerless nave. This provides corroboration that the nave and tower are contemporary, and further evidence of this is the equal thickness of the tower wall and the nave west wall measured outside the tower, which is thicker than the nave side wall. An originally towerless church would be expected to have west and side walls of about the same thickness. The ground stage of the east wall in the tower was probably built flat for the sake of simplicity of construction of the tower arch.

There are convincing grounds for attribution of the same date to the 'Saxon' features of the Beachamwell tower as to Great Dunham church barely ten miles away which, because of its considerable use of dressed limestone for features of Saxon style is now usually regarded as of post-Conquest date. There, in the square tower is long-and-short quoining in Barnack stone and two-light belfry openings in which round heads arched in flint with some Roman brick are supported on through-stones set on mid-wall shafts. These features make striking parallels with the north-west nave quoin and the belfry openings at Beachamwell.

The dating suggested above relies heavily on the assumption that limestone was not available in the area before the Conquest. While it can convincingly be shown that Caen stone was not imported into East Anglia until the late eleventh century, the earliest use of Barnack is less certain; it has been thought to have travelled in pre-Conquest times as far from the quarries near Stamford as Ramsey and Bury St Edmunds, and so it is not impossible that it might also have reached destinations in West Norfolk accessible via the western waterways. It is nevertheless perhaps unlikely that it would have been brought for minor churches.

Herringfleet

The tower at Herringfleet has a similar belfry to Haddiscoe, but the openings facing south, west and north lie beneath the semi-circular arch of an outer order with shafted jambs and cushion capitals. Bands of billet moulding outside the shafts and in the arch confirm the belfry as Norman. Two intermediate round-headed openings in the belfry stage at south-west and north-west framed with post-medieval bricks are probably much later.

The church has dressed stone quoins at all corners of the nave and chancel. They are, or were, Caen stone but many have been replaced with a colder grey stone, particularly the lower ones that would have been more vulnerable to deterioration. At 3'7" thick, measured both outside the tower and at the tower arch apex, the nave west wall is almost a foot thicker than the side walls and only an inch or two less than the tower wall. Within the ground stage of the tower, the east wall in which the plain round-headed tower arch is formed is flat, though at first-floor level and above, the inside of the tower is fully circular with unbroken continuity of its flint coursing on the east side; this curved wall, self-evidently thinner than the flat wall at the tower arch position below, would clearly not have been the west gable of a previously towerless church, and proves that the nave and tower must have been built together. The lower section of the wall was presumably made flat to simplify construction of the tower arch. This is another instance where a flat east wall at ground-floor level within a tower does not indicate that the tower has been added to the nave.

The first-floor stage has two slit windows facing north and south, and three more above them at north, south and west; all have stone dressings externally with arch-lintel heads cut from semi-circular stones in the lower ones and from rectangular stones in the upper. Internally all these windows have splayed reveals and the two lower ones have flint jambs and stone arch voussoirs (47) but the upper three have jambs of stone as well as the arches; shuttering board-marks on the arch soffits between the outer and inner stone

dressings and uninterrupted continuity of flintwork coursing around and above the inner dressings show that the stonework was part of the original construction and not inserted later. Jamb stones of the round-headed upper door in the tower east wall are shaped to a slightly obtuse angle to conform to the wall curvature.

Although displaying features considered as characteristic of Saxon style such as the quadrant fillets between tower and nave and the through-stone belfry lights, a post-Conquest date for this church and tower is clearly indicated by the Caen stone quoins of the nave (which are unlikely to be later insertions), the extensive use of dressed limestone in the tower, and the Norman arch feature of the belfry openings as well as their billet mouldings.

47. Flint jambs and dressed stone voussoirs in the round-headed arch of a first-floor window inside Herringfleet tower, showing uninterrupted continuity of flintwork above

Gissing

Three double-splayed circular flint windows in the tower and a tall tower arch are features that have caused this tower to be attributed as Saxon even though it has several Norman features that appear to be original parts of the tower. A Norman west window with zig-zag incised face decoration externally (48) and stone dressings inside shows no evidence of later insertion, the adjacent flint coursing running uninterruptedly right up to the stonework jambs of the opening; twin Norman belfry openings have chamfered imposts, the outer ones extending through the full thickness of the wall to act as the springings for the single arch behind the twin openings at the face of the wall, and both sides of the tower arch have stone dressings with Norman arch mouldings facing the nave (some of whose voussoirs, though, have been renewed).

The case for a Saxon attribution depends on an unproved preconception that double-splayed circular flint windows were never used after the Conquest and a consequent assumption that all the Norman features of the tower and the nave must therefore be later insertions or alterations, but since there is no evidence that the Norman features are not contemporary with the walls in which they appear, but, on the contrary, convincing evidence for them being original features, the inference is that the double-splayed windows are an instance of the use of a characteristic Saxon feature in an essentially Norman building.

The similarity of the flintwork of the west wall and the tower and the continuity of its coursing where the tower meets the nave establish that the nave and tower were built

48. Two-light Norman stone window with chevron decoration, in the west wall of the tower at Gissing.

together. The nave is about 21 feet wide with 3'2" thick side walls and a west wall four feet thick. Its west quoins of Barnack stone and the north and south doorways are its chief Norman evidence. The quoins are of typical Norman size and proportions and the adjacent flint walling shows no evidence of the stones having been inserted after the walls had been built. Likewise, the Norman stonework of the south door shows no evidence of later insertion, the flintwork coursing running up to the outer jamb stonework without apparent disturbance. At certain points, particularly at the right-hand jamb, weathering has eroded the jointing of the stonework to the extent that the original mortar in which the stones were bedded can be identified – it is quite distinct from later re-pointing – and continuity of mortar of the same composition and colour can be traced in the adjacent wall flintwork for some way beyond the doorway jambstones. Later pointing in these areas is easily distinguished from the original mortar in which the flints were set, and much of it has fallen out through ineffective adhesion to the original mortar and flints. This uniformity of the mortar of the doorway and the nave wall proves that the south door is an original feature of the nave, and consequently that the nave is Norman. The same can be shown for the south-west nave quoins. As the tower was contemporary with the nave, it must also be Norman.

Ladbrooke's drawing of the 1820s shows four small windows high up in the nave south wall that are no longer there, having presumably disappeared when the wall was heightened. One of them is circular and drawn with voussoirs around it. This has prompted a belief that the nave could be Saxon, but the visible evidence for a Norman attribution is more convincing.

To summarise: on the strength of the visible evidence, the realistic conclusion must be that the nave and tower are Norman and the circular windows in the tower and the one shown in the nave in Ladbrooke's drawing are instances of the use of a Saxon feature in a Norman building, rather than that the nave and tower are Saxon and all the Norman features in them have been altered to Norman style or inserted after the Conquest.

CHAPTER 10

TOWERS WITH WALL SURFACE MODELLING

There are only four round towers on which shallow surface modelling executed in flint without the use of dressed stone has been used as exterior wall decoration. Two themes have been adopted – narrow projecting strips of flint (lesenes) and recessed blank arcading.

On the towers of Kirby Cane and Thorpe next Haddiscoe a series of plain vertical strips of flint about eight inches wide and projecting about three inches from the wall face, are spaced at intervals around the tower circumference; those at Kirby Cane (49) extend from ground level to a height of about four feet but at Thorpe (50), they are a feature of the middle section of the tower.

49. Projecting flint lesenes, or pilaster-strips, extending to about four feet above ground level around the base of Kirby Cane tower

50. Projecting flint lesenes on the middle stage of the tower at Thorpe-next-Haddiscoe.

At Tasburgh (51) and Thorington (52), blank arcading encircles the tower, comprising sequences of round-headed panels formed in rubble flint and recessed about three inches from the wall face. At the latter, the recesses span about 2'6" on average, and the pilasters between them are about a foot wide but at Tasburgh the arched recesses and the pilasters are approximately the same width – both about 2'8"; this equal spacing allowed for an upper tier to be set with the recess and pilaster positions reversed relative to the lower tier. The upper tier, however, has no arches, having apparently been truncated for the later addition of a lancet-style belfry. Narrow flint-framed windows within the flint blind arcading and another lower down, a tall tower arch formed without dressed stone, and the remnant of an earlier nave west wall with flint quoins suggest that stone for dressings was unavailable when the tower and church were built; this, and the workmanship suggest a late Saxon date.

It has been suggested that the flint strips at Kirby Cane and Thorpe may be truncated pilasters of former blank arcading similar to that at Tasburgh and Thorington, but this is considered unlikely because of their narrowness; at Thorpe, with the spaces between them being as much as 3'7", this would have resulted in an ill-proportioned arcade with wider arches on narrower supports than at Tasburgh or Thorington. At Kirby Cane, there could not have been arcading above the strips because the plane of the recessed walling between them is that of the tower wall itself. In association with a plain, tall round-headed plastered tower arch, they probably confer a pre-Conquest date to the lower stage of the tower, and being simple projections from the wall face, these vertical strips seem to be an equivalent in flintwork of typical Saxon stone stripwork or lesenes as seen for example on the towers of Earls Barton (13) or Barnack churches.

51. Blind arcading in flint on Tasburgh Tower. An upper tier apparently has been truncated by the addition of a later belfy.

52. Blind arcading in flint on Thorington tower.

Thorpe next Haddiscoe

The tower (50) has two stages, both of coursed flint rubble, separated by a dressed stone string course; the lower stage is about twice the height of the belfry stage and has a slightly larger diameter. At first floor level three narrow windows framed with dressed stone have semi-circular heads cut from single stones with a simple concentric double-groove decoration; over two of these, small carved stone corbels project. Above these windows, segments of the tower wall circumference are recessed about three inches, separated by vertical flint lesenes in the wall plane, about eight inches wide, that extend nearly to the top of the lower stage, their topmost two feet or so tapering in width. Four of the recesses contain blocked slit windows framed in dressed stone with undecorated stone arched lintels. Double belfry openings at the cardinal points in the upper stage have shafted jambs and central knopped balusters with cushion capitals and chamfered and quirked imposts supporting semi-circular arches bearing simple concentric mouldings. Between tower and nave, quarter-round fillets capped with a conical stone finial surmounted by a carved head, extend above the original nave west wall roofline.

The stonework in the tower windows is probably Caen, and internally, the first-floor windows have radial flint arches above which the walling shows no disturbance such as would be expected had they been later insertions, and the flintwork of the splayed reveals, which courses with the internal walling, is in undisturbed contact with the backs of the external stone dressings: this effectively proves that the windows were built with the wall and that the stonework is part of the original construction and not a later insertion. The stone finial features that cap the quarter-round fillets between tower and nave walls must also have been contemporary and built with the fillets and bonded with them into the tower wall; it is improbable that these curious minor embellishments would have been later additions, and so they tend to confirm a post-Conquest date for the lower stage of the tower.

A double-splayed circular window high up in the gable of the nave west wall, and part of the flat western face of this wall visible within the tower shows that the tower is likely to have been added to an earlier towerless church.

On an assumption that the flint lesenes and recessed panels on the tower are the lower parts of decapitated blank arcading like that at Tasburgh and Thorington, from which the arches were removed for the addition of an upper stage, it has become almost universally accepted that the belfry stage is a Norman addition to an earlier, Saxon, lower stage, replacing the arches of blind arcading and a former Saxon belfry; but there is no direct evidence to substantiate this. There is no sign of the start of any arching at the tops of the lesene strips, but, like the tower fillets, they taper off, gradually dying back into the wall face; this implies that if arches of conjectured blind arcading had been removed for the construction of the belfry stage, appreciable alteration to the topmost three feet or so of the lower stage would also have been required. The presumption of such apparently unnecessary work seems rather implausible, and there is no change in the quality of flintwork at the level where this supposed alteration would have started, to suggest that it might have been done.

If, in fact, the present belfry did replace an earlier one, that would imply that there had been three distinct building campaigns: firstly, a towerless church, with Caen stone quoins and doorways (unless they are later insertions); secondly, the tower, with Caen stone windows, fillets, conjectured blind arcading and presumably a belfry stage, and thirdly demolition of the assumed earlier belfry and the arches of the blind arcading, alteration of the top of the lesenes to a tapered shape and the building of a Norman belfry.

However, having regard to the probability that Caen stone was not available in East Anglia before the Conquest and was unlikely to have been used on minor churches before its use at the Cathedral in the last decade of the eleventh century, it seems unlikely that three building campaigns in which this stone was apparently used would have been undertaken within the short timescale implied by the Norman style of the conjectured third campaign.

Since the recessed panels on this tower are nearly a foot wider than the blank arch recesses at Tasburgh and Thorington, and the average width of the lesenes is considerably less than the pilasters there, it tends to suggest that the arrangement at Thorpe is more analogous to the Kirby Cane theme than to blind arcading. The likelihood, therefore, is that the tower's builders had never intended to form blind arcading like that at Tasburgh and Thorington but rather, perhaps, to create an effect similar to that created by the flint lesenes around the base of Kirby Cane tower, about five miles away. This supports a probability that the present configuration represents the original form of the lesenes and that consequently there never was any blind arcading at the top of the tower's lower stage.

If this were so, there would be no reason for thinking that the tower was built in two phases, particularly in view of the unconvincingly short interval between the two phases that that would imply. It is therefore much more likely that the whole tower was built in one operation. This idea is supported by the consistency of the style of ornament on the arches of the first floor windows and the belfry openings and by the uniformity of the flintwork on the two stages of the tower (This is better seen in photographs taken before the present pointing was done, in for example, Cautley's[1] and the Taylors'[2] books).

If the whole tower (except the later parapet) is of a single build, and if the Caen stone features of the lower stage are original work and not later insertions, then they and the belfry date the tower as no earlier than the last decade of the eleventh century; the flint lesenes, nevertheless, suggest a Saxon tradition and so the tower could be regarded as a late product of the Saxo-Norman Overlap and be attributed to the early twelfth century, a date that would not be inconsistent with the belfry details.

The nave has dressed stone quoins at the south-west and north-west corners and simple Norman north and south doorways, also of stone, the former blocked. If these were to be regarded as original features, it would imply that the tower was considerably later than suggested above, because the double-splayed window in the nave west wall proves that this wall must be earlier than the tower. It seems more likely, therefore, that the stone quoins and doorways have been inserted into earlier nave walls, and this may have been done when the tower was built, having in mind the similarity of the imposts of the belfry openings to those in the north doorway.

The blind arcading theory is an interesting idea with no actual evidence to support it. It has been repeated so often without scrupulous examination that it seems to have passed into the domain of accepted fact.

Thorington

The flint tower is circular to the top of the belfry stage above which the battlemented stepped parapet is octagonal and built in brick. Up to about a third of the way up the belfry openings, the tower flintwork is coursed rubble with erratics, but above this it is uncoursed.

The ground stage contains a modern Norman-style window in the west wall. On the external wall face at first-floor level, a sequence of eleven blank round-headed arches forms blind arcading around the tower from south-east to north-east (52). They are recessed about three inches and average just under two-and-a-half feet in width, with pilasters about a foot wide between; arches and pilasters are formed entirely in flints without any dressed stone.

Within this arcading three small windows at south, west and north are faced with dressed stone and have semi-circular heads cut from single stones; the two facing west and north are off-centre in the arched recesses in which they occur. Internally, they have splayed reveals and heads, with flint jambs and rere-arches. The soffit mortar of the heads, which shows board-marks of the shuttering on which the rere-arches were built, can be seen to be actually adhering to the backs of the stones which form the external facings of the windows, proving that the external stonework was built concurrently with the backing arch.

The belfry stage has belfry openings at the cardinal positions, each with a semi-circular dressed stone outer arch above the twin openings of a recessed, stone inner order. Below the imposts of the outer arch, dressed stone is used on the jambs for part only of their height, their lower two feet or so on all the four openings being formed in flint; this change occurs at about the same level as the change in the external tower fabric. Internally, the jambs and backing arches of the belfry openings have been reconstructed in brick, much of which is similar to that used in the parapet although some looks modern.

On the evidence of the blind arcading and in the belief that such work executed in flint without dressed stone could not have been Norman, it has been widely assumed that the tower is Saxon with an added Norman belfry. However, as there is comparable blind arcading without dressed stone in the undisputed Norman square tower at Corringham, Essex (53), this allows the definite possibility that the Thorington tower could be Norman.

It seems certain that the belfry stage is not a replacement for an earlier one or an addition to an originally lower tower because, firstly, there is no discontinuity in the external wall fabric at belfry cill level and, secondly, in a conjectured tower no higher than the present belfry cill level, there would have been insufficient space for belfry openings in the wall above the blind arcading, nor is there any evidence of any. Hence, the tower's original height was probably no less than the height of the present tower excluding the brick parapet, and the present belfry openings are probably original, though perhaps partially restored.

53. Blind arcading in rubble stone on the square Norman tower at Corringham, Essex

Although the present belfry openings are clearly Norman, the lower two feet or so of the jambs of each one are flint, and as these flints are unlikely to have replaced stonework, it is probable that the upper jambs and outer arch, which are stone, may also originally have been flint; this would have been stylistically and technologically in keeping with the flint details of the blind arcading. Again, at Corringham, Norman dressed stonework occurs in the inner order of rubble-framed belfry openings and elsewhere in East Anglia there are other examples of Norman flint-framed belfry openings, e.g. those at Wortham, and the rere-arches of the Norman belfries at Thorpe-next-Haddiscoe, Little Saxham and Gayton Thorpe.

The brick jambs and arches of the belfry openings internally and the change of flintwork quality in the external wall fabric at the level where the jambs of the belfry openings change from flint to stone are evidence that there has been considerable renovation to the top of the tower, but the internal brickwork clearly indicates that this was later than Norman times. It looks as though the upper two-thirds of the belfry stage was substantially rebuilt when the brick parapet was built in the sixteenth or seventeenth centuries, and that the upper jambs and arches of the outer order of the belfry openings, conjectured as having originally been in flint, were replaced with stone at that time.

54. Blind arcading on the square Norman tower of South Lopham church, showing the asymmetrical placing of a blocked loop, as at Thorington.

On the evidence of their external dressed stonework, the three round-headed windows which occur within the blind arcading can be dated as Norman, but were they built with the tower or inserted later? A window with splayed jambs and a splayed arch head which has been built on shuttering, as these have been, could not have been formed in an existing flint wall four feet or so thick without considerable disturbance to the existing wall outside and in, as has been described in Chapter 5. Here, no derangement of the blind arcading is apparent and internally there are no signs of disturbance to the flintwork or disruption of its coursing above and at the sides of these windows which might suggest that they were not built as part of the original wall.

However, as two of the windows are off-centre within the panels of the blind arcading, the Taylors argued that they were insertions, believing that no builder would have placed them so oddly; but the same reasoning could apply to later insertion. Comparable windows located asymmetrically in arcading on the Norman tower at South Lopham church (54) show that odd placing of small windows was not contrary in principle to Norman practice. It follows that if the Norman windows at Thorington were part of the original tower wall, the blind arcading must also be Norman.

On balance, the evidence and reasoning for a Norman attribution for this tower probably outweigh the grounds for belief that it might be Saxon.

---

[1] Cautley, *Norfolk Churches*. Adlard. 1949

[2] H M and J Taylor, *Anglo-Saxon Architecture,* Vol.II. C.U.P. 1980

[3] Ditto. Page 613

CHAPTER 11

NORMAN ROUND TOWERS

For minor churches in East Anglia, the introduction into the area of limestone in significant quantities and its use for dressings was probably the most important technological advance attributable to the Normans, and although there may be some instances where they used it to enhance existing features formerly of flint or where they inserted new doorways in existing walls, it is probably safer to assume that Norman features of dressed stone in flint walls are likely to be contemporary with the walls in which they occur unless there is evidence to show that they are later insertions.

About forty or so round towers can be considered as Norman if the term is used to denote those in which the lower part, i.e. the original structure, was, as far as can be ascertained, built after 1066 AD but before the end of the twelfth century; this number includes towers of the Saxo-Norman Overlap since by definition they are post-Conquest. The total is rather more than might from first sight seem to be Norman because, as a result of later alterations or additions many towers are not immediately recognisable as such. Conversely, one or two with Norman belfries like Titchwell or Bexwell have earlier work below.

It is in towers that lack obvious external Norman features such as those for example at Rushmere, Rickinghall Inferior or Fritton, Norfolk described in the next chapter, that it may seem difficult to establish their Norman origin, but it can usually be traced or deduced from Norman evidence in the nave if the tower is contemporary with the church, by the evidence of changes in the tower's external fabric, or by characteristics of the tower arch.

One of the means by which towers that are contemporary with their churches can be differentiated from those that were added later, is a continuity of flintwork coursing in the tower and the nave west wall. Where this is apparent, as for example at lower levels at Quidenham (33), Rushmere and Fishley, or where other evidence described in Chapter 6 shows that tower and nave are contemporary, the tower can be convincingly established as Norman if the nave's western quoins are dressed stone, of Norman pattern and original. Typical Norman quoin stones are about nine inches to a foot high, of squarish proportions, and, having little difference in the lengths of their exposed faces, the bonding with adjacent flintwork is fairly scanty. They are invariably of Caen or Barnack stone, the former being found more in locations accessible from the eastern waterways. In some cases, for example at Rushmere or Fishley, weathering has in places eroded later pointing to the extent that the original bedding mortar of the stones can be identified and be seen to extend well into the adjacent flintwork proving that the quoins were part of the original wall and not inserted later.

In general, Norman flints are often, but not always laid coursed; earlier flintwork typically might be of larger irregular pieces, uncoursed and with wide mortar joints, whereas that of the immediate post-Norman period is usually more closely packed and laid uncoursed, showing comparatively less mortar in the surface jointing. The typical regular coursing of Norman work is recognisable in the lower part of the three towers mentioned, in contrast to the flintwork above it, revealing the levels at which later work was superimposed on the Norman walls.

As the minimal aesthetic gain to be obtained from later insertion of plain stone dressings into an existing plastered tower arch would hardly seem to justify the difficulties of what would be an awkward structural undertaking – still less, the insertion of stone imposts only, it follows that the use of plain unmoulded limestone dresssings for the jambs and arch voussoirs of a round-headed tower arch is a strong indication of Norman work because such stonework is likely to be an integral part of the arch's original construction rather than later decorative enhancement; the same applies to arches with stone imposts only, whether comprising single or multiple stones. Sometimes, as at Heckingham (37), proof can be seen that the dressed stone is contemporary with the formation of the arch in that the board-marks of the shuttering on the arch soffit can be seen to be contiguous with the backs of the voussoir stones that form the arch dressings, showing that the arch masonry and the facing stonework were built on the same shuttering – if the facing stones had been inserted subsequently, there would be discontinuity between the board-mark pattern and the stonework.

Typically, the stone imposts of Norman tower arches are plain with a simple chamfer on the lower edge, but in the stone-dressed tower arch at Breckles they have carved ornament that has been attributed by Pevsner as early eleventh-century. The circular stage of the tower, however, seems to be Norman, apparently being of one build with the nave whose south-west corner has Barnack stone quoins of characteristic Norman proportions. The putlog-hole bridgings in the tower walls are also Barnack stone and in the upper part of the circular stage facing south, west and north, large rectangular stones are set, each perforated with a nine-inch-diameter circular hole, now blocked with flints; at the corresponding positions internally, and also on the east, the openings are also blocked flush with the wall, but straight jamb stones about two feet high and three feet apart, are still in situ. The tower could be an early Norman one on which Saxon masons were employed for the carved tower arch imposts. The low height of the circular stage and absence of belfry openings in it (the holes in the four perforated stones seem far too small to have served as bell openings) suggests that the octagonal belfry replaces an original Norman one.

With the odd exception, notably the two-light west window at Gissing (48), Norman stone windows in round towers were narrow single-light openings. Their external jambs usually consist of multiple stones often with chamfered edges around the opening, and the heads are usually of the arch-lintel type in which a semi-circular 'arch' is cut into the lower edge of a single stone. The shape of this arch stone may be semi-circular as in the first-floor windows at Little Saxham (55), or rectangular as at Kilverstone (56); both kinds occur in Herringfleet tower and there are many other examples. Less common are true turned arches with separate wedge-shaped voussoirs as were used at Seething (57) and in the chevron-ornamented west window at Little Saxham. Internally these Norman windows are single-splayed, generally with flint jambs and arches but at Kilverstone the jambs only are dressed stone (though in the north window they change to flint halfway up), the flint arches they support being set back on the reveals and showing shuttering board-marks on their soffits. In a few other towers, dressed stone is used internally in the jambs and in the arches – the west windows at Little Saxham and Gissing and several at

Haddiscoe, Herringfleet and Seething – and at Snailwell the internal jambs are dressed limestone with arch voussoirs of similar stone but only roughly-hewn. At Little Saxham and elsewhere the internal stone dressings can clearly be seen to be part of the original tower wall construction because shuttering board-marks on the arch soffit are contiguous with the backs of the stones and there is no derangement to the coursing of the walling flintwork above and at the sides of the stonework.

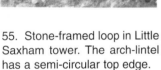

55. Stone-framed loop in Little Saxham tower. The arch-lintel has a semi-circular top edge.

56. Stone-framed loop in Kilverstone tower. The arch-lintel has a straight top.

57. Stone-framed loop in Seething tower. The arch here is formed with voussoirs.

Of the Norman round towers, there are about a dozen that today still have recognisably Norman belfries. Gissing, Thorington and Thorpe next Haddiscoe have already been reviewed and Gayton Thorpe is discussed in a later chapter. Snailwell and Kilverstone have double belfry openings with the centre shaft, jambs and sub-arches formed with dressed stone set at the outside face of the wall and backed internally by a larger arch encompassing the two lights. Merton (58) has the same kind, though with exterior jambs of flint; unfortunately, bad repairs to their heads using flints and odd pieces of brick and stone, have made the original construction of the sub-arches uncertain but comparison with its counterpart at Kilverstone (9) of the remnant springer stone on the capital of the central stone shaft of the west opening suggests that originally the Merton arches may have been of stone. Hengrave and Wortham, described below, and Piddinghoe, Bexwell, Blundeston and Holton have belfries with single-light openings; at the latter three, described in later chapters, the Norman belfry is surmounted by a later one.

Little Saxham is without question the finest Norman round tower and its belfry is in a class of its own (X). In the four main directions, twin openings form the inner of three orders each with circular colonnettes with cushion capitals supporting the moulded stone arches. Between the openings, are pairs of blank arches with similar stone colonnettes and arches, all rising from a billeted string course. The tall tower arch is formed with dressed stone and south of it is a low round-arched recess, one of whose stones is common to the tower arch stonework.

Reportedly,[1] the internal arches that span the twin lights of the belfry openings at Little Saxham and those of the upper windows below the belfry are formed with flints, by contrast with the stone internal dressings of the lower window and upper door. At Blundeston also, the lower windows and upper door have stone dressings internally but above them the original six Norman belfry openings and the small sound-holes between are framed and arched in flint internally. Again, at Herringfleet (see Chapter 9), two tower windows have flint jambs internally while dressed stone is used for others in the same stage, and at Seething (see below) blocked openings with internal flint jambs are found above lower windows that have internal stone dressings. These examples illustrate that it was not an uncommon Norman practice to use stone dressings in some internal openings and flints for others in the same tower.

Wortham

Standing some 50 feet or more high, the tower is in a semi-ruinous state and is open to the sky. In the west wall a gaping void indicates the position of a former large west window, some of whose internal dressed jamb stones remain in position. Just above this, a small rectangular opening must be part of a twentieth-century repair, as an early photograph[2] shows the rift in the west wall as larger than now and encompassing the area in which the small opening is located. At belfry level, another large breach in the west wall leaves no trace of the west belfry opening.

58. Double belfry opening at Merton. Backed by a single internal arch, the badly-repaired arches at the wall face were probably originally stone. Note the likeness of the shaft capital and springer stone to their counterparts at Kilverstone, 9.

The tower's internal diameter is said to be 20 feet and the external diameter is given in the church guide as 29 feet. These measurements establish it as the largest flint round church tower in the country, its nearest rivals being Great Leighs in Essex which has an internal diameter of about 17 feet, and West Dereham in Norfolk at 17'4" but that is built of ferricrete.

There are three small offsets in the tower's external profile, at about 13 feet above ground level, at approximately 30 feet and at about 6 feet higher at belfry cill level. Measured at the west window void, the wall thickness is 4'7" at the north jamb and 4'4" at the south. Below the window void in the west wall, a large stone coffin slab is set vertically, flush with the flintwork. With no apparent disruption in the surrounding flintwork and the uniformity of the mortar setting of the flints adjacent to the slab with that of the walling generally, it appears that the slab was incorporated when the wall was built. Low in the wall to the north-west of this, also flush with the wall face, is set a 5'6" long x 6" thick horizontal slab of Barnack stone, its face curved to the tower wall profile. Internally, the tower walls are of similar material to the exterior.

59 Flint-framed belfry opening of Wortham tower.

Near the top of the tower there are three single-light belfry openings, at south, north and east, estimated to be about three-and-a-half feet wide. These openings (59) have semi-circular arches with radially-laid rough-dressed limestone voussoirs internally and externally, and their jambs are formed with flints and occasional pieces of squared limestone; the reveals are not splayed. The east opening, visible within the tower, is blocked at the east face and externally is covered by a later wooden bellcote. The south opening has a cinquefoiled, pointed stone window inserted at the external face beneath the semi-circular arch.

In the tower's east wall, a tall wide tower arch of roughly parabolic shape, framed in flint and now blocked, can be seen; presumably a smaller Norman arch between nave and tower disappeared when it was inserted. Its apex cuts into the lower part of the former upper door, also blocked, which has a semi-circular arch of radially-laid stone voussoirs and jambs of similar construction to the belfry openings.

The tower walls are of characteristic Norman style and consist of coursed rubble flints and non-flint erratics, with occasional pieces of limestone here and there in the fabric. To the south of the tower, the fabric of the nave west wall where un-repointed can be seen to be similar to that of the tower and the coursing of the flints seems to coincide with the tower coursing.

It has been thought though, that the tower once stood independently as a watch tower or defence tower, before the church was built; T.H. Bryant (op. cit.) records that it is said to have been one of the watch towers for the Abbot of Bury. However, these theories are considered unlikely, firstly, because the coinciding flintwork coursing of nave and tower suggests that they were built together, and secondly, it is noticeable that the external curvature of the lower part of the tower wall straightens as it nears the nave wall, whereas higher up, at about the original nave roof level, it reverts to fully circular shape. If the tower had originally stood on its own, it would have been fully circular from ground level.

The likelihood that the tower was built as a bell tower rather than a defence or watch tower is confirmed by the size and design of the belfry openings. Their width, height and parallel reveals clearly identify them as belfry openings rather than look-out or defence windows indicating that the tower was built as a bell tower.

The radially-set voussoirs in the semi-circular arch of the upper door and in the internal and external arches of the belfry openings, though formed in rough-dressed stone rather than ashlar, are Norman in style; a post-Conquest date is corroborated by their use of limestone, and further evidence for a Norman date is provided by the slab of Barnack stone built into the wall, though its purpose is obscure. As no ashlar or carved stonework is used in the tower, the likelihood is that it is early Norman work, but having in mind the probability that little, if any, Norman ecclesiastical building was undertaken in Suffolk before the Norman work at the Abbey at Bury in the later years of the eleventh century, an early twelfth-century date seems more likely.

Seething

The tower is circular to the top but clearly of two separate stages, differentiated at roughly two-thirds of the tower's height, i.e. at about nave ridge level, by a noticeable break in the tower wall profile, above which the walls taper. The lower stage fabric is well-coursed rubble flint in typical Norman style but the upper stage flintwork differs and incorporates medieval brick.

The tower arch between nave and tower is round-headed with stone jamb and arch dressings both sides; it has stone imposts returned on the nave wall face and in the tower. It is 5'9" wide in reveal and 10'7" high to impost level and the arch is 4'6" thick at the crown, the same thickness as the tower wall. Above the arch, the tower east wall is a flattened curve.

At first floor level in the lower stage, an upper door in the tower east wall has flint jambs and reveals and a semi-circular head formed in flint but three narrow round-headed single-splayed windows at south, west and north, are framed with dressed stone inside and out (57). Internally the window embrasures are splayed to about two feet wide and board-marks of the shuttering on which the arch flintwork was built are continuous between the inner and outer stone voussoirs, showing that these openings and the stonework are contemporary, nor is there any evidence inside or outside of disturbance to the fabric above the arches that might suggest that they were later insertions into an existing wall; on the contrary, the well-coursed flintwork above these arches, particularly internally, is clearly undisturbed original work, indicating that the windows and their stonework must have been built with the wall. The lower stage of the tower and the fillets between it and the nave can therefore be confidently dated as Norman, an attribution supported by the Norman character of the tower arch.

Within the tower, at a level estimated to be about the same level as the external profile change, the inner face of the walling of the upper stage is set back a few inches, forming a ledge; above this level, a difference in the internal fabric is noticable in that, like the outside of this stage, it also incorporates medieval brick. In this top stage, as on the outside, there has been much repair in post-medieval brickwork but sufficient original work remains to indicate that the four belfry openings in the cardinal orientations have, or originally had, medieval bricks in their jambs and arches internally. Externally, those facing west, east and north have original stone jambs but renewed arches of post-medieval brick. The south opening is entirely of post-medieval brick with a semi-circular arch and is formed within a large area of walling rebuilt in the same kind of brick.

At south-west, north-west, north-east and south-east in the tower wall internally, pairs of vertical straight joints about three feet apart extend downwards for about four feet from the ledge at the top of the lower stage; they seem to be the lower jambs of four blocked openings, whose heads were evidently sacrificed when the upper stage was built. These interior jambs were formed with flints but as the blocking material of the openings is flush with the wall, it is not possible to tell whether the embrasures were splayed or straight. External examination of the tower walls at the corresponding positions reveals indications of blocking which, if unsuspected, could easily be overlooked or dismissed as repairs.

From the evidence of these headless blocked openings, it seems that the present upper stage replaces an earlier one which had been taken down to a level part-way up these openings; they were then built up solid as the base for the present upper stage, which on the evidence of the medieval bricks within its fabric and in the internal arches of the belfry openings, is post-Norman and probably not earlier than late thirteenth century. The non-cardinal orientation of the blocked openings and their relatively low position suggest that they were more likely to have been small tower windows than original Norman belfry openings. If so, the tower's original height with a Norman belfry might have been about the same as now.

60. Seething. Remnant of the original nave west wall, robbed of its quoins, seen between the later, thinner buttressed west wall of the widened nave on the right, and the fillet and tower on the left.

Externally, the condition of the nave west wall each side of the tower shows that the nave has been widened by the building of later side walls a few feet further out than the original alignments. When this was done, the western returns of the new side walls were not built as thick as the original nave west wall and the difference in thickness can be seen at set-backs of about 10" where they join the thicker original wall which measurement has shown was about 3'3" thick. Betwen 9" and 16" only of this original wall remains each side of the tower and the original south-west and north-west quoins have gone, leaving deformed and out-of-plumb angles where the quoins would have been at the junctions of the later walls (60).

As the edges of the extremities of the old nave west wall where they meet the later walls are so out of true and devoid of any material larger than the normal walling flints, they are clearly not former quoins but simply the residual wall from which the quoins have been robbed. The logical presumption therefore is that the original quoins were ashlar stone, because, had they been flint, it is likely that they would have been left in situ, like on many other similarly widened naves. If the old quoins had been stone as seems likely, that would confirm a Norman date for the church.

The flintwork of the fillets between the old nave west wall remnants and the Norman tower seem to course with the wall's flintwork, thus corroboratng a Norman date for the original nave.

Suggested Dating

C.12: Original church and tower built.

*C.13 or early c.*14: Present belfry replaced original Norman belfry. Nave widened. Possibly the chancel east wall rebuilt using quoins from west end – perhaps replacing an apse.

C.18: Extensive repairs to belfry stage with post-medieval brick.

Hengrave

The tower is circular to the top and is faced with rubble flints and non-flint erratic cobbles in a typical inland-Suffolk mix, fairly evenly coursed, and to a greater or lesser extent showing stratification (61). Three quite distinct 'lifts' of walling are noticeable; from ground level up to a height of about seven and a half feet, very marked stratification is apparent in which ten well-defined flintwork bands, three, four or five courses high, are clearly distinguishable. In this section, two wood putlog-hole bridgings are visible. Stratification virtually ceases in the next section up to about the cill level of the first-floor windows but the material is no different from that below. At the first-floor window-cill level there are six putlog holes bridged with limestone and upwards from this level a significant amount of limestone appears in the walling and there are other putlog holes at belfry level. Stratification again becomes noticeable but not as sharply defined as in the ground stage. The battlemented parapet and a few courses below it are later. It is more likely that the noticeable fabric differences in the three lifts of the tower walls represent seasonal constructional breaks rather than different building episodes. Although the lower

61. Pronounced stratification of the lower courses of flintwork on the tower of Hengrave church. Their continuity has been disturbed by recent repairs around and above the circular window.

section shows more distinct stratification and the upper part includes limestone, and some areas of apparently later pointing tend to create superficial differences, the basic walling material is constant throughout and the coursing of the flints is pretty consistent. It is probable therefore that the whole tower except for the parapet was built at one time.

Two circular single-splayed windows, facing west and south, in the ground-floor stage have external stone frames and plastered splays inside. The diameter of the aperture is 1'5" externally and 2'9" at the inside wall face. The west window has recently been restored and reglazed, but some of its stonework is Barnack and may be original because this variety of stone was no longer available after the quarries were worked out in the late fifteenth century. The south window stonework is probably Ketton stone and is Victorian or later.

First-floor windows at south, west and north have rectangular stone frames externally; the stonework of the south and north ones is probably Barnack and original, but the west one is modern except its cill. Internally the north window has tooled jambs and head and unsplayed reveals. The south and west ones are not visible behind the organ.

At belfry level there are five single-light stone-framed windows about one and a half feet wide. Those at south, west and north are round-headed, their stone heads cut from large single stones. Only the south one is glazed; the other two are blocked and the clock has been mounted in the west one. Internally, all three have different amounts of dressed stone in their jambs, and have arches turned in flint; the south and west arches are round and the north 'triangular', but surprisingly its external stone head which can be seen at the back of the blocked recess is a four-centred pointed shape rather than truly semi-circular like the south one. The two windows at south-east and north-east have pointed heads and the disturbed exterior flintwork around them shows that they have been inserted. Internally, they have no stone in their jambs or head, and the roughness of their flint reveals and heads without any form of turned arch confirms the external evidence that these openings were broken out through an existing wall. The north-east one is blocked.

There is no sign of an upper door. Had there been one at first-floor level, it would, no doubt, have disappeared when the Perpendicular tower arch, about seventeen feet high to the apex, was inserted. Within the belfry stage, the east wall is flat and contains a possible indication of the north slope of an earlier roofline which would imply an original nave roof ridge level at about halfway up the belfry windows. This corresponds with the external trace of an old nave roofline visible just above the ridge of the present lower-pitched nave roof. These indications, and the flattened curve of the tower's east wall externally, suggest that the tower was added to an earlier towerless church, with the top part of the tower built on its nave west wall. Such fabric of the nave west wall as can be seen differs from that of the tower.

The use of Barnack stone in the west circular window, the first-floor windows and the round-headed belfry windows, and its random occurrence in the wall fabric suggest a post-Conquest date unless one is prepared to believe that all this stonework has been inserted into earlier walls. There can be little doubt though that the three round-headed belfry windows with their stone dressings were built with the tower walls and not inserted later – one has only to contrast their internal construction techniques, i.e. dressed stone built in the jambs and arched flint heads, and the conjunction of their exterior stone dressings to the surrounding flintwork, with the equivalent rough details of the south-east and north-east pointed windows that have been shown to be obvious later insertions.

Although the round-headed pattern of the three original belfry windows suggests Norman style, their particular design is probably a Transitional pattern of the late twelfth century or early thirteenth, and this is corroborated by the pointed shape of the stonework seen in the north window recess. The rectangular first-floor windows which appear to be part of the original structure are perhaps more indicative of the thirteenth century than the late twelfth.

A Transitional date is supported by the stratification in the walling flintwork which, as mentioned earlier, seems to have been a feature of the twelfth and thirteenth centuries with no instances reliably dateable earlier than Norman.

It is interesting that both wood and stone putlog hole bridgings occur in the tower walls. No great significance need be attached to this; it appears that for reasons unknown, when the tower had reached first-floor window-cill level, some random limestone had become available and the larger pieces were selected for use in putlog holes.

[1] Goode W J. Op. Cit. 1994
[2] Bryant T H. *County Churches, Suffolk*. George Allen, 1912

CHAPTER 12

PARTIALLY REBUILT TOWERS

In addition to those early towers that must have collapsed and were rebuilt in later medieval times, there are several whose circular stage seems to have been partly rebuilt, following perhaps a partial collapse or degeneration of the tower. These can often be identified by a change in the fabric of the tower's circular stage that is not easily comprehensible as other than a different building phase.

Where a difference in the material or in the size of the flints or a change in coursing is found in the circular stage in association with an absence of a belfry contemporary with the lower part, it is a strong indication that the work showing the different characteristics replaces an earlier superstructure.

There are at least thirty round towers, wholly circular or with octagonal tops, in which, below the belfry stage, variations in the external fabric other than repair work can be seen. On some of them, the fabric discontinuities may have a deliberate decorative intent or they may represent seasonal building stints; about ten feet (3 m.) has been suggested as the height of round tower walling which would have been built in one year, and the fabric changes on Bessingham (4) or Roughton (41) towers for example seem to conform roughly to this. At Hengrave, the consistency of the basic walling material and of its coursing suggest continuity of construction and hence that the noticeable flintwork differences at three levels in the tower wall probably arise from seasonal constructional breaks rather than different building episodes. Surprisingly few other towers show this kind of subdivision.

Since repairs, later pointing and remnants of old rendering often tend to obscure any differences, or fortuitous flintwork variations may suggest discontinuities where in fact there are none, it is not always easy to recognize fabric differences that could be indicative of different dates but the examples described below show that careful examination can establish whether the two parts of a circular stage in which such differences occur are separate phases of building. This can be important for dating.

In the following descriptions, the expression "lower stage" means the part of the tower nearest to the ground and "middle stage" means the part of the circular stage between the lower stage and the present belfry.

Aldham tower, described in Chapter 8, provides a defining example of how separate building phases can be identified by variations in a tower's external wall fabric. There, three different types of brick used in the lower, middle and belfry stages, and a different kind of flintwork in the belfry stage clearly differentiate three distinct building episodes.

At Fritton, Norfolk, the fabric of the lower stage of the tower of St Catherine's church is of typical Norman coursed flint whereas the middle-stage flintwork is smaller, less regular, more closely packed and contains occasional medieval bricks. A single-light west window framed with medieval brick in the middle stage has a shallow 'triangular' head comprising two bricks propped against each other at a shallow angle, and at corresponding levels on south, north and east, blockings of similar-sized openings can be detected. These four features were no doubt the former belfry openings of a post-Norman belfry which apparently replaced an original Norman one before the addition of the present fifteenth-century octagonal belfry and they corroborate the indication of the different fabric that the middle stage was a later build.

At Fritton in Suffolk a striking change from dark knapped flints mixed with a few bricks and squared stones in the lower part to white knapped flints in the top third or thereabouts of the tower of St Edmund's church (XIV) is a strong indication that the superstructure above the level of the fabric change is a later building phase. Nevertheless, although windows formed with post-medieval bricks seem to be original features of this upper stage's construction rather than insertions into it, the belfry openings above them have stonework apparently of the fourteenth century. How this may have come about is considered in Chapter 16.

As at the top of Little Snoring (16) and Welborne towers (see Chapter 4), a fabric change in the middle stage of Bedingham tower (23) suggests that its original upper parts have disappeared. A tall, narrow, round-headed tower arch formed without stonework is convincing evidence that the lower stage of the tower is probably pre-Conquest, but the different tower flintwork above nave roof level and the absence of any evidence of former belfry openings in that part suggests that the middle stage has been rebuilt, probably when the octagonal belfry was added. Clearly, without belfry openings, the present circular stage never stood as a finished tower.

At Wickmere (XI), a change from ferricrete to flintwork and a different style of workmanship in the tower walls at about the level of the ground-floor window suggest that from that level the tower, originally perhaps of the eleventh century, may have been rebuilt in the fourteenth.

About halfway up the tower at Titchwell (62), a slight set-back in the wall defines the start of a taper in the walls and a marked change in the fabric, which together suggest that the work above this level, including the Norman belfry, is likely to be a separate building phase. The lower part of the tower could therefore be pre-Conquest, and the fabric change may in this instance represent a break in construction at the time of the Conquest rather than a rebuilding of the upper stage.

The short round tower at Howe (IX) has no belfry openings in its upper part and at about ten feet below the top, the tower fabric changes to more regular, coursed flintwork, suggesting that from that level, the upper part may have been rebuilt, and the absence of belfry

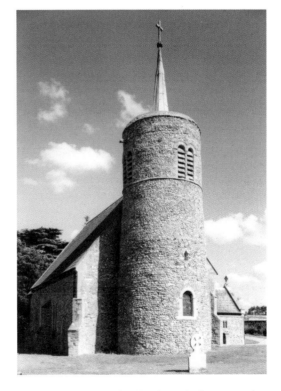

62. A slight set-back about halfway up the lower stage of Titchwell tower coincides with a marked change in the wall fabric.

openings tends to confirm this. The tower's present height cannot therefore be taken as indicating its original height.

Similarly at Barmer, a change in the quality of the flintwork suggests that this short tower may have been rebuilt from about eleven feet above ground. It has no proper belfry openings – only three small stone-framed rectangular apertures facing south, west and north at about two-thirds of the tower's height. In Ladbrooke's drawing of 1831 a taller tower with a circular belfry stage is shown with a lancet belfry opening; the post-Norman

date that that implies is endorsed by the tower's lower flintwork and a pointed tower arch with dressed stone facings.

Worthing is another truncated tower; random bricks in the upper half and crude square brick-framed belfry openings suggest that that part was rebuilt, perhaps in the eighteenth century, but a splayed base might imply that the whole tower has been rebuilt on an earlier foundation.

Although there is no marked difference in the fabric of the lower and middle stages of Kirby Cane tower, they can be established as different builds by a band of medieval brick that completely encircles the tower at about 23 feet (7 m.) from the ground. Since insertion of a level course of bricks into existing uncoursed flintwork would have been impracticable, with no structural purpose and minimal aesthetic effect, this brick course is probably the starting level of a later building phase. Features below

63. Blocked loop formed with medieval bricks above the level of the brick band that encircles the tower at Kirby Cane.

the level of the brick band suggest an eleventh-century date, but above it, loops formed with medieval bricks (63) clearly indicate post-Norman construction.

In addition to those towers mentioned above which show evidence of reconstruction below the belfry stage, there are others with a circular post-Norman belfry that is clearly later than the lower stages, whether pre- or post-Conquest, and must, therefore, have replaced an earlier one of which no evidence now remains. Circular belfries at Morningthorpe, Long Stratton, Bruisyard, and Yaxham, where a small flintwork variation at belfry cill level is discernable, are probably fourteenth-century or later replacements, while the post-Norman one at Seething has extensive eighteenth-century repairs. Those at Geldeston and probably Norton Subcourse were rebuilt in the nineteenth century, and, of course, a number of earlier belfries were replaced by octagonal ones.

Rickinghall Inferior

The tower is circular for about three-quarters of its height and has an octagonal belfry stage crowned with a battlemented and finialled parapet.

For most of the height of the circular stage, the fabric is reasonably-coursed, fairly large flint rubble containing a generous proportion of non-flint erratics and is similar to the nave west wall, but the fabric of the top seven or eight feet below the stone string course at the base of the octagon is noticably different from that in the lower part, the flints being smaller, more closely packed and uncoursed. Within this upper section, on the east, north and to a lesser extent on the south where residual rendering partly obscures the flintwork, irregularities in the external flintwork provide indications of internal blocked openings, and at the corresponding position on the west, there is a stone lancet window with a trefoil head.

A dressed stone weathercourse moulding built into the tower's curved east wall defines an earlier nave roofline; it consists of two sloping members, the upper ends of which terminate about a foot or so below the level of the point where they should meet. A short horizontal length of similar moulding connects the top ends of the sloping members at precisely the level at which the change of fabric occurs (64).

The octagonal belfry stage has knapped flint walls with stone quoins and flushwork in the parapet; the two-light belfry openings in the cardinal faces have cusped Y-tracery.

The tower arch has a semi-circular head and is faced with stone. It has one-piece stone imposts for the full width of the reveal with short returns on the nave side but flush in the tower; they are of normal chamfered profile, with two grooves on the face. The arch is 5'2" wide and about 12'6" high, and measured at the crown of the arch, the tower east wall is about 3'9" thick; at the west window, the wall is 3'6" thick.

An upper door in the east wall of the tower at first floor level internally is three feet wide x 7'3" high and is blocked with flint at the nave face leaving a recess in the tower about 2'9" deep. It has straight reveals with jambs of

64. At Rickinghall Inferior, the apex of a dressed stone weathercourse in the tower wall has been truncated at the level at which a later belfry was built, replacing the original one. That later belfry's openings were blocked when the present octagonal belfry was built.

flint and a semi-circular head formed with radially-laid roughly shaped stone voussoirs. The arch is set back on the reveals and the board-marks of the shuttering on which it was built are clearly visible in the soffit mortar which can be seen to be contiguous with the backs of the voussoir stones. The first floor west window internally has splayed reveals and flint jambs and a semi-circular arch head formed with radially-laid roughly shaped stone voussoirs, and like those in the upper door, the soffit mortar of the arch is contiguous with the backs of the voussoirs.

At the level where the external change of material occurs, there is a corresponding change in the internal fabric and a set-back in the internal wall. Below this set-back, the internal walling is similar to the exterior, but above it the material is smaller, rougher and partially rendered.

Within this top section of the circular stage there are, or were, four openings at the cardinal positions, those at south, east and north now being blocked with flint flush with the internal wall face, and the one on the west remaining open as a window. These openings measure about 2'3" wide x 5'8" high at the internal wall face and, though their heads are rounded, they are not truly semi-circular – more a pointed shape with a rounded apex; this is a shape commonly seen in the rere-arches of pointed tower windows, particularly those formed with medieval bricks. The jambs and arches are formed with thin red tiles except at the bottom on some of the jambs where squared stones are incorporated. At the springing level of the arches the tiles are laid at angles whch progressively steepen towards the apex and although some show tendencies reminiscent of "Tredington fashion" (see below), in general they can be seen as relating to the curvatures of arches of pointed shape, and in fact the arch tiles of the south opening show no abnormal deviations.

There is compelling evidence that the top seven or eight feet of the tower's circular stage is a later build than the lower part: this evidence includes the different flintwork in the top section both externally and internally, the internal reduction of wall thickness at the level where these changes occur, and the difference in internal constructional methods of the jambs and arches of the first floor west window and upper door in the lower part from those of the upper section openings – flint jambs with stone heads and round arches in the lower part, and tile jambs and heads with round-apexed pointed arches in the upper part. Also, the absence of tiles in the fabric of the lower part, by contrast with their abundance in the blocked openings of the upper section, tends to suggest that tiles were not available when the lower part was built, and this implies different building dates.

Further corroboration for a later build for the upper circular section is provided by the curtailment of the two sloping members of the weathercoursing at the precise level at which the change in the tower fabric occurs and the absence of apex weathercourse stones in the east wall of this section. There is no rational reason why nave roof weathercoursing should terminate with a horizontal member as it does here, and so the sloping weathercourses must originally have met at a normal pointed apex; the absence of their apex stones and their apparent truncation below apex level at the level where the change of material starts suggests that an original upper circular section of the tower which had contained the apex stones of the weathercourse was removed and therefore that the present upper circular section is not part of the original tower, but a replacement of an earlier belfry, built at a later date than the lower part of the tower containing the weathercourse.

Because of the practical constructional difficulties of inserting a curving and sloping stone moulding into an existing flint wall, and because it had clearly been in situ when the upper circular section was built, the stone weathercoursing built into the tower east wall is almost certainly contemporary with the tower lower stage. Since dressed stone as used for the weathercoursing was unlikely to have been available before the Conquest, its presence confirms a post-Conquest date for the lower stage.

I
The carstone round tower at Bexwell.

II
Beeston St Lawrence round tower.

III
The round tower of the derelict church at Great
Hautbois.

IV
Stone string courses on Haddiscoe round tower.

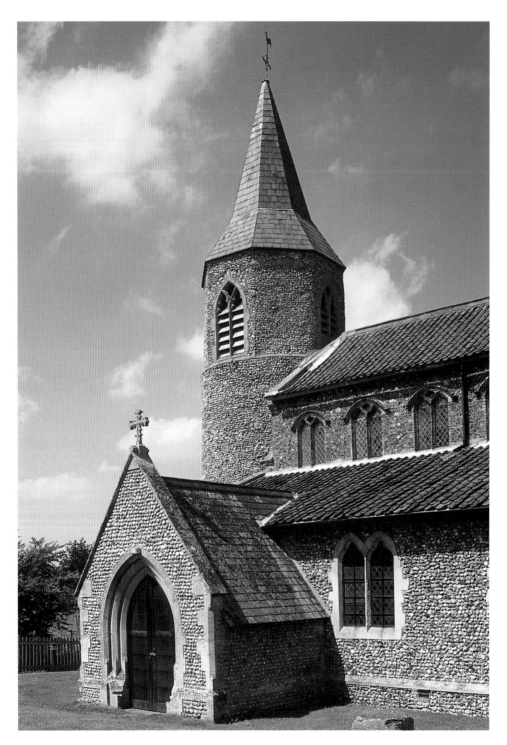

V
The octagonal belfry of Croxton round tower has flint corners.

VI

Irregular megalithic ferricrete quoin stones used on the angles of the octagonal tower of the derelict church at Edgefield.

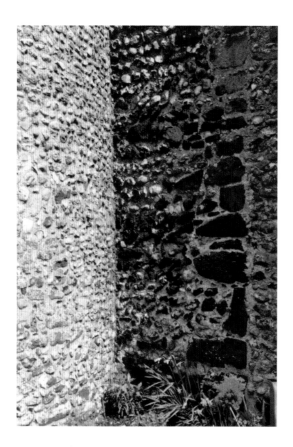

VII
The junction between the tower, on the left, and the nave west wall at Gresham church, showing the different flintwork of the two walls.

VIII
The north reveal of the tower arch of the ruined church of Burlingham St Peter. The amount of medieval brick in its construction dates it, and hence the fallen round tower, as post-Norman.

IX
The short round tower at Howe. Its upper part may have been rebuilt.

X
The belfry stage of the fine Norman tower of Little Saxham church.

XI
Wickmere. A change in the tower's fabric just above the west windows sill suggests that all above that level is a later build than the lower part of the tower.

XII
Fishley round tower. Lancet belfry on top of former Norman belfry, the openings of which are clearly visible blocked in brick.

XIII
The buttressed round tower of Ramsholt church.

XIV
The tower of St Edmund's, Fritton, near Yarmouth.

XV
St Edmund's, Fritton. The nave east gable and east wall of the south aisle.

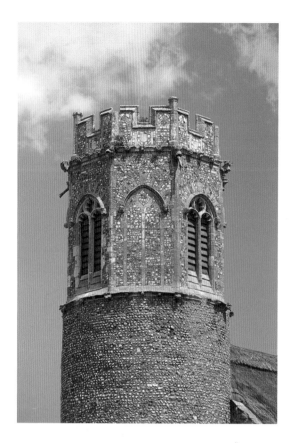

XVI

The octagonal belfry stage of Potter Heigham tower. The level of the first row of putlog holes in the octagon is defined by one visible in the knapped flint about a foot above the stone base of the belfry.

XVII

The octagonal stages of Thorpe Abbotts tower showing the first row of putlog holes in the octagon just above the lower string course.

XVIII
Hassingham tower, with a contemporary octagonal lancet belfry.

XIX
Circular feature formed with bricks in the west wall of Rushall tower. Originally, probably a small lancet window with a medieval brick frame, it was altered later, perhaps to form the setting for a clock.

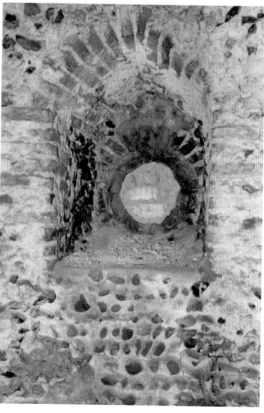

XX
The internal embrasure behind the circular brick feature in the west wall of Rushall tower. The opening, with an arch of pointed shape, is formed with medieval brick. The later circular brickwork within the original opening can be clearly seen.

XXI
Southease round tower, Sussex.

XXII
Great Shefford round tower, Berkshire.

On the evidence of the tower arch, the stone arches to the upper door and first-floor west window shown by the contiguous board-marks to be original construction, and the stone weathercourse, none of which show any evidence of having been inserted into earlier walls, it is considered that the lower five-sixths of the circular stage of the tower is Norman; its coursing and the larger size of the flints and erratics are typical of Norman work, and this is quite distinct from the much smaller, uncoursed and closely-packed flintwork of the upper circular section that is characteristic of the thirteenth and fourteenth centuries.

All the evidence suggests that an original upper circular section of the same date as the lower part of the tower was, for reasons unknown, taken down and a new circular belfry built, probably in the thirteenth century, with single-light lancet type belfry openings having their inner arches and jambs framed with Roman or medieval tiles. When the octagonal belfry was added later, probably in the fourteenth century, these thirteenth-century belfry openings were blocked except for the west one in which a small window was inserted although its present stonework may be Victorian.

The term "Tredington fashion" is often used to describe the arrangement of arch voussoirs when laid non-radially and at irregular angles relative to the curve of the arch, such as those of rubble stone over blocked openings in the nave walls of Tredington church. Baldwin Brown attributed them as Saxon, and arches of that kind have since been widely regarded as indicative of Saxon workmanship. However, in the flintwork tradition of East Anglia, the practice of setting voussoirs of brick or tile above window openings at odd angles relative to the arch curvature has been found to extend well beyond Saxon times, and so tile voussoirs which may be less than perfectly radially laid, such as those in the blocked openings in the upper circular section of Rickinghall tower, are not an infallible indication of Saxon work.

Bexwell

Bexwell church tower (I) is built of carstone. It is circular for three-quarters of its height and has an octagonal top. Careful examination of the walls of the circular stage reveals that they are built with two different types of carstone, in two distinct styles of stonework, with the change from one to the other occurring roughly halfway up the circular stage.

The lower part is built with a type of carstone with a fissured surface, used in random-shaped pieces of all sizes and laid uncoursed, whereas the upper part uses a type with a pitted surface in more evenly-sized blocks, many of them squared, which are laid in definite, regular courses. This difference is particularly noticeable in the south wall, most conspicuously at a stepping between the two techniques.

Unlike the tower at Bessingham (4) for example, where abrupt changes of material occurring at definite levels probably indicate seasonal building stints, the irregular levels at which the changes of material and workmanship occur on the Bexwell tower seem to rule out that possibility, and they probably define the junction between the truncated original walls of an unfinished or partially collapsed early tower and a later added or rebuilt upper part.

The possibility that these changes of material and style of wall construction in the tower's circular stage could indicate two distinct building phases is reinforced by a comparison of the heads of two blocked circular openings in the lower part with those of the ten blocked round-headed former belfry openings in the upper part. The arches of the blocked circular openings are formed with thin, irregular, undressed pieces of carstone of varied lengths in quite a different manner from the arches of the former belfry openings which are framed externally by two orders of carstone stonework; the inner order is recessed two or three inches from the wall face and the jambs and heads of both orders are formed with even-sized, reasonably well-dressed stones and rough but definitely wedge-shaped voussoirs. The openings are about fourteen inches wide and inside the tower are framed with jamb stones and voussoirs similar to the exterior ones but in a single order only and perhaps more roughly dressed. The openings are all blocked with medieval bricks except for the easternmost which is blocked with carstone.

The carstone used in the circular part of the tower and for the belfry arches is not a freestone and cannot be dressed with such accuracy as is possible with say, Barnack or Caen limestone. Its texture makes sharp edges impossible to achieve and it is understandable therefore, that although its original general character is still apparent, after centuries of weathering and repointings, carstone that may originally have been squared and shaped will not now be sharply defined.

The present west upper doorway, located roughly at the level of the change in walling style, is a later alteration of a single-splayed window; the opening is about 1'9" wide and is splayed within the tower. Above the crudely reconstructed external arch of the opening, carstone voussoirs are visible with corresponding ones internally. The apparent radius to which the external carstone voussoirs are laid and the presence of the smaller altered arch below them give reason to suppose that this window-head was originally of two orders like the former belfry arches. The present external jambs of small pieces of hard carstone, matching neither the upper or lower stone types, do not bond with the adjacent walling, presumably having replaced the original jambs when the window was converted to a doorway.

The church walls contain several types of carstone but the oldest walls, i.e. the nave west wall and the west parts of the side walls are mainly of the same type as the lower part of the tower. This, the nave west wall measurements and the flattened curve of the east wall within the tower suggest that the nave and lower part of the tower were contemporary. At high level in the north wall of the nave, near the west end, a double-splayed round-headed window has an arch similar to those of the two circular blocked openings in the tower.

The change of walling material and the different methods of shaping and laying the stone in the lower and upper parts of the circular stage of the tower, the difference between the arch voussoirs of the blocked circular windows and those of the ten former belfry openings, and the single splay design of the first floor tower window (now the upper west doorway) in contrast to double-splayed windows in the lower part of the tower and the nave are all convincing evidence for the proposition that the upper circular part was a different build from the lower part and the nave.

Double-splayed windows are widely accepted as being features of late Anglo-Saxon work (and indeed some can be shown to be Norman), and so, if the nave and lower circular part of the tower are considered as late Saxon, then it is unlikely that the upper circular part will be earlier than Norman.

The squared and coursed walling of the upper part of the tower, the wedge-shaped arch voussoirs of about the same width as their radial length in the belfry openings, and the double order of stonework around the belfry openings with a recessed inner order, all point to Norman workmanship and it therefore seems probable that the upper part of the circular stage, which includes the west upper doorway and the ten round-headed former belfry openings, is a Norman addition built onto the lower walls of a partially collapsed or unfinished late Saxon tower. The later octagonal belfry was probably added in the fifteenth century.

Rushmere

The tower is circular to the top and can be seen to be in three distinct stages, clearly defined by the flintwork of the walls. The lower stage, from the base to about nine feet above the ground is of coursed rubble flints; the middle stage which occupies more than half the tower's total height is of more closely-packed uncoursed flints and contains a few medieval bricks; the belfry stage, surmounted by a shallow brick parapet, has coursed flintwork containing medieval bricks which course with the flints and in places are laid in short consecutive stretches.

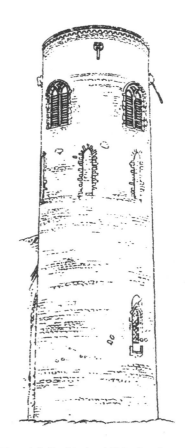

The only window in the tower below the belfry is a tall narrow lancet facing west; it is located mainly in the lower part of the middle stage and has a renewed stone frame externally. A drawing of 1829 (65) by J.C.Buckler[1] shows a shorter pointed window apparently inserted within the outline of a taller lancet shape, and the present window may therefore be a true representation the original arrangement.

Higher up in the middle stage above the level of the nave roof ridge, there are traces of six blocked openings. Their shape on the outside is indeterminate but Buckler's drawing shows them as lancets and this is confirmed internally where they can be clearly seen to have pointed heads (66);

65. J.C.Buckler's 1829 drawing of Rushmere church tower.

the heads and the internal jambs are framed with medieval bricks, and there are also internal putlog holes bridged with similar bricks in the walls below the blocked openings.

The four two-light belfry windows at the cardinal positions in the top stage are of dressed stone and have simple Y-tracery beneath semi-circular arches. Internally they have stone jambs and the west opening has its original medieval brick rere-arch; the others have modern brick repairs.

There are flint fillets between the tower and church, and the coursing of the tower flints can be seen to be continuous across the fillets and in the nave west wall. The quoins at the south-west and north-west corners of the nave are of squared Caen stone of typical Norman proportions and size, and many of their joints have been weathered back to such an extent that the visible mortar is likely to be the original bedding mortar in which the stones were set. This mortar can be seen to be uniform with that of the flintwork in the nave west wall, fillets and tower.

66. One of the six blocked lancet belfry openings below the present belfry, within the tower of Rushmere church.

The tower's internal diameter is eight feet and its wall thickness measured at the west window is 3'7". Internally, the tower east wall is curved and at the tower arch apex its thickness measures slightly less than the nave west wall thickness measured outside the tower, which is the same as the tower wall thickness. The tower arch is plastered and about six feet wide and 9'9" high to the arch springing level. It has no imposts but the springing of the pointed arch is set back an inch or two on the jambs.

The nave is about 14'6" wide and the thickness of its side walls is about a foot less than its 3'7" thick west wall. The north wall for most of its height, the south wall west of the porch and its lower part east of the porch have similar flintwork to the tower's lower stage.

Assuming that an original round-headed tower arch followed the tower's inner curvature as the present pointed one does, its thickness at the crown, like the present one, would have been less than the nave west wall thickness measured outside the tower; the nave and tower must therefore have been built together, because if the tower had been added, the internal curvature of its east wall clearly could not have been intruded into an existing nave west wall without unnecessary and improbable disturbance to it. Contemporary construction of the nave and the lower stage of the tower is confirmed by the continuity of the flintwork coursing in the nave west wall, fillets and tower walls, and further supporting evidence is provided by the nave west wall having been built to the same thickness as the tower wall – if the church had originally been built without a tower, it is unlikely that it would have had a 3'7" thick west wall.

The uniformity of the mortar setting of the quoin stones with that of the flintwork in the adjacent walling provides evidence that the quoin stones are likely to have been original components of the nave walls and not later insertions. The style and material of the quoins themselves establish the nave walls as Norman, and since nave and original tower were built together, the remaining part of the original tower, i.e. the present tower's lower stage must also be Norman.

PARTIALLY REBUILT TOWERS

The marked change in the character of the tower's flintwork at about nine feet above the ground suggests that the tower was rebuilt from that level, presumably following a partial collapse of the upper parts of the Norman tower. The different flintwork, the blocked former belfry openings with pointed arches, and the use of medieval bricks in these windows and in the fabric of the middle stage clearly denote a different building phase from the lower stage and suggest a late thirteenth- or early fourteenth-century date. It is suggested that the assumed collapse of the Norman tower also caused damage at the tower's junction with the nave west wall to the extent that the original tower arch had to be rebuilt, thus accounting for its present pointed shape. It is significant that the springing of the pointed tower arch is at approximately the same level as the external fabric change.

It is to be expected that there would have been a reasonable interval between completion of the tower's middle stage with its six belfry windows and the building of the later, present belfry. The round-headed, Y-traceried belfry openings are therefore probably rather later in the fourteenth century than their design might suggest. Alternatively, is this tower evidence that medieval bricks came into use in East Anglia earlier in the thirteenth century than has generally been supposed?

We can only guess at the reasons for the different building dates of the circular stages of these towers: a partial collapse of the tower, a prolonged delay in the progress of the work, or the replacement of an existing belfry with a new one – these are just three possibilities. Whatever the reasons may have been, one thing is certain: the present height of a circular stage below the belfry cannot be a safe indication of the original height of any round tower in which there is evidence of rebuilding.

There are cases however where changes in the external fabric do not necessarily indicate different building phases. On the tower of Burgh Castle church, for instance, there is a marked difference between the flintwork of the lower and middle stages. While the lower stage flintwork contains only a small number of knapped flints, they are predominant in the middle stage and give it an entirely different, much darker appearance. However, at the transition from one to the other there is no distinct boundary between the two stages; the different facings are so gradually and skilfully merged as to suggest that in spite of the differences both stages are part of one continuous build; if so, the knapped flints and medieval bricks in the middle stage confer, at the earliest, a fourteenth-century date.

---

[1] Gage J. Op. Cit. 1831

CHAPTER 13

TOWERS WITH CIRCULAR BELFRIES SURMOUNTING EARLIER ONES

Mention was made in Chapter 12 of towers in which circular post-Norman belfries had apparently replaced earlier ones. But the original belfry was not always demolished, and several circular post-Norman belfries are built directly on eleventh-twelfth- or thirteenth-century ones.

The former belfry openings in the Norman flint tower at Fishley (XII) have been blocked in red brick. The blocked areas show that the original openings were probably about 3'6" wide overall, and above the impost stones, still in situ, indications in the flintwork suggest that at the wall face there would have been a pair of small arches rather than a single one. The present circular belfry, faced with brick, with trefoiled lancet openings is clearly a later addition.

Below the belfry stage in the tower at Brooke, blocked round-headed openings facing north and south and indications of a smaller one at the same level facing west may have been original belfry openings of a lower tower. Two small round-headed stone windows at ground-floor level and a tall round-headed tower arch confirm that the tower is earlier than the present belfry which has medieval bricks in its fabric and in the surrounds of its single-light pointed openings.

Similarly, the amount of medieval bricks in the fabric as well as the pointed belfry openings of the circular belfries at Holton (77) and at Blundeston (70) leave no doubt that they are later additions surmounting clearly recognisable Norman belfries beneath.

Rushmere tower, described above, is probably the only case where a circular belfry surmounted an earlier post-Norman one that had itself apparently replaced a Norman belfry.

At Kirby Bedon, St Mary's, now in ruins, the tower received a new belfry in the early fifteenth century, probably when the nave was heightened; its remnants stand precariously on a brick string course above an original late-thirteenth-century belfry in which the brick-dressed arches of the blocked pointed openings are clearly visible.

Hales

Accepting that the church's Norman stonework is contemporary with its construction and not, as has been proposed, a wholesale enhancement of an earlier structure, the contrast between its mature mid-twelfth-century Norman details and the partially-blocked double-splayed circular windows in the lower stage of the tower makes an attribution for the tower problematical. The tower (67) displays three distinct constructional technologies: the lower stage contains two double-splayed circular windows, blocked externally but internally showing impressions of basketwork centering on which the flintwork splays were formed (68); by contrast, at first- and second-floor stages internally, round-headed openings, splayed at the lower level and unsplayed above, have radially-laid arches of flint or undressed stone and occasional dressed stones in their jambs; the circular belfry stage has lancet belfry openings with stone dressings, and its internal flintwork is different from that of the two lower stages and incorporates medieval brick.

67. Hales. Virtually no external traces remain of the double-splayed windows in the tower lower stage.

The first-floor windows have stone exterior dressings. The unsplayed second-floor openings at the cardinal orientations must originally have been belfry openings: the eastern one is blocked but this does not show in the tower east wall externally; the other three have been partially blocked and narrower stone lancet windows inserted within the blocking, but although this is obvious inside (69), the external flintwork surrounding these windows shows no signs of 'making good' where the openings were reduced and previous dressings removed.

The present belfry, clearly an addition, has an unusual arrangement of belfry openings: two separate lancets side by side face west and east, and a single one with cusping in the head faces north; the equivalent opening facing south has been blocked. Despite the different internal fabric of the belfry stage, the tower's exterior flintwork is surprisingly

68. Blocked double-splayed circular window inside the lower stage of Hales tower, showing impressions of conical basketwork shuttering around which the window was built.

69. Former round-headed belfry window in Hales tower, later blocked and provided with an inserted lancet loop.

undiversified. This, and the lack of external evidence of the alterations to the former belfry openings suggests the possibility that the middle stage was refaced when the present belfry was added – perhaps even the whole tower, since external blocking of the ground-stage double-splayed windows is not obvious.

As has been shown earlier, only when the body of a church has been rebuilt is it likely that it will be later than the tower. Here, at Hales, the double-splayed windows in the tower's ground stage and a blocked triangular-headed upper door in the east wall at first-floor level seem to suggest that the parts of the structure in which they occur could be earlier than the Norman church details. That being so, the implication is that there was previously an earlier church than the present one, and on that assumption, the evidence suggests the following chronology.

Phase I. A small Saxon church with a round tower, perhaps of the early eleventh century.

Phase II. The church was demolished and a new one built by the Normans, perhaps wider than the original one. The lower stage of the tower was retained, but the upper part rebuilt from first-floor level, with three stone-dressed first-floor windows and round-headed belfry openings at second-floor level, no doubt with exterior stone dressings. The different technology of the openings of the tower's ground-floor and first-floor windows – basketwork shuttering on the ground floor and boarded shuttering on the first floor as shown by the board marks on the arch soffits – could imply different building dates. The dentilled imposts of the tower arch suggests that it may also have been altered at this time. No part of the original nave west wall outside the tower would have remained – the present nave side walls are three feet thick and the present nave west walls, being shorter than this, are in fact the ends of the side walls, which would have been bonded to the earlier ground-floor tower remnant. This would probably all have been mid-twelfth-century work.

Phase III. The present lancet belfry was probably added in the fourteenth century. Stone-dressed lancets were built into the former Norman belfry openings at south, west and north, the eastern opening being blocked, and this stage may possibly have been refaced.

Barsham

The tower is circular to the top and is in three stages: the lower stage occupies just over half the height and terminates at an offset in the outer wall at approximately the level of the nave roof apex. The middle stage is about nine feet high and rises from the offset to a level about two feet below the cills of the belfry openings, and the top stage comprises the belfry and a parapet capped with moulded bricks.

The lower stage fabric is roughly-coursed flint rubble but the flints in its top few feet are larger and more widely spaced than below. The middle stage flintwork is generally similar to the lower and areas of inconsistent flintwork in the cardinal faces, though not conspicuously obvious, signify former openings that have been skilfully blocked. The belfry stage flintwork is smaller and contains several bands of bricks in its lower half and much random brick in the upper part. Belfry openings of two-light width at the cardinal positions have stone frames and arches of Tudor shape, but mullions and tracery are gone, leaving just remnant cusps in the arch stonework. These belfry windows and the extent of brick in this stage clearly defines it as a later addition that can probably be safely dated as late fifteenth- or early sixteenth-century.

The lower stage contains a restored Decorated-style ground-floor west window and at about halfway up at first-floor level there are three stone-faced lancets at south, west and north.

Internally, the embrasures of these first-floor windows have splayed reveals and heads formed in flintwork; the soffit-mortar of the heads shows the board-marks of the shuttering on which the arches were built and it can be clearly seen to be actually in contact with the backs of the stones which form the external facings of these windows (31), providing proof that the embrasures and the external stonework were built together. Nor are there any signs of disturbance to the internal flintwork or disruption of its coursing above and at the sides of these windows that might suggest that they were not built as part of the original wall. The date of the wall and the windows can therefore be regarded as the same and the lancet shape of their external stonework provides a positive post-Norman date – perhaps the late thirteenth century or early fourteenth. Clearly they are too low and too small to have been belfry openings and as there is no evidence of blocked openings above them in the lower stage, it seems likely that, unless it replaces an earlier one (for which there is no evidence) the present middle stage was the original belfry.

In the middle stage, at second-floor level internally, there can be seen dressed, splayed jambstones of four former openings at the cardinal positions, though the east one is noticeably off-centre to the north. The level of their cills coincides with the external offset between the lower and middle stages, and the openings are blocked with flintwork leaving internal recesses about eight inches deep and five feet wide measured across the stonework, while the lengths of wall between are about 3'8". The stone jambs are about seven feet high and the heads of the recesses are now renewed with low modern brick arches. They must have been belfry openings, since openings of this size at this height in a round tower for any other purpose would be unprecedented; it follows therefore that their blocking would have been contemporary with the construction of the later, present belfry.

At the base of the middle stage at south and north, two small brick-framed slit windows were formed within the flintwork that blocks the former belfry openings and they both have horizontal brick heads externally and inverted V-shaped brick heads internally.

The tower has an internal diameter of 10'6" and its wall thickness measured at the west window is 3'11". The tower east wall is circular within the tower and 3'8" thick at the apex of the tower arch whereas the nave west wall measured ouside the tower is about three feet. The tower arch opening is double-splayed on plan and is about 4'6" wide at its narrowest point; the archway is 9'9" high to the apex with a pointed head towards the nave that, owing to the splayed plan shape, develops into a Tudor shape towards the tower.

There is convincing evidence that the tower was added to an earlier towerless church; a small blocked window near the apex of the nave west wall confirms that the church once stood without a tower, and it is recorded in the church guide that a thin probe can be inserted between the tower wall and the outside face of the nave west wall for a distance of at least a metre. This means, of course, that unless the original towerless church had a west doorway, the tower arch would have been formed when the tower was built. The double-splayed ground plan of the arch however, is probably as originally formed when the tower was added as there seems no reason why this should have been altered since. The pointed arch, whether in original form or altered, can therefore probably be taken as an indication of a post-Norman date for the opening because the double-splayed plan form is quite untypical of Norman or earlier work – tower arches of those times usually went straight through a wall. The tower arch plan, therefore, gives an initial suggestion of a post-Norman date for the tower.

The technological contrast between internal flint jambs and arches of the first-floor windows and the stone dressings of the blocked former belfry openings poses the question as to whether the lower and middle stages were contemporary or whether the middle stage was later than the lower. There is no evidence that the middle stage replaces an earlier belfry and the similar quality of its external flintwork to that of the lower stage suggests that they were probably of the same build. Difference in size of the openings may account for the constructional contrast between the first-floor windows and the former belfry openings.

Blundeston

Although circular to the top with no string courses, the tower (70) was originally only three-quarters of its present height. The original part is built of reasonably well-coursed rubble flints and has stone-framed round-headed windows at first- and second-floor levels and six former stone-framed belfry openings with small apertures between, also stone-framed.

Internally, the first-floor window and upper door have dressed stone jambs and arches and the soffit mortar of the window arch and its flintwork reveals can be seen to be contiguous with the internal and external stone dressings, thus establishing them as integrally built with

70. Blundeston tower. Later widening of the nave southwards caused the tower to become off-centre.

the wall; the second-floor windows are blocked flush with the inner wall face and not easily detected, suggesting the possibility that internal dressings may have been robbed for reuse, and the original belfry openings, now blocked, have rubble jambs and radially-laid rubble arches. The ground-floor west window is a Tudor brick insertion into a former round-headed opening, now plastered internally, but dressed stone arch voussoirs are still just visible above the floor in the unplastered first-floor wall.

These round-headed openings in dressed stone, and a round-headed tower arch are convincing evidence for a Norman attribution for the original tower.

An added belfry, surmounting the Norman one, has much medieval brick in its fabric and pointed lancet openings at the cardinal orientations; their dressings are small square stones, some of which might well be material from the blocked second-floor windows.

The tower is off-centre relative to the nave because the church was widened by demolition of the nave south wall and rebuilding it further south. As a result of the larger roof that this necessitated, the height of its ridge reached almost to the level of the top of the original belfry openings, and this was, no doubt, the reason for the addition of a higher belfry. The three-light lancet-style window in the widened nave west wall and the single lancets of the belfry suggest a late thirteenth-century date for these alterations although the amount of brick in the heightened nave west gable and the raised belfry might indicate that they are a little later.

CHAPTER 14

WHOLLY REBUILT MEDIEVAL TOWERS

It is inevitable that in addition to those round towers such as Ashmanhaugh, Brandiston and Weeting in Norfolk and Belton and Spexhall in Suffolk known from records to have been rebuilt in the last two centuries following collapse of an earlier tower, others must have fallen and been rebuilt from ground level in earlier times. Many post-Norman round towers were probably new additions to existing towerless churches, others were built at the same time as their churches but some can be shown to have been built as replacements of earlier towers, and a few such towers are described below.

As mentioned earlier, unless the arch between nave and tower had formerly been the west door of a towerless church, it is to be expected that it would have been formed at the time the tower was built, whether tower and church were built together or whether the tower had been added to an existing church. There are however instances where it can be shown that the tower arch had not been a west door but that it nevertheless apparently pre-dates the present tower, implying that the contemporary tower to which it must originally have given access probably collapsed, to be replaced by the present one.

Repps with Bastwick

The tower is circular for about three-quarters of its height, with an octagonal belfry. Its material is mainly cobble flints with a few large erratics; it is roughly coursed but not very obviously so. It has a small ground-floor west window with modern stone external facings, shown as a pointed lancet in Ladbrooke's drawing of the 1820s, and at first-floor level, brickwork blocking of former openings slightly east of south and north can be seen; internally they have flint jambs and arches, the arch flints laid radially or nearly so. In the east wall at this level there is evidence of an upper door, now blocked with modern brick. There are no signs of other or blocked openings in the internal wall below the present belfry.

The octagonal belfry (71) has flintwork similar to that in the circular stage; it has stone quoins at the angles and twin pointed-trefoil bell openings in the cardinal faces, shafted between the lights and with a quatrefoil in the apex. These are recessed within an outer order comprising a pointed arch springing from square abaci on shafts. Each section of wall between the belfry openings is decorated with two bays of blind arcading with pointed arches and pierced stone tympana. The belfry terminates with a stone table course carried on closely-spaced semi-circular corbels above which the battlemented parapet stage has medieval brick quoins and similar bricks randomly distributed in its flintwork.

The belfry stage is circular internally and there is no variation in the internal fabric at the level where it joins the circular stage. The belfry openings have pointed flint arches with occasional medieval bricks in them and in the reveals.

The tower arch is round-headed, 4'4" wide and about eleven feet high; it has a plastered finish and simple chamfered imposts in the reveals only. Being eleven feet high, it is unlikely originally to have been a west entrance to the church and so it can be assumed that it was built as a tower arch; this naturally implies that a tower would also have been built at the same time, whether as part of the original church or as an addition. The flat east wall within the tower is an indication that the tower was probably added to an existing church, but although the tower arch is round-headed implying an eleventh- or twelfth-century date, the tower has no corroborative evidence to establish that it is contemporary – the 'Norman' west window is unreliable because its stonework is obviously modern. The two blocked openings in the tower wall at north and south, located at a height barely above nave eaves level are far too low to have been belfry openings, and as there is no evidence of any other former openings below the present belfry, the

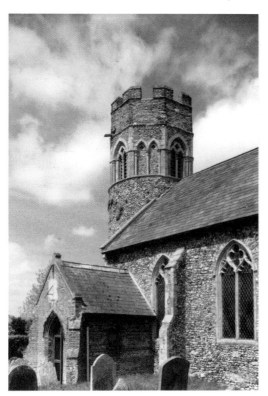

circular stage could never have stood as a finished tower. This means either that the present octagonal belfry replaces an earlier one or that it is contemporary with the circular stage. Whereas the circular stage has no reliably datable features that might support the possibility of there having been an earlier belfry of the eleventh or twelfth-century, the fact that internally the circular shape continues into the octagon with no variation of the wall fabric where the exterior change of shape occurs is convincing evidence that the circular and octagonal stages were built in one operation, and the whole tower, except the parapet stage, can therefore be dated by the belfry details as thirteenth-century.

71. Repps tower. Medieval brick in the parapet stage shows that it is probably later than the rest of the tower.

It seems, therefore, that the explanation of the apparent difference in age between the tower arch and the tower must be that the present tower replaces an earlier one, unless tower arch and tower were products of the Transitional style between Norman and Early English of the late twelfth/early thirteenth century, when contemporary use of round and pointed arches was not uncommon.

Ramsholt

This tower (XIII) is one of only two buttressed round towers, the other being at Beyton. Its three external buttresses extend for its full height and are located at north, south and west. With a width of 2'9" and projecting more than four feet at their bases, they are of four stages and have dressed limestone quoins and weatherings at the steppings. The fabric of the tower and buttresses is mainly septaria with some flint and a few medieval bricks. There is little doubt that they are medieval because their colour and size are quite uncharacteristic of Roman bricks.

The three single-light, pointed belfry openings at south-west, north-west and east are framed with stone externally and a ground floor window facing south-west is similar; internally it has splayed reveals, stone dressings and a pointed head. All these openings have exterior arches of plum-coloured medieval brick above their stonework and the ground floor window has in addition a relieving arch in similar brick above. Bricks of the same kind are also used for the putlog holes whose spacing can be traced for the full height of the tower, being particularly striking on the east face. The internal fabric contains brick and has brick putlog holes.

A stone weathercourse in the east wall of the tower defining an earlier nave roofline extends across the east faces of the north and south buttresses and there is a clear difference in the walling material above and below it on both buttresses and tower. These two buttresses are in effect part of the nave west wall, and measurements taken inside and outside show this wall, inclusive of the buttresses, to be about seven feet thick! By comparison, the nave side walls are about 2'9" thick.

The tower wall is about four feet thick and measures about 3'7" at the apex of the tower arch, above which the east wall of the tower is curved. The tower arch comprises two arch elements, clearly of different dates. The nave-side element is a plain Norman round-headed stone arch, 2'11" wide and 6'9" high to the crown and only eight inches thick; it has chamfered imposts with eleven-inch returns along the nave wall face, but damage to their back corners suggests that returns on the tower side could have been cut off flush with the back face of the arch stonework. The tower-side element (38) is a little wider and taller, 3'4" wide x 8'5" high to the apex, just wide enough to provide two-and-a-half-inch rebates for a door and just high enough to the springing to allow a round-headed door to be fully opened to 90°. It has a Tudor-style depressed pointed arch and a plastered finish.

Since there is no reason to suppose that they are not part of the tower's original fabric, the medieval bricks in the putlog holes, window arches and here and there elsewhere in the walls, must be regarded as convincing evidence for a post-Norman attribution for this tower.

The pointed arches and stone dressings of the belfry openings and the south-west ground floor window are clearly post-Norman and there is no evidence to suggest that they are earlier altered openings or later insertions; in fact, the brick arches at their heads are pretty conclusive indications that they were built with the wall because later insertion, particularly of the relieving arch above the arch over the ground floor window, could not have been accomplished without improbable disturbance to an existing wall.

The characteristics of the buttresses proclaim them as no earlier than the thirteenth century, and so if they can be shown to have been built with the tower, that would irrefutably confirm it as post-Norman. The following indications substantiate the probability that tower and buttresses were one build; individually they are convincing, collectively they are surely conclusive.

1. The walling material of tower and buttresses appears to be the same. If these Gothic buttresses had been built on to an earlier tower, it is likely that a difference in the fabric of tower and buttresses would be apparent.

2. The fabric of the buttresses contains dark plum-coloured medieval bricks of the same kind as appear in the tower putlog holes and window arches.

3. The continuous stone weathercourse built into the tower east wall and into the east faces of the north and south buttresses, and the difference of the fabric above and below it that is apparent on the tower wall and the buttresses, are sure indications of their

original unity of construction.

4. The dispositions of the ground-floor window facing south-west and the belfry openings at south-west, north-west and east seem to have been determined by the locations of the buttresses. If these openings had pre-dated the buttresses, it is likely that they would have been more conventionally located, particularly the ground floor window; thus their unusual placing suggests that the openings, walls and buttresses are all of the same build.

5. If the buttresses had been added to an existing tower, the north and south buttresses would more logically have been aligned on the north-to-south diameter. The manner in which they have been integrated into the nave west wall suggests that they were part of a major reconstruction at the nave/tower junction, rather than simple additions to an existing tower.

The imposts of the Norman tower arch, returned on the nave wall face and perhaps originally on the tower side as well, and the absence of a rebate on the nave side seem to preclude this arch from having been the west doorway of a towerless church, and so it must have been built as a tower arch. This implies that there was a tower when it was constructed, and the fact that the arch is only eight inches thick does rather suggest that it was inserted into an existing opening which must have been earlier. On an assumption that the present pointed archway on the tower side is the earlier opening into which the Norman arch was inserted, it has been argued that that opening, and consequently the tower, are pre-Conquest.

However, the tower's post-Norman evidence is so overwhelming and the shape of the arch in the tower behind the Norman arch is so un-Saxon, that there must be another explanation; the following interpretation is suggested as a plausible alternative.

The present pointed archway in the tower is unlikely to be the opening into which the Norman arch was inserted, for four reasons. Firstly, whereas the Norman voussoirs are about six inches deep on face, only about two-and-a-half inches of stonework now shows at the jambs facing the tower (i.e. the present door rebates), indicating that the Norman stonework couldn't have been inserted into so narrow an opening without cutting into its jambs; secondly, the size of the pointed archway, being precisely the minimum to accommodate a round-headed door fitted to the Norman arch, tends to suggest that it was formed to suit such a door, and consequently was later than the Norman arch; thirdly, if the impost mouldings had originally been returned on the west faces of the Norman arch, this would obviously imply that it had been set into a wider opening than the present one, and fourthly, the shape of the pointed archway surely cannot be Saxon; it is not the shape regarded by the Taylors as cruck-shaped[1] and is in fact the profile seen in the rere-arches of the pointed nave dorways, much more Gothic than Saxon.

Having in mind the size of the stones of the Norman arch, it is suggested that the opening into which it had been inserted was probably wider than the present 3'4", perhaps about 4'6", and no doubt higher, and that this conjectured wider opening was the tower arch of an earlier tower. That early, probably pre-Conquest tower fell, perhaps bringing quite a lot of the nave west wall down with it, to be replaced by the existing tower and nave west wall, built in the late thirteenth or early fourteenth century. The very existence of this buttressed tower design suggests the probability of an earlier calamity and subsequent constructional determination to ensure that it would not happen again. The positioning of the north and south buttresses and the consequent massively thick nave west wall tends to show that considerable work was done in the area of the nave/tower junction.

The present pointed archway behind the Norman arch was probably built up against the west face of the Norman arch, within the span of the conjectured original wider tower arch opening, as part of the major reconstruction of the nave west wall undertaken when the present tower was built. The impost returns facing the tower were probably cut back at that time to allow the hanging of a door.

Little Bradley

Built with even-sized, coursed flintwork containing a high proportion of brown-stained cobble erratics, typical of the walls of many churches in this part of East Anglia, the two-stage tower is circular to nave ridge level, above which the belfry stage is octagonal with Perpendicular belfry openings in the cardinal faces. In the 3'9" thick walls of the circular part, three slit windows light the ground floor; they are formed in flints internally with flat boarded heads and have modern round-headed dressed stone frames outside.

Internally the tower east wall is flat for the width of the tower arch plus about six inches each side and it is the same thickness as the nave west wall measured outside the tower. This and the apparently unbonded junction between the two structures confirm that the tower is a later addition to the nave. Where the curved wall of the tower meets the flat wall, it is possible to insert a probe into open joints between them, in particular for about three inches along the buried face of the tower arch impost return.

A solid oak doorframe, probably of the fifteenth century, having curved corner spandrels carved on the nave face with mouchette and quatrefoil motifs, has been set in the tower archway (72); notches were cut out of the stone imposts to allow the jamb-posts to be fixed up to the reveals of the opening, and above the frame the tympanum is infilled with plastered brickwork that is clearly contemporary with the doorframe. The present door is modern.

No evidence of an upper door shows in the nave but the east wall of the tower, curved above first floor level, contains an upper door recess with flint

72. Heavy medieval oak doorframe and threshold fitted into the Norman tower arch at Little Bradley church. The tympanum infill above the frame is plastered medieval brick.

jambs. It is nineteen inches deep x 2'4" wide but only 4'6" high to the springing of a segmental arch formed with medieval bricks. This arch does not go through the full thickness of the wall but only spans the recess, being built up against the back face of flintwork blocking in the opening at the nave wall. Opposite, in the west wall, there are indications of a possible blocked opening but no evidence of any others. The rere-arches of the belfry openings are built with medieval bricks similar to those in the arch of the upper door recess.

The tower arch, of similar design to the chancel arch, has plain stone jambs and a round arch faced with dressed stone, and a simple splayed plinth within the reveal but not returned on the wall faces. Chamfered imposts appear to be from single blocks of stone through the full wall thickness and the impost mouldings are returned along both faces of the respond walls. The tower arch is 3'9½" wide and 7'10" to the crown.

The stonework in the tower arch (and in the similar chancel arch) is without doubt Norman, and as the tower wall partially covers this stonework and the impost returns within the tower, the tower cannot be earlier than this, nor, for the same reason is it likely to be contemporary with it.

Since the present tower arch opening, irrespective of whether converted from an original west doorway without stone dressings, has projecting imposts in reveal and impost returns on both sides of the nave west wall, it would have been unsuitable for the hanging of a door, and must therefore from its inception have been intended as a tower arch. Formation of a tower arch obviously implies that a tower was built at the same time, presumably with its walls meeting the nave wall beyond the ends of the impost returns. However, on the clear evidence of the tower walls covering the impost returns on the west side of the nave wall, it seems as though the present tower is unlikely to be the one for which this tower arch was formed. If that is so, the implication is that an earlier tower either collapsed or was demolished and a new one was built at some time after the construction of the dressed stone tower arch.

There is no reason to suppose that the circular stage of the present tower is a late Norman replacement of an earlier fallen tower, apart from the possibility that the modern round-headed external stonework of the three slit windows might reflect what was there before; internally though, their splayed jambs and cills of flint and flat board-marked heads, some with boards still in place, tend to tell against a Norman attribution as these embrasures, if Norman, would be expected to have had splayed arched heads like the one in the Norman chancel extension. Externally, the unweathered condition of the stonework of these tower windows and the neat diagonal splays at the outside corners of their heads betray their modern origin. Furthermore, if the tower had been contemporary with the chancel extension, its flintwork would be expected to have been similar, but it is coursed whereas the chancel extension is uncoursed.

It seems therefore that the tower is post-Norman, with the circular stage and the octagonal belfry being contemporary. Evidence to support this conclusion is the fact that the internal flintwork of the octagon looks as if it could be of the same build as the circular part; there is no sudden change of quality and where undisturbed by later repairs, some areas of apparently original mortar are virtually uniform and continuous over curved and octagonal walls. Externally, although the pointing of the octagon flintwork makes it look at first sight quite different from the mainly unpointed flintwork below, both stages are coursed with similar flints, and when the octagon walls are compared with a band of similarly-pointed walling on the circular part, the likeness shows that the two stages could be contemporary.

But most convincing perhaps, is the evidence of the fifteenth-century oak doorframe in the tower arch. It is no light screen like those in many closed-off tower doorways, but has 5" x 4" jamb-posts, a 5" x 3½" head and a hefty 10" x 4" threshold, and the tympanum space above the frame is substantially filled with plastered brickwork. It seems clearly to have been intended for an external door. This raises the question of why such a door was required at that stage in the church's life; was it because, as conjectured, suddenly there was no tower and a sturdy door became necessary to secure the church? If so, the date of this doorframe not only establishes the probable date of an earlier tower's demise but also implies that the whole of the present tower is fifteenth-century or later.

The closing-off of the upper door provides further evidence that is consistent with the suggested date for the present tower. The original upper door opening through the nave wall was clearly taller than the present recess; it can be seen that the flintwork that blocks the opening at the nave face extends upwards behind the present low segmental medieval brick arch. This arch, and the curved tower east wall that it supports, were obviously built after the upper door had been blocked and there is no trace above the brick arch of the outline of the original taller upper door, nor is there any discontinuity with the adjacent tower walling. The similarity of the bricks in the arch over the recess to those in the belfry window arches implies that both tower stages were part of the same building campaign. It is suggested that the sequence of events was as follows: (1) when the original tower was added, the upper door with flint jambs was formed in the gable of the nave west wall/tower east wall; (2) the upper door opening was blocked with flints at the nave wall face, probably when seats were installed in the nave; (3) the original tower collapsed, causing collateral damage to the nave west wall gable; (4) the remains of the collapsed tower were cleared to ground level and an oak frame and external door inserted into the tower arch opening; (5) a new tower was constructed including substantially rebuilding the nave west wall from first-floor level, including a brick arch on the lower part of the reveals of the former upper door opening, built up against the flint blocking in the recess. Whereas in the ground stage of the present tower the east wall is flat, above first-floor level this wall is curved.

One further question needs explanation: why was the blocked former upper door opening bridged with a brick arch, leaving a low recess, instead of being entirely built up solid? The answer, perhaps, lies in the change from a flat east wall in the ground stage to a curved wall above. It seems that in the re-building of the tower east wall from first-floor level, advantage was taken of the 2'4" wide opening at that level in that position to make the transition from the flat wall below to the curved one above.

All these indications point to the likelihood that the tower replaces an earlier one and that its circular and octagonal stages are contemporary and no earlier than the fifteenth century.

Cockley Cley

All Saints' church at Cockley Cley comprises nave, chancel, north and south aisles, south porch and the remains of a circular western tower that collapsed in August 1991. That tower was itself apparently a replacement of an earlier tower. The following description is a precis of an analysis prepared by the author shortly after the collapse[2].

In the late thirteenth or early fourteenth century, major alterations were apparently undertaken at this church which at the time seems to have had a conventional Norman plan consisting of a nave about twenty feet wide, a chancel probably narrower by about three feet and a round tower centrally on the west wall. The alterations, comprising the building of a wider chancel with a chancel arch off-centre southwards relative to the nave, a south arcade and aisle, the related raising of the nave walls and the reconstruction of the tower, were probably all contemporary as there is considerable evidence for their interdependence.

The tower was circular to the top and is of particular interest because of its unique flintwork decoration. Two neat bands of black knapped flints about nine inches high incorporated within its lighter flint rubble fabric encircled the walls at about twelve and 24 feet above ground level. They are probably one of the earliest examples of the use of different kinds of flint as architectural decoration. They can still be seen in the standing ruin (73).

73. Decorative knapped flint bands incorporated within the rubble flint wall of Cockley Cley tower.

Photographs taken before the tower fell show that it had a single-light west window with a cusped pointed arch and hoodmould directly below the lower knapped flint band and, above this, just below the upper band, a narrow stone window of Norman type with an arched lintel. On the south side, there was a similar but shorter window below the lower band. At about four feet above the upper band, the tower had a shallow offset, part of which is still visible on the north side of the standing remains. Four two-light belfry openings had cusped Y-tracery that was probably medieval though the belfry had been extensively restored internally in brick in the nineteenth century; above these a stone string course formed the base for an octagonal battlemented parapet. Internally, the tower was completely circular and the easternmost part of the inner circumference lies an estimated six inches behind (i.e. to the east of) the external plane of the nave west wall, strongly suggesting that tower and nave walls were of homogeneous construction. The low, pointed, tower arch is off-centre from the tower axis by about seven inches to the south, and the tower itself relative to the axis of the nave is off-centre to the north.

The possibility that the whole tower was rebuilt as part of the major restorations undertaken in the 1860s is discounted, mainly on the grounds that its flintwork is markedly different from the known Victorian flintwork of the north aisle and because no bricks as used in the restored (but now fallen) belfry stage are to be seen internally in any part of the remaining structure below this level as might be expected if it had been rebuilt at the time of the nineteenth-century belfry restoration. Furthermore, evidence of a former nave roofline on the east face of the tower above the present Victorian roof indicates that the existing tower was standing when this roof was built.

As to the possibility that the tower was re-cased during the nineteenth century or earlier, or that the knapped flint bands were inserted into an earlier wall, close inspection of the walls in section at the fracture faces revealed no evidence of a later facing having been applied. The facing flints generally and the knapped flints in the bands were integrally bonded with the core of the walling and the mortar was of uniform colour and texture through the full thickness of the wall. This provides conclusive proof that the facing flintwork is contemporary with the building of the tower, and that being so, the decorative bands assume prime importance in its dating.

Earliest instances of walls entirely of cut flint (as opposed to fortuitous cleft or broken pieces amongst rubble) seem to be late thirteenth-century, and decorative themes which exploit the contrasts between cut and natural flints seem to appear no earlier than the fourteenth. A dating for the tower of Cockley Cley church of circa 1300 at the earliest therefore seems appropriate and would be consistent with its pointed tower doorway and the cusped Y-tracery of its belfry openings. Corroboration for this date, revealed by the collapse, is given by the clearly evident unity of construction of the tower south wall and the upper part of the nave west gable (74) which, with the nave side walls, was heightened when the south arcade and aisle were built. They are datable by their own features as circa. 1300 and it follows therefore that the tower must also have been built at that time. Further support is conferred by the lack of any indications of earlier bell openings or tower arch.

74. Where the fallen tower south wall joined the raised gable of the nave west wall (above the two flat built-in sloping stones), the flintwork shows their construction to be integral.

The collapse of the tower's south wall exposed about a square yard of the surface of the nave west wall that is completely flat and coated with a smooth mortar rendering. This flat rendered area, about fifteen feet above ground level, is of more or less square shape with a twelve-inch-wide leg extending diagonally downwards from the bottom left corner towards the inside of the tower, terminating at the former ceiling level of the ground floor stage.

At this flat mortared area, the tower flintwork has parted cleanly from the west face of the nave wall. Above this, up to the top of the wall, only the outer flints of the tower wall have parted from the nave wall, but rather less cleanly. Other than at these two places, substantial sections of the tower wall above and below the flat mortared area have not separated at the nave wall face but remain attached and appear to be homogeneously bonded into it.

On the evidence of the flat area, it has been argued that the tower was added to a church already standing. This is considered unlikely for three reasons. Firstly, if the tower had been added to a pre-existing flat nave wall, it is likely that either the east face of the tower internally would be flat, or if circular, the inner circumference of the tower east face would fall outside (that is, to the west of) the external plane of the nave wall, indicating a facing applied over it. But the tower's eastern internal curvature lies inside the line of the west face of the nave wall; had the tower been added to a pre-existing nave, accommodation of its internal curvature in this way could not have been achieved without improbable structural disturbance of the nave wall. Secondly, the fact that substantial sections of the tower south wall have remained attached to the nave wall suggests homogeneous construction of tower and nave walls. Thirdly, the rendering on the mortared area appears to be trowelled up to the edges of surrounding flintwork still attached to the nave wall and does not appear to be continued behind it. This suggests that its extent is limited to the area exposed by the collapse.

The curvature of the tower east wall internally and the evident homogeneity of the tower and nave west wall indicate a close structural affinity between them. However, the coarser texture of the nave west wall and its thickness suggest that it was earlier than the tower. These apparent contradictions can, however, be reconciled by the proposition that the present tower replaces an earlier one built concurrently with the nave.

It is suggested that, for reasons unknown, an original Norman tower came down and the present tower with its knapped flint bands and Y-traceried belfry openings was then built on the original tower base, the new walls being bonded into the original retained remnants of the former tower and the raised nave west wall. The original tower arch would have disappeared during this operation and the new tower doorway would have been formed in its non-axial position within the tower to minimise the difference in alignment of the chancel and tower arches arising from the contemporary rebuilding of the chancel off-centre southwards. Resetting of the Norman features from an earlier tower into the new tower fabric would explain the apparent anachronism of Norman windows in a manifestly later wall, while their very presence could be understood as evidence for the prior existence of an earlier tower.

What then could be the explanation of the flat mortared area on the nave west wall exposed by the collapse? Could it have been the side of an opening or recess in the former tower that was blocked when the new tower was built, leaving no trace internally or externally in the reconstructed wall? Might that opening perhaps have been a recess for a sanctus bell, the diagonal leg at the bottom being a shaft to lead the bell rope to the ground floor of the tower?

---

[1] Taylor H M and J.Op. Cit. Vol.1 page 51

[2] Hart S N *Cockley Cley Church Tower – A constructional Analysis.* pp 185-195 in *Norfolk Archaeology Vol XLII Part II.* Norfolk and Norwich Archaelogical society. 1995.

CHAPTER 15

TOWERS WITH A CIRCULAR BELFRY ON A STONE STRING COURSE

Because of the deficiency of limestone in East Anglia before the Conquest, a string course of dressed stone between a round tower's lower stage and a circular belfry is a sure indication that the belfry is post-Conquest and in the absence of grounds for thinking that the stage below the string course originally stood as a complete tower or that the belfry is a replacement of an earlier one, the probability is that it is contemporary with the lower stage.

Of the eighteen fully-circular medieval round towers that have a stone string course below the belfry, six have a belfry that is clearly later than the lower stage. The nineteenth-century belfries at Geldeston and South Ockendon surmount lower stages that have also undergone considerable restoration, but medieval brick in its lower fabric and putlog holes suggest a post-Norman date for the former. The Norman belfry at Titchwell was probably contemporary with the upper part of the lower stage that has already been mentioned as probably being later than the tower base, and at Holton, the eight Norman belfry windows on the string course that were probably contemporary with the lower stage are surmounted by a post-Norman belfry. At Beyton, the absence of any former belfry openings in the two lower stages of the tower suggest that the mean little belfry above the upper string course is probably an eighteenth-century replacement of an earlier one; the tower's integral buttresses, the intermediate string course and the stone plinth

75. Pseudo-Norman belfry above original Norman tower windows at South Elmham All Saints.

76. South Elmham All Saints church. A drawing of circa. 1818 by Isaac Johnson.

weathering are strong evidence of a post-Norman date for the lower stage.

Only at South Elmham All Saints (75), where the present round belfry is a modern construction on the Norman lower stage, is there any evidence outside or inside of possible former belfry openings below the string course, which on this tower is only about 25 ft. above the ground. Just below it, three stone, single-light, round-headed windows, about 3'9" high alternate with three smaller ones, comparable to those in the Norman belfry at Blundeston. However, their low position and the rather complicated history of the tower suggest that they were not belfry openings. A drawing by Isaac Johnson of circa. 1818 (76) shows the lower stage rather taller than now, well above the nave roof level, and with an octagonal belfry, and so it might seem that these windows could have been belfry openings before the nave's shallow clerestory and the octagon were added. The octagonal part though, was apparently removed in the 1830s and the circular part above the level of the nave roof, said to have had belfry openings which were blocked with red brick, received a tall embattled parapet[1]. It seems therefore that an original circular tower did have belfry openings above nave roof level, i.e. above the level of the existing alternating large and small Norman windows, and that since the latter were apparently located in the chamber to which the upper door gave access, they were more likely just to have been tower windows, with a Norman belfry above. Later, the Norman belfry was surmounted by an octagonal one that was itself subsequently removed, and the original upper circular part above nave roof level with its blocked belfry openings seems to have disappeared when the upper stage was reconstructed with a string course in 1912.

In the towers that have no evidence of former belfry openings below the string course, the likelihood that the stage below the string course might originally have stood as a complete tower can be eliminated, but the question remains as to whether the present belfry is contemporary with the lower stage or whether it replaces an earlier one. As well as Titchwell (62), five other towers have Norman belfries above a string course – Haddiscoe (IV), Herringfleet, Gayton Thorpe (78), Little Saxham (X) and Thorpe-next-Haddiscoe (50). Only at Thorpe-next-Haddiscoe are there grounds for it to have been thought that the present belfry might have replaced an earlier one, although persuasive arguments remain for regarding it as part of the original tower (see Chapter 10). All except Gayton Thorpe have belfry flintwork similar to the lower stage and small, dressed-stone, round-headed windows in the lower stage, and all have round-headed tower arches except at Thorpe next Haddiscoe where it has been altered.

The other seven towers in this group have post-Norman belfries – lancet openings at Frostenden, Syleham, Weybread and Bartlow, and two-light openings with Y-tracery at Eccles, Threxton and Bardfield Saling. They all have uniform flintwork in both stages, and have pointed tower arches, and in none of them is there any evidence of earlier features or such differences in detail, fabric or construction between the two stages as would suggest that the belfries are later than the lower stages.

Holton St Peter

The chancel wall is of small, very rough, uncoursed flint rubble and appears to be the oldest fabric. West of the porch, the lower three feet or so of the nave south wall is similar but above this, the flints are much larger and are laid coursed, and this style continues in the nave west wall, fillets and tower. The nave has south-west and north-west quoins of

Caen stone and a Norman south doorway.

The flintwork of the chancel walls and possibly the small area low down in the nave south wall west of the porch is so different from that in the west wall, fillets and tower that it may be surviving fabric of an earlier building phase. Be that as it may, the Caen stone quoins, the coursed flintwork in the west wall, fillets and tower, and the south door together provide persuasive evidence that the nave and tower are Norman, although most of the nave south wall to the east of the porch has been rebuilt.

At about two-thirds of the tower's height, eight round-headed stone-framed original belfry openings (four blocked) rest on a continuous stone string course, and below this are three similar windows at south, west and north, and at a lower level, two more at south and north. From about two feet or so above the eight original belfry openings, the height of the tower was increased by the addition of a new belfry in perhaps the fifteenth or sixteenth century. Its fabric is different from the lower part and contains much brick, and the four belfry openings seem originally to have been two-light but have now lost their tracery and mullion (77).

A major reconstruction seems to have been undertaken to the Norman belfry when the later one was added whereby much of its walling was rebuilt and four of the windows were blocked though their external stone frames were retained; upwards from about three feet below the string course level, the internal wall contains much brick set in a different mortar, entirely obscuring four of the eight windows at this level, leaving visible only those at the cardinal points. Some of the jambs and arches of the retained cardinal windows were also re-formed with bricks although others retain original flintwork. Examination at the corresponding level outside shows that three feet or so of flintwork below the string course does differ slightly from that in the lower part of the tower, though not containing bricks like the inside.

The similarity of the bricks in the reconstructed interior to those in the added belfry's external walls suggests that the two developments were parts of the same building operation.

A Saxon attribution has been claimed for this tower on an assumption that the string course was a later insertion and that the stone dressings of its windows were Norman enhancements of flint openings, but it is much more likely that all the Norman stone features in the tower are contemporary with its construction. If the eight early belfry windows had originally been of flint, they would have had individual cills and it is probable therefore, that had they later been faced with stone, simple cills like those of the

77. Detail of Holton St Peter church tower showing a remnant of the built-in stone weathercourse in the east wall.

lower windows would have been used since insertion of a continuous string course cill into an existing flint wall would have been very exacting. The stone windows and string course are more likely therefore to be original construction than insertions, thus confirming the tower as post-Conquest.

Similarly, the weathercourse in the tower's east wall indicating an earlier nave roofline must have been built into the wall at the time of construction because insertion of a sloping and curving feature of this kind so neatly into existing flintwork is hardly a practical proposition, particularly where there seems no reason why it would have been necessary; countless other round towers show that thatch and later roofing materials have satisfactorily been butted to curved tower walls without a weathercourse.

Internally, the east wall in the tower is curved, and as its thickness at the apex of the tower arch is five inches less than the nave west wall thickness measured outside the tower, the tower and the nave west wall must have been built together, because otherwise, unnecessary disturbance to an existing wall would have been required to accommodate the internal curvature of the tower in this way.

The tower arch is pointed and tall – about eleven feet high to the springing and the apex is only two or three inches below the ceiling of the tower's first floor. The upper door recess in the tower east wall, originally at the level of the first floor, is now partially built up at the bottom and blocked at the nave face; it is only visible from within the tower.

It appears that in post-Norman times the tower arch was altered from its original Norman form to a pointed arch and considerably heightened. It has dressed stones on the nave side in the lower 5'3" only of both jambs that could be those of an original Norman arch formed in the nave west wall when the tower was built. When the arch was heightened, the raised part was formed without dressed stone and plastered, the original stone jambs in the bottom part being left in place. The dressed stone is unlikely to be repairs to the present tall arch because firstly, it seems unlikely that identical repairs to both sides of an internal archway to this height would have been necessary, and secondly, if repairs to the lower jambs of an existing plastered arch had been necessary, it is more likely that they would have been made to match the rest of that arch rather than introducing dressed stonework.

The apparent conversion of a dressed stone Norman arch to a tall pointed one suggests that a requirement for tall tower arches, conventionally considered a characteristic feature of Saxon towers, continued into the post-Norman period.

Gayton Thorpe

The tower (78) has a 9'3" internal diameter and four-foot-thick walls, but pronounced flattening of the external circumference on the east above the nave gives the upper part of the tower a marked D-shape. The lower six feet or so of the tower is built mainly of roughly-squared blocks of carstone and silver carr; above this the walling is flint rubble, and from about six feet below the belfry the flintwork style noticeably changes, containing larger pieces with cleft faces. A stone string course with chevron decoration forms the base of the circular belfry stage, above which the belfry wall material reverts to flintwork not significantly different from that on the main body of the tower.

The tower's lower stage has two round-headed windows facing west, both double-splayed. The smaller lower one differs from the normal type of double-splayed window in

78. Gayton Thorpe church. Because of later widening of the nave, the tower is off-centre, and three carstone quoin stones in the nave west wall to the left of the tower indicate the nave's original width.

that its narrowest point is not at the middle of the wall but only about fifteen inches from the outer face. It has narrowly-splayed reveals outside and inside, a rough round facing arch externally and the head soffit internally is splayed at two different angles. The inclusion of bricks in its external jambs and the distorted profiles of its internal and external heads are indicative of the opening having been broken out through an existing wall rather than having been built on shuttering. The larger upper window has wide splayed flint reveals and its round arched heads inside and out both show board-marks of the shuttering on which they were built strongly implying original construction with the walls. It has a Barnack stone 'frame' set in the aperture near the centre of the wall. Ladbrooke's drawing of the 1820s of Gayton Thorpe church shows a single west window in the tower in place of the two we now see and it appears to be a pointed lancet, set flush with the wall face without any splays – possibly an eighteenth-century Gothick insertion in the upper window recess (frontispiece).

The four two-light belfry openings are of two orders formed in limestone. Shafts in the outer order, each flanked by a vertical band of chevron, support a round arch with chevron decoration; in the recessed inner order, sections of interlacing, round arcading produce the pointed arch shapes of the lights. The motif of interlacing round arches can be seen in the west front of nearby Castle Acre Priory which may well have been the inspiration for the Gayton Thorpe belfry. Internally the belfry openings have jambs of dressed limestone but their round arches, encompassing both lights like the outer order externally, are formed with large flints roughly radially laid, with an occasional piece of carstone, demonstrating that flint arches were used by Norman builders.

The tower arch, which passes straight through the wall without rebates, is plastered on the nave side and faced within the tower with dressed stone; its squared jambs, some of carstone and some of limestone, are six, eight and ten inches high. The radially-laid arch voussoirs don't appear to be wedge-shaped although it isn't possible to be certain because of rather wide, coarse pointing at the joints. The arch springs from one-piece, chamfered limestone imposts returned within the tower but not on the nave side. The squared stones in the jambs and head of the arch, the chamfered limestone imposts and the arch proportions suggest early Norman construction.

At the sides of the opening where the tower walls meet the nave west wall, they partly cover the jamb stonework, imposts and the lower voussoirs of the arch. Above the tower arch, the wall is flat, and above first-floor level the original gable line of the nave west wall can be seen, with the upper part of the tower east wall built directly on it. This evidence proves that the tower was a later addition to a previously towerless church. It has been suggested that the tower arch stonework was inserted after the tower was built but that can be dismissed as impracticable.

There is no evidence within the tower of any blocked early belfry openings or other windows but at first floor level, there is a blocked upper door in the nave west wall; it is formed in flint, without stone, and has a triangular-shaped head whose sides are set back about two inches on the jambs. At about six feet below the belfry level there is a change in the character of the internal flintwork corresponding with the external flintwork change referred to above.

The tower is off-centre southwards relative to the nave, and in the nave west wall north of the tower, three eight-inch-high squared and dressed carstone quoin stones similar to those of the square Norman tower at Flitcham about five miles away, indicate the original position of the north-west corner of the nave. Their proportions and dressed finish are typically Norman in style and they are quite uncharacteristic of pre-Conquest quoins; they show that the nave was widened later by the rebuilding of the north wall about 3'6" further to the north, accounting for the off-centre position of the tower.

Almost all commentators have called this tower Saxon with a Norman belfry; but can we be certain that the lower stage is Saxon? In attempting to date the church and tower, it is necessary first to try to establish the sequence of construction, and then from this and other evidence, seek to arrive at probable dates.

The tower arch stonework and fact that the impost mouldings are returned along the west face of the nave wall, formerly the outside wall, but not on the nave side to allow hanging of a door are strong indications that the opening was originally an external west doorway to the church before the tower was added. If the opening had been formed as a tower arch when the tower was built, it is more likely that that the stone imposts would have been returned to enhance the nave face of the wall rather than the tower side.

When the tower was built, thus closing off the west entrance, a door or doorways would have been formed in the nave side walls if they hadn't already existed. The north door would have disappeared later when the nave was enlarged and the south door perhaps converted to its present pointed shape at the same time, or there may not have been a south door originally.

Although the balance of the evidence seems to favour a Norman attribution for the nave, a Saxon attribution for it has nevertheless been claimed, on interpretation of the three former north-west quoins as Saxon and a rebuttal of a Norman attribution for the stone tower arch on the grounds, firstly, that the stones used are bigger than those used by Normans, secondly that the imposts are single stones (said to be a Saxon practice in contrast to Norman use of multiple ones) and thirdly that the voussoirs are not wedge-shaped. This Saxon claim can be challenged on the grounds that the three former squared north-west quoin stones are quite unlike any of the East Anglian types of quoining normally recognised as Saxon, and all the objections to a Norman attribution for the tower arch can be refuted by reference to instances in undisputed Norman arches elsewhere of stones of the sizes used here, of single impost stones and non-wedge-shaped voussoirs.

The triangular-headed upper door (which, of course, would have been unnecessary before the tower was built) and the two double-splayed flint west windows (or at any rate, the larger one) tend to suggest earlier work than the stone-dressed tower arch and quoins, but on the evidence described above, the tower's lower stage is clearly later than the arch. So, contrary to a commonly held belief, features formed with flint without dressed stone have been used at a later date than features using it, and if the arch is Norman and the tower's lower stage later, it clearly isn't pre-Conquest. Though triangular-headed openings have been widely considered to be exclusively Saxon features, examples are to be found in Norman buildings – as mentioned earlier, a blocked upper door with a triangular flint head can be clearly seen in the east face of the nearby square Norman tower at Flitcham (25).

Theoretically, the Norman belfry could be a replacement of an earlier one, but in view of its apparent closeness of date to the Norman tower arch, this seems improbable, and since there would presumably have been a reasonable lapse of time between the building of the nave with its Norman west doorway (now the tower arch) and the erection of the tower whose walls partially cover it, it seems more likely that the whole tower was of one build and thus that the upper double-splayed flint window and the stone belfry are contemporary. That being so, it confirms that double-splayed windows and triangular-headed openings, though recognised as features typical of Saxon workmanship, persisted well into the Norman era.

A striking feature of this tower is the distinct change of material and workmanship at the lower level where, at about six or seven feet above ground, we see quite a sudden change from carstone and silver carr to flintwork. It is not inconceivable that the change of flintwork style at a similar distance below the belfry stringcourse could be an intentional aesthetic artifice to echo the change of material at the ground stage.

A dating based on this evidence and interpretation might be as follows:

Late 11th Century: Towerless church built with 3'3" thick nave walls, dressed and squared carstone quoins and a stone-framed west entrance.

12th Century: Tower built; upper doorway formed; north and/or south nave doorway(s) formed if not already in existence.

Post-Norman: Nave widened by rebuilding north wall approx. 3'6" further north. South door formed if not already existing; if existing, altered to pointed.

If the upper door with a triangular head and double-splayed windows are considered more indicative of a pre-Conquest date for the lower stage of the tower than the grounds for a Norman attribution, then the dating for the church and tower might be:

Early c.11 (say): Saxon nave with 3'3" walls and small squared dressed carstone quoins, and an unrebated west door opening with stone dressings and chamfered limestone imposts.

3rd Quarter c.11: Saxon tower and upper door under construction. By the Conquest, tower had reached the level of the change of flintwork. Work ceased.

C.12: Upper part of lower stage of tower completed in different flintwork and belfry added.

Post-Norman: Nave enlargement and south doorway insertion or alteration to pointed.

---

[1] Church Guide, All Saints' Church South Elmham Suffolk. Churches Conservation Trust 1996. Series 4 no.55

CHAPTER 16

TOWERS WITH KNAPPED FLINT WALLS

Although early flint walls contain some flints with severed faces, such flints are likely to result, not from skilled knapping, but from reducing larger flints to manageable sizes, breaking off of awkward projections or the inclusion of broken pieces. It was not until the late thirteenth century that walls were faced entirely with flints with cleft or split faces, and the early fourteenth before skilfully knapped flints were used. If therefore, the circular stage of a round tower contains cut or knapped flints of greater precision and in greater proportion than is normal in early work, it is unlikely to be earlier than the fourteenth century.

There are a few fully-circular towers in which the numbers of knapped flints in their walls and the manner in which they are distributed give reason to believe that they are part of the tower's original fabric, and thus attributable as no earlier than the fourteenth century. In none of them are there any Norman or pre-Conquest features: they include Keswick and Tuttington (79) in Norfolk, and Burgh Castle, Lound, and Fritton in Suffolk. The same can be said for the circular stages of several towers that have octagonal belfries, whether contemporary – Edingthorpe, Horsey, Potter Heigham, or later – Old Catton and Surlingham, for example.

Fritton, Suffolk

To the architecturally inquisitive, first sight of this church poses an immediate conundrum: why is the tower not central to the nave and how does it manage to have apparently genuine fourteenth-century belfry openings above first-floor brick windows of perhaps four centuries or more later that seem to be contemporary with the wall in which they are set? Answers to these anomalies can only be found by considering them in

79. Extensive knapped flints at random and in irregular bands in the facing of Tuttington church tower.

conjunction with alterations made to the rest of the church.

The tower (XIV) is wholly circular, though the upper stages show a marked flattening of the curvature on the east and west faces. The facing of the lower two-thirds consists substantially of black knapped flints with some medieval bricks randomly distributed and several large, roughly-squared blocks of semi-dressed stone including six stone 'ties' more or less evenly spaced one above the other in the west face. It has a stone lancet west window on the ground floor with stone jambs and an arch of medieval brick internally. The upper third of the tower, from just above the first-floor window cills is faced with light knapped flints rather larger than the black ones below, and first-floor windows at south, west and north, shown by their internal construction to be contemporary with this stage, are formed with post-medieval bricks and have pointed arches. Above, two-light belfry openings facing east and west have Decorated stone tracery, and single pointed belfry lights facing north and south have stone dressings.

Since there is no evidence for a pre-Conquest or Norman tower, the church was probably originally towerless. Pevsner's suggestion[1] that a tower was intended above the chancel is considered unlikely because the Norman arch between chancel and apse that would have supported its east wall is only fifteen inches thick. The eleventh- or twelfth-century chancel with an apsidal east end is about 12'4" wide internally and, deduced from the eight-inch inset of the chancel wall relative to the nave north wall at the chancel arch, the original nave width would have been about 13'8". Chancel apse buttresses and original nave quoins are of Caen stone which indicate post-Conquest dates for chancel and nave. The nave walls were formerly lower than now, as is shown by the height of the original north-west quoin stones and a change in the flintwork of the north wall above the level at which they terminate.

An enlargement of the church seems to have been carried out in the mid-fourteenth century: the nave north wall was heightened and Decorated windows inserted into it; the nave south wall would have been correspondingly raised and a new roof constructed over the higher nave. Arches would have been formed in the nave south wall to create a south arcade and the south aisle would have been built, having Decorated windows in its south wall and a low-pitched lean-to roof and end walls. Convincing evidence of the original level of the aisle roof and its low pitch is given by the flintwork change in the extended west wall south of the tower, and rather less clearly in the corresponding east wall south of the chancel. The possibility that at this time the original nave south wall was totally demolished and a larger roof then built to span the increased width of the church can be excluded because, had this been so, the nave east gable would have been built homogeneously with the extended east wall of the nave south of the chancel and could not have been of the type of brick used, and the flintwork of the extended west wall south of the tower would have been of uniform style for its full height.

At about the same time as the south aisle was built, the tower arch was formed in the nave west wall and the tower built on the original nave/chancel axis; the tower would have been rather lower than now, with the cill level of the belfry openings just above the ridge of the new nave roof. The belfry was, no doubt, faced with flintwork similar to that in the lower stage and the Decorated tracery and stone dressings of the belfry openings were probably those now in the present belfry.

The evidence for a post-Norman date for this original tower is overwhelming: knapped flints of the quality of those in the external facing of the lower stage were not used until the early fourteenth century; the internal construction of the stone lancet west window shows it to have been built with the wall and not inserted later; the belfry window styles are fourteenth-century; the tower's internal cantilevered projection over the nave west wall above the tower arch implies that the tower was added; and the medieval brick construction of the tower arch and, most conclusive of all, the extent of medieval brick in the ground-stage internal fabric puts a post-Norman date beyond doubt.

The chancel arch was presumably originally Norman and seems to have been altered to its depressed shape in the fourteenth century. During the fifteenth, Perpendicular windows were inserted into the chancel, two each side.

The nave east gable (XV), embracing the full width of the church and built entirely in post-medieval brick laid in Flemish bond with tumbled-in gable parapets, shows that the next major alteration was probably not until the eighteenth or nineteenth century, when the fourteenth-century nave roof and the low monopitch aisle roof were replaced by the present larger roof spanning the full width of nave and aisle. The arcade wall would have been demolished, the aisle south wall was slightly raised and the west end wall of the former aisle was built up to the gable profile of the new larger roof with closely-packed small flints that are noticeably different from those in the lower part of the wall. An apparent former small window blocked with brick in the raised wall seems to have been altered to a stone trefoil in Victorian times.

As a result of the wider roof, the nave ridge line became offset southwards from the chancel/nave/tower axis, and since the wider roof would now have been higher than the then existing belfry openings, that belfry was taken down as far as its cill level (i.e. to the level where the flintwork changes from dark to light) and the tower then rebuilt from that level, faced with light knapped flint. First-floor windows framed with bricks were incorporated at about the starting level of the raising, above which, in the taller tower, the new east and west belfry openings, which have brick jambs, re-used the stone tracery of the original belfry windows. The stone dressings of the single-light ones facing north and south are probably also the original material reset.

The post-medieval bricks in the first-floor tower windows and in the jambs of the belfry openings can easily be understood to be contemporary with the large brick gable on the east end of the nave.

There are three windows on each side of the nave, all of similar fourteenth-century patterns but the eastern pairs on both sides are taller than the single western ones. On the north side, the jambs and cills of the taller windows look original but with most of their tracery restored; on the south, the stonework of all three looks too crisp and unweathered to be of medieval age and they were probably renewed when this wall was raised for the larger roof, the two eastern ones probably originally having been the same height as the western one. The north vestry of 1855 contains a reset, very weathered window of the same pattern, of the smaller size – an original one from the south wall, perhaps?

The widened nave at this church provides interesting comparisons with Brampton, Blundeston and Beeston St Lawrence where naves have been widened southwards and larger roofs have replaced original nave roofs, but direct analogies cannot be drawn because the circumstances at each are different.

Potter Heigham

The church comprises a 16'1" wide nave with north and south aisles, a chancel of about the same width as the nave, a south porch and a circular west tower with an octagonal belfry stage. Apart from fillets between tower and nave, a feature that has been said to be exclusively Saxon but, in fact, also occurs on post-Conquest towers, this tower exhibits no early features; on the other hand there is considerable evidence to show that the circular stage is probably contemporary with the fourteenth-century octagonal belfry.

The circular stage of the tower and the fillets are faced with a variably-coursed mixture of rounded water-worn cobbles and knapped flints; the latter occur within the cobble work mainly in irregular drifts and they are well cut, closely laid and on the whole, evenly sized and show a proficiency of knapping not found in flint walls before the end of the thirteenth century. The extent of the knapped flints and the way they are laid does not suggest that they are repair insertions, and this flintwork is similar to and continuous with that in the fillets and the west walls of the nave and the aisles.

Where the west walls of the fourteenth-century aisles join the west wall of the nave each side of the tower, there are no signs of the original nave quoins, and continuity of the flintwork where the aisles join the nave suggests that the nave west wall received a facing of flintwork to match the aisles when they were built, covering the original nave corners. This is supported by the fact that the nave west wall measured outside the tower is about nine inches thicker than the original nave side walls.

All this flintwork is entirely different from the uncoursed rubble flint of the north and south chancel walls that is probably the oldest visible flintwork on the church. This difference seems to rule out any likelihood that the tower and church are contemporary, implying therefore that the tower is a later addition to an originally towerless church. The continuity of the flintwork of the west walls of the nave and aisles and its similarity to that of the tower and fillets suggests that tower and aisles were built at the same time. The two-light ground floor west window in the tower has cusped Y-tracery of the fourteenth century, and though windows in this position in many towers are later insertions, this one is likely to be contemporary with the wall.

The tower walls are about 3'9" thick measured at the west window and at the tower arch, above which the tower's east wall is curved internally. The wall at the tower arch apex is appreciably thicker than the original nave west wall, confirming the probability that the tower was added to an earlier church, having been positioned so as to achieve a tower wall of uniform thickness for its full circumference in order to give a fully circular shape on the east externally above the nave.

There is no evidence in the nave or within the tower of an upper door in the tower east wall, nor are there any signs of earlier blocked belfry openings in the tower wall below the present belfry either externally or internally; this is a strong indication that the octagonal belfry is contemporary with the circular stage unless, of course, the present fourteenth-century octagonal stage replaces an earlier belfry. That seems unlikely though, because of the proximity of its date to the deduced date of the circular stage implied by the evidence described.

The octagonal belfry (XVI), faced externally with knapped flints, has two-light belfry openings at the cardinal faces; the lights have cinquefoil heads with a quatrefoil reticulation unit in the apex, a design typical of the Decorated period of the fourteenth-century which is reproduced in flushwork in the diagonal faces. Internally, the belfry openings have dressed stone jambs and arched heads of medieval brick.

The different facing flintwork of the circular and octagonal stages of the tower does not necessarily imply different building periods, and corroboraton of the likelihood that the octagonal and circular stages are contemporary is provided by the first row of putlog holes in the octagon which can be seen in the flushwork panels about a foot above the stone table-course which forms the base of the octagon. As shown in Chapter 8, if the octagon had been an addition to an earlier circular stage, its first row of putlog holes would have been just below the start of the "new" work, not just above it; hence, the level of these putlog holes is an indication of unitary construction where the change from circular to octagonal occurs.

The tower arch is tall (11'4" to impost level) and about 6'3" wide with a pointed head and there is no evidence to suggest that it has been altered from an earlier pattern. It has a double-splayed plan profile with stone dressings on the nave face; at the centre of the double splay there are chamfered stone responds twelve inches wide, continued above the moulded imposts as matching arch voussoirs. The imposts are of a design similar to those of the chancel arch and to the capitals of the nave arcade piers and are judged to be of the fourteenth-century. This, and the similarity of the tower flintwork to that of the aisle west walls, seem strong grounds for assigning the same date to the tower as to the arcades and aisles .

Of a small stone window frame in the west wall of the tower, only part of its cill, its left jamb and one curved voussoir stone remain and so it is difficult to be sure whether it had a round or pointed head. However, a square rebate along the inner edges of the stones is similar to those on thirteenth-century lancets elsewhere, and so this little window probably did have a pointed head. In any event, if the tower is of the fourteenth-century date suggested, the window might be a re-set early window from the north wall of the chancel. No definite evidence of it shows internally except possibly the remnants of the arch of a blocked opening.

Old Catton

South of the tower, the lower part of the nave west wall and a short length of the south wall are of uncoursed rubble flints with large flint quoins at the south-west corner; this is the only visible remnant of the original nave and probably dates from the eleventh century. Above this ancient nave corner, the clerestory stage of the south wall is faced with coursed knapped flint with medieval brick quoins and probably dates from the fifteenth century.

The tower (80) is circular for about two-thirds of its height, with an octagonal belfry stage and a battlemented brick parapet. A little below halfway up the circular stage, there is a distinct change in the facing flintwork: the lower section, on a splayed knapped flint base, is faced entirely with roughly-coursed knapped flints and medieval brick headers arranged in a loose but regular open chequer pattern, a style that can be shown to be a fourteenth-century practice by comparison with the unbuttressed square tower of Mattishall Burgh church whose lower stage has similar, though not identical walling. The facing of the upper section comprises fairly regular uncoursed flintwork more than half of which is knapped flint of a standard not found before the early fourteenth century and its similarity to that in the porch west wall (originally the aisle wall) suggests the same date for the aisle. Two west windows in the circular stage, one in each section, are probably contemporary with the tower. Both are lancets framed externally with cant bricks; the bricks of the lower one course well with the flintwork in which they are set, and they match those used in the open chequer patterning. Internally, the upper one, opposite the upper door, has splayed flint jambs and a segmental double-ring medieval brick arch head.

The internal diameter of the tower is 10'9" and the wall is 3'11" thick measured at the west window. The tower arch to the nave is pointed, 3'10" wide in reveal and 7'11" high to the apex. This arch is moulded on the nave side and dies into plain splayed jambs without imposts; the wall thickness at the arch is 2'6", but behind it, in the curvature of the tower's east wall, a taller rere-arch with a depressed pointed head, about eighteen inches higher, adds a further ten inches, giving a combined thickness of about 3'4" at the apex. This double-arch configuration, one arch through the nave wall and one in the tower's curved internal wall, is indicative of the tower having been added to an existing nave, and their pointed shapes date them as post-Norman.

The most significant feature relevant to the dating of the tower, however, is the level of the blocked upper door in the east wall: the head of this opening is only about three feet below the top of the circular stage – considerably higher than is usual for upper doors in round towers – and so, unless the original nave had been exceptionally high, the nave must have been heightened when or before the upper door was formed and the tower built. It seems possible therefore that the tower was built and the nave heightened, though without a clerestory at that stage, as interdependent elements of a major alteration that may also have included creation of one or both aisles that were subsequently rebuilt

80. Old Catton church tower, Norwich.

in the nineteenth century. A mid-fourteenth-century date as derived for the tower from the considerable evidence described above, would therefore also be applicable to the early nave alterations.

It is clear that the present height of the circular stage was never the tower's full original height because its upper compartment does not appear to have been a belfry: there is no evidence inside or out of any blocked former belfry openings and in any case it is improbable that the upper door, whose head is only two or three feet below the top of the circular stage, would have given access directly into a bellchamber. It follows therefore, that the present belfry is either contemporary with the circular stage, or it replaces an earlier one. The latter alternative seems more likely because just below the top of the circular stage, the flintwork changes to a predominantly cobble type, outside and in, and contains putlog holes lined with medieval bricks. It is as if the topmost few courses of the circular stage had been rebuilt, weathered with a course of cant bricks, in preparation for a new belfry, and certainly suggests the start of a different building phase from the work below it. The present octagonal belfry is therefore more likely to be a replacement of an earlier original one of the same date as the circular stage.

The belfry walls are of roughly coursed flints, mainly knapped and with a few brick headers, and the quoins are formed with medieval bricks. The two-light Perpendicular belfry openings in the cardinal faces are square-headed and framed in brick with simple panel tracery and mullions of moulded brick; plain brick dummy windows in the diagonals are infilled with squared knapped flint. There is reason to believe that as well as being later than the circular stage, the belfry could also be later than the fifteenth-century clerestory, because not only are the belfry openings formed with brick in contrast to the stone windows of the clerestory, but the bricks in its quoins and dressings are yellow, whereas red bricks are used in the clerestory quoins. The brick details of the belfry openings suggest that it could be sixteenth-century.

Based on the evidence recorded, a constructional chronology might be:

11th Century: Original towerless church built.

Mid-14th Century: Nave enlarged and heightened, with upper door formed in heightened west wall; tower built; tower arch formed.

15th Century: Clerestory added; west bay of south aisle converted into porch.

16th Century: Original fourteenth-century belfry replaced by present one.

19th Century: Aisles rebuilt, transepts built.

Brome

The knapped flint facing of the circular stage of Brome tower is a modern renewal of the facing of a tower said by Pevsner[1] to be Norman, but its octagonal belfry reportedly of 1875 and certainly looking very Victorian, is built of rubble flints with corners of brick that have every appearance of being medieval. It poses the question: have the eight Victorian belfry windows been inserted in a medieval octagon, or have medieval corner bricks been skilfully reused?

[1] *The Buildings of England, Suffolk.* Second edition revised by E Radcliffe. Penguin, 1974.

CHAPTER 17

ROUND TOWERS WITH CONTEMPORARY OCTAGONAL LANCET BELFRIES

As has been mentioned earlier, where the circular stage of a round tower with an octagonal belfry stage has no evidence of former belfry openings nor any evidence of Norman or earlier features but contains post-Norman evidence such as a pointed tower arch or medieval bricks in its fabric, there is clearly a likelihood that the octagon, unless it can be shown to be a later replacement of an earlier belfry, could be contemporary with the circular stage.

The earliest towers with these characteristics are probably the few that have octagons with lancet-type belfry openings and in most of those there is sufficient post-Norman evidence in their circular stages to imply the same date as their lancet belfries.

The closely-packed rubble flintwork of the circular stage of the tower at Hassingham (XVIII) could, before recent repointing, be seen to be similar to that in the octagonal belfry. A date probably no earlier than the late thirteenth century is suggested by the remnants of a medieval brick-framed west window below the present one (81) and by the regular pattern of medieval brick putlog holes in the circular stage. Their spacing seems to rule out the possibility that the circular stage ever contained belfry openings and implies, therefore, contemporary construction of the two stages. A round-headed nave south door with chevron and billet decoration, and limestone quoins at the west corners confer a Norman date for the church, and a flat east wall above the tower arch within the tower tends to confirm that the tower is a later addition. The tower arch has a Tudor head and may have been altered from an Early English one and perhaps heightened when the Perpendicular west window that has a similarly-shaped head was inserted.

At Horsey, brick putlog holes and knapped flints in the external wall of the tower's circular stage and the pointed tower arch internally imply a date no earlier than the late thirteenth century. The low height of the circular stage – only to nave roof ridge level – suggests that it never stood as a complete tower, nor is there any evidence in its walls externally or internally of blocked openings, although four holes left in the internal walls following removal of old floor timbers from the upper part of the circular

81. Remnant of an early window framed with medieval bricks, below a later inserted window in the west wall of Hassingham tower.

stage have been mistaken for Saxon windows! The octagonal belfry stage, with medieval brick corners, has flintwork that is not dissimilar to the circular stage, and its lancet-style belfry openings, being compatible in date with the pointed tower arch, suggest that the round part and the octagon represent a single building phase.

Again, the absence of any early features or evidence of former belfry windows in the circular stages of the towers at Acle and Mautby suggests that they could be contemporary with their lancet octagonal belfries, but this is less certain because, although they have pointed tower arches, the circular stages lack definite post-Norman evidence and much of the original character of these two towers has been weakened by later restorations.

West Somerton

The circular stage of the tower is about two-thirds of its total height, and in the octagonal belfry stage (82) single-light lancet-type belfry openings in the cardinal faces are framed with stone externally and have medieval brick jambs and rere-arches internally. In the other faces, stone replica lancets are filled with squared knapped flints set flush with the external face of the stonework and behind these internally, undisturbed continuity of the wall fabric shows that the blank lancets are not merely blocked openings but were built as decorative features. The external fabric of both stages is similar, comprising flint cobbles, roughly coursed, and a few medieval bricks randomly

distributed. The walls display a distinct and regular pattern of putlog holes framed and bridged with medieval bricks. The internal fabric is similar and neither in the external flintwork nor in the tower, is there any evidence of blocked former window or belfry openings. Within the tower, the internal shape is circular to the top, though at the level of the external change of shape, an offset reduces the thickness of the octagon wall.

There are two windows in the circular stage, both facing west. The two-light ground-floor window is probably Victorian, and a difference in the external flintwork below this window and a corresponding recess internally suggest that there may originally have been a west door in this position. The other window, a few feet below the top of the circular stage, is a small lancet framed externally in medieval brick with a rough fan-like brick relieving arch above. Internally, this window has medieval brick jambs and its pointed brick arch extending through the full thickness of

82. West Somerton. Lancet style octagonal belfry contemporary with the tower's circular stage.

the wall confirms it as having been built with the wall. In the tower east wall at first floor level internally, a large upper doorway is also arched with medieval bricks and is clearly an integral part of the tower's construction.

The tower has an internal diameter of 8'9" and a wall thickness of 4'1" measured at the west window which is about the same as at the apex of the tower arch. The pointed tower arch is about fifteen feet tall and 5'8" wide in reveal with semi-octagonal responds and chamfers towards the nave and a plain plastered rere-arch behind.

Although the circular part of the tower has been called eleventh- or twelfth-century with an added thirteenth-century belfry, there is no visible evidence to support the early dates for the lower stage, or to show that the two stages are of different periods. On the contrary, the extensive use of medieval bricks that are manifestly features of the original tower wall construction, in both stages externally and internally in the putlog holes, occasionally amongst the flints, in the small lancet and in the upper doorway, provides solid evidence for dating the wall no earlier than say, the last quarter of the thirteenth century, a date which would be compatible with the style of the belfry openings and the small lancet window.

Features revealed by the stripping of the external rendering from the nave wall in 1989 indicate an earlier date than the twelfth century for the nave and so the pointed tower arch, likely to have been cut through the nave west wall when the tower was added to the church and being clearly later than the twelfth century, corroborates a post-Norman date for the tower.

Grounds for belief that the circular and octagonal stages are contemporary are the similarity of the materials and workmanship in the two stages, both externally and internally, not only of the walls but also of the construction of the belfry openings to the first-floor window embrasure and upper door opening. The most convincing evidence that the circular stage never stood independently without the belfry stage is the uninterrupted pattern of the external putlog holes in the circular stage, proving that there never were any belfry openings where they would be expected if the circular stage had originally been an earlier tower without the present belfry.

Topcroft

The tower has four stages and a battlemented parapet. The ground stage, only about nineteen feet high, is circular; it has an internal diameter of 9'9" and its five-foot thick walls are faced with regular uncoursed rubble flint. The top three stages are octagonal and the internal circular shape of the ground stage is maintained in the two lower octagonal stages which are faced externally with material similar to the ground stage, and have angles formed with medieval brick. Their internal walls contain quite a lot of medieval brick – headers and stretchers – which are clearly part of the original fabric and not repair insertions.

In the lower octagonal stage there is a stone-faced lancet window with a medieval brick relieving arch above; internally, this window has an arch of medieval brick through the full thickness of the wall and medieval brick jambs except for a few flints at the bottom, and there is no evidence to suggest that it is a later insertion. There is no upper door.

In the next octagonal stage there are eight single lancets framed with medieval brick and internally they have medieval brick jambs and arches of similar construction to the single window below; there is no evidence to suggest that they might have been altered from an earlier pattern.

The present belfry which occupies the top stage, and the parapet were probably added in the fifteenth century; they are faced with knapped flint with stone quoins at the angles. Feigned two-light windows in the diagonal faces of the belfry suggest that the present single-light belfry openings of similar proportions in the cardinal faces have lost their mullions and tracery. Each of the octagonal stages is separated by stone string courses.

Whereas usually the upper part of a round tower above the nave can be seen to be built on the nave west wall, at Topcroft (35) the first octagonal stage of the tower at nave roof level is clearly separate from the nave west wall and is not built on it, but the east face of the octagon is built up against the west face of the nave gable. This, and the considerable wall thickness of 5'10" at the tower arch apex seem to indicate that the tower was independently built against an existing church, and because of this apparently premeditated relationship between the octagon and the nave west gable, the concentric circular ground stage would have been positioned accordingly and must therefore have been built at the same time as the octagon. This conclusion is corroborated by other evidence: firstly, the external flintwork of the circular stage is similar to that of the octagon, and secondly, the tower arch is pointed, suggesting that its formation was contemporary with the lancet windows in the octagon; being of a plain plastered finish unembellished with dressed stone, this arch is more likely to be original than an aesthetic updating of an earlier arch implying the same date for the circular stage of the tower to which it gives access.

The tower arch is off-centre to the north within the tower with the result that the south jamb of the opening covers a larger area than the north. This, and the greater than normal wall thickness at the tower/nave junction arising from the tower's thick walls and its placing vis-à-vis the nave may have been to provide enough room for a stair within the walling south of the opening; but there is no stair. There is, though, a deep cupboard in the south-east quadrant of the tower wall internally which might have been the entry to a now-blocked stairway.

The tower's three lower stages can probably be dated as a thirteenth-century addition to a previously towerless church. It has however been suggested that the two lower octagonal stages were built in the thirteenth century to replace a collapsed earlier upper round section, but in view of the evidence described, it seems more likely that they were a contemporary continuation in octagonal form of the lower circular shape.

It has alternatively been suggested that, because they are circular internally, the two lower octagonal stages must have been the upper part of a circular Saxon tower that has been cut back externally from its original shape to the present octagonal form, and that the eight brick-framed lancet windows were originally round-headed Saxon belfry windows altered in the Early English period. This fanciful idea can be dismissed, firstly and essentially because of the constructional impracticability of altering the external shape of an existing flint tower, secondly because the lancet windows show no evidence inside or out of having been altered and thirdly because the circular internal walls contain medieval bricks which were not made until after the Norman period.

CHAPTER 18

ROUND TOWERS WITH CONTEMPORARY OCTAGONAL BELFRIES WITH TWO-LIGHT BELFRY OPENINGS

Most of the towers of this kind are fourteenth-century. Some, namely Theberton, Potter Heigham, Shimpling, Ilketshall St Andrews and Thorpe Abbotts (XVII) have flushwork replicas of the belfry openings in the alternate facets of the octagon. At Poringland and Bylaugh, these facets are in proudwork and at St Benedict's, Norwich, (21) in brick flushwork; Rockland St Peter (88) has recessed blank windows and Repps (71) has blank arcading. Other octagons, with plain wall between the belfry openings, include Sedgeford, Hasketon, Croxton (V), Rollesby, Stuston, Edingthorpe, Wramplingham, Little Bradley and Morton on the Hill before the tower's collapse in 1959.

Although all of these towers except Morton on the Hill and those at Repps and Little Bradley, described earlier, have pointed tower arches and none of them have any evidence of former belfry openings in the circular stage, they have often been described as having a later octagonal top, without regard to the possibility that the two stages might be contemporary. For this reason, several are described below, with fuller explanations of the grounds on which the opinion for contemporary construction of their circular and octagonal stages are based.

Thorpe Abbotts

The key to the dating of this tower lies in first establishing the chronology of the nave, and this is best traced in the nave north wall. This wall is built of fairly well-coursed flint rubble; the north-east corner is formed with rubble flint quoins which are only marginally larger than the walling flints and almost course with them, and the west end has Barnack stone quoins. At about the mid-point of the wall, there is a blocked round-headed door whose arch and jambs are formed with flints, and near the west end, a pointed door with Barnack freestone dressings. The wall contains two two-light windows of about the same size – one near the east end with Y-tracery and the other with Perpendicular tracery a little to the east of the pointed door. Above the windows, the wall appears to have been raised, as a single row of medieval brick putlog holes can be traced at about window-head level and the upper quoins of the nave north-east corner change from flint to stone. There are no other medieval bricks in the north wall fabric.

At about 19'6" from the west corners of the nave, vertical straight joints can be detected in the flintwork of the north and south nave walls below the cills of the windows at these positions. There is a discernable difference in the flintwork on each side of the straight joints and the flints immediately to the east of the joint line are slightly larger than the average walling flints and are set in vertical alignment directly one above the other in similar fashion to the flint quoins at the north-east corner of the nave. The fact that they are found on both the north and south nave walls at precisely the same distance from the west end of the nave must surely establish them as surviving flint quoins of the west corners of an originally shorter nave, and they confirm that the western end of the nave north wall in which the pointed north doorway is located is a separate and later build from the eastern part. On the evidence of the blocked flint door and the flint quoins, the eastern part of the nave wall is probably eleventh-century; the westward extension to the originally shorter nave that has been established by identification of its flint west quoins, is datable by the pointed north doorway as thirteenth-century.

The tower walls are different from the nave wall; they are roughly-coursed with evenly-sized rubble flints, non-flint erratics and a few medieval bricks; many putlog holes framed and bridged with medieval bricks are visible. The tower is circular for about two-thirds of its height, the upper part being octagonal. The circular stage has a plinth weathered with medieval cant bricks on edge, and facing west, a cinquefoiled cusped lancet stone window on the ground floor has a medieval brick ray arch above it (now partly obscured by crude modern pointing) and higher up, narrow rectangular stone windows face south and north though the latter is blocked internally. A circular stone string course forms the base for the octagon which is in two stages separated by another stone string course (XVII); their flint fabric is similar to the circular stage and the angles are formed with medieval bricks. The lower octagonal stage is about eight feet high and its walls are plain except for a single narrow rectangular stone window in the west face similar to the south-facing one in the circular stage. The belfry stage above has two-light belfry openings in the cardinal faces and flushwork replicas in the diagonals.

Internally the tower walls are plastered up to second floor level which occurs at about 2'6" below the level of the external change of shape from circular to octagonal; above second floor level the internal flintwork is small cobbly rubble similar to the external fabric, with brick putlog holes. The circular shape is maintained internally nearly to the top of the lower octagonal stage and there is no change of material or workmanship internally at the level of the external change of shape.

Apart from the blocked north window, there is no evidence in the external flintwork of any other blocked openings in the circular stage; any internal indications that there might have been or possible evidence of an upper door are lost behind the internal plastering; the plastering however, does not extend into the reveals of the rectangular south window and its jambs can be seen to be medieval brick of similar construction to those of the rectangular window in the circular internal wall of the lower octagonal stage.

Clearly the tower cannot be earlier than the nave extension, and in contrast to the medieval bricks in the tower's fabric and features, the complete absence of such bricks in the thirteenth-century walls of the westward nave extension implies that the tower is a different, later build, and perhaps of the same date as the raised section of the nave walls defined by the single row of medieval brick putlog holes at window-head level in the north wall.

The low height of the tower's circular stage and the absence of any evidence of former belfry openings near the top precludes the likelihood that the circular stage ever stood as a finished tower, and so, unless the octagon replaces an earlier post-Norman belfry, the circular stage and octagon must have been built together. Replacement of an earlier belfry by the present octagonal one seems no more than a theoretical possibility because the deduced post-thirteenth-century date for the circular stage seems unrealistically close to a probable date for the octagon. Also, if the octagonal stages *had* been a later addition, it is likely that at the level at which the new shape starts externally, either some variation in the flintwork workmanship would be apparent internally or the internal walls would have been built octagonally for the full height of both octagonal stages, but neither of these circumstances applies in this tower.

On the other hand, there is considerable convincing evidence for the octagon being contemporary with the circular stage. The most telling is the continuity of the circular shape internally within the octagon up to within two feet or so of the top of its lower stage with no variation whatever in the internal flintwork where the change of shape occurs externally. This evidence of continuity of construction at the junction of the circular and octagonal stages is confirmed externally by the vertical spacing of the putlog holes at that level as described in Chapter 8. Further evidence for a single build is the similarity of the construction of the rectangular stone windows in both the circular stage and the octagon, and the similarity of flintwork in both stages.

If, as the evidence suggests, the circular and octagonal stages are contemporary, the tracery in the belfry openings can suggest a dating for the whole tower. The trefoiled heads of the lights with a straight-sided quatrefoil reticulation unit in the apex are characteristic of the mid- to late fourteenth century when Decorated tracery was giving way to Perpendicular. The narrow rectangular stone windows are inconclusive as diagnostic features but they appear in a few other round towers which are also probably fourteenth-century such as Weybread and Rockland St Peter. On balance, a late fourteenth-century date for the whole tower seems likely.

Hasketon

The tower is circular for about two-thirds of its height, above which it is octagonal, and both stages are faced with even, uncoursed, well-packed rubble flints. The octagon, much repaired with brick at the top, has dressed limestone quoins and two-light Y-traceried belfry openings in the cardinal faces whose cill level is about ten feet or so above the stone weathering between the round and octagonal stages.

The circular stage has a two-light ground-floor west window with Y-tracery, which, though appreciably restored, contains sufficient original stonework to authenticate the tracery pattern. At first-floor level in the circular stage, three lancet windows at south, west and north have stone dressings both externally and internally to their jambs and pointed arches. They have splayed internal reveals widening from nine inches at the external aperture to 2'8" at the inner wall face and are 5'4" tall (the glazing opening). Internally the tower changes from circular to octagonal at about the same level as on the outside, though the flintwork above and below this level is similar.

An upper door in the tower east wall at first floor level has a pointed head with dressed stone jambs and arch and shows no evidence of having been altered. Above its stone arch, and set directly on the voussoirs, longer flints laid non-radially take the form of a relieving arch. An interesting detail, if not unique certainly unusual in the upper chambers of round towers, is a chamfer on the inner edges of the internal voussoirs of the upper door and first-floor lancets, with mini-broaches on the springer stones of the arches.

The tower has no Norman features; it has an internal diameter of nine feet and walls about 5'4" thick. The pointed tower arch is a very tall one without imposts but it has dressed stone jambs in nave and tower; its thickness of about five feet at the apex by comparison with a nave west wall thickness of 2'10" measured outside the tower suggests that the tower was a later addition to a formerly towerless church.

The pointed arches of the tower arch and the upper door, neither of which have any evidence of later alteration, indicate a post-Norman date for their formation, which of course would be the date of the tower's construction. The width of the lancet windows' internal splays is identical to the upper door width, and the similarity of their construction and voussoir details to the upper door implies that it and the windows are contemporary. The absence of external or internal disturbance to the flintwork surrounding the lancets or the upper door indicates that all were part of the tower's original construction and were not inserted later. A theory that the windows were originally Norman belfry openings subsequently modified to lancet shape can be dismissed on three counts: firstly, they show no evidence whatever of having been adapted from Norman openings; secondly, they are at the same level as the upper door and it is highly unlikely that that an upper door would have opened directly into a bellchamber; and thirdly, it is improbable that the Normans, or later builders, would have built a tower with a belfry below the level of the nave ridge, which at the time the upper door was formed must have been at least at this height.

Because, then, the three lancets are not altered Norman belfry openings, nor for the same reasons later ones, the level at which the shape changes from circular to octagonal could not have been the top of a finished tower, since such a tower would have had no belfry. Consequently, the present octagonal stage or an earlier, post-Norman belfry must have been part of the original complete tower. Since a post-Norman belfry earlier than the present one is unlikely, it follows that the present octagon must be this tower's original belfry. The circular and octagonal stages are therefore contemporary.

Further corroboration for the date of the circular stage and that it was contemporary with the octagon comes from the ground floor west window; it has the same tracery pattern as the belfry openings, and although considerably restored, retains some original stonework. Because many early round towers have had later ground-floor west windows inserted, this feature has come to be regarded as notoriously untrustworthy for dating, but in some of the later towers the ground-floor west window was clearly part of the original tower structure, and Hasketon tower seems to be one of those cases. The Y-tracery of the west window and belfry openings suggests that the tower may have been added to a Norman nave in the late thirteenth century or early fourteenth, though this window pattern was used for a long time after it first appeared in the late thirteenth century.

Standing about 60 feet high, Hasketon tower is one of the tallest of all round towers and its wall thickness of more than five feet is an indication that a tower of considerable height had been envisaged from the outset. This is further evidence, albeit circumstantial, that the circular and octagonal stages are contemporary.

Sedgeford

St Mary's at Sedgeford is probably the only medieval church with a round tower that was built from the outset with an aisled nave. The present aisles, though, are wider than the original ones and extend westwards beyond the original nave west wall, embracing the tower (83).

The evidence that the original church was built with aisles is provided by the north and

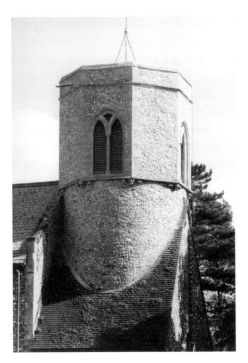

83. Original aisles at Sedgeford were replaced with wider ones extending westwards to embrace the round tower. It is the only one where this has occurred.

south arcades. Firstly, they occupy the full length of the nave between its original west wall and the chancel, with no residual lengths of former side walls each end such as are usually seen where an arcade has been cut through an outside wall later, and the depth to which the capitals of the west responds can be seen to have extended into the west wall is an indication that responds and west wall were built together; secondly, had the nave originally been without aisles, some evidence of its west corners would be expected to have survived behind the arcade responds, as there would have been no reason to remove them, but there is no such evidence – only the scars of where the nave west wall was later removed; thirdly, since the size of the arcade column bases averages about 3'7" square, the implication is that they were built as individual footings for the columns rather than being residual sections of former side walls of that excessive thickness – where an arcade has been formed by cutting arches through an existing wall, the columns usually stand directly on retained sections of that wall; and fourthly, as both arcades are identical (except for a single octagonal column in the centre of the north arcade) and therefore almost certainly contemporary, this implies that they were more likely to have been part of the nave's original construction because arcades that have been inserted later usually show differences reflecting different insertion dates. The circular columns and capital mouldings suggest a thirteenth-century date. Lastly, there is no evidence in the church or tower of any work that can be authenticated as earlier than the arcades. (Indications of a blocked upper door, said by Pevsner to be twelfth-century, are so indistinct as to be unreliable for dating.)

The original aisles of which there are now no traces, were almost certainly narrower than the present ones, with the slopes of the original nave roof (before the later clerestory) probably continuing down over the aisles at the same pitch. This was a normal arrangement in early aisled plans.

The tower's circular stage has been called Saxon, Saxo-Norman and Norman, but contrary to those attributions, there is considerable evidence to show that the whole tower is the same date as the nave, i.e. thirteenth-century. The main evidence for this is the ground-floor plan shape within the tower (84). Its north-south diameter is about 10'3", but where its side walls meet the back of the stonework jambs of the pointed tower arch, its width is 11'2", giving the floor plan a hairpin shape; looking upwards though, the internal shape is completely circular at the level of the first-floor, the underside of which coincides with the apex level of the outer chamfers of the tower arch.

The transition of the tower's ground-floor shape to circular at first-floor level has been achieved by oversailing the walling in the spandrel areas of the tower arch and it must have been built like that from the outset because alteration of a supposedly previously circular tower plan to its present shape and widening of a conjectured originally narrower tower arch to the present size would have required so much cutting away of existing walling as to render such an undertaking impracticable, if not impossible. Realistically, the relationship of the tower's plan shape to the tower arch could only have resulted from preconceived design and construction of tower and tower arch together. Likewise the height, width and thickness of this tower arch, and the incorporation of a hoodmould in

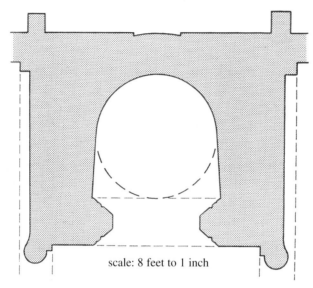

scale: 8 feet to 1 inch

84. Sedgeford tower plan showing hairpin ground-floor shape and circular shape above at the apex level of the tower arch.

the wall above it facing the nave are collectively more indicative of the arch having been built with the nave west wall than having been cut through it later. Hence, the obviously post-Norman tower arch places the tower's circular stage also as post-Norman.

Objection to dating the tower arch as contemporary with the nave arcades may be made on the grounds that the tower arch impost mouldings are a later style than the moulded capitals of the arcade columns. But this can be explained by the fact that the inner order of the tower arch is a later insertion into an originally double-chamfered wider arch without imposts. Proof of this is shown by the clumsy and unconnected manner in which the back faces of the impost mouldings of the inner, added order meet the inner face of the original double-chamfered arch (85); also, the jamb stonework of the inner order does not course with the outer double-chamfered stonework in accordance with traditional masonry practice, nor has the radius of the inner arch been struck from the same centre as the outer chamfers and so can be seen to follow a different curve from them.

The tower has no Norman evidence to show, and the claim for a Saxon attribution for it relies on a triangular-headed window in its west wall and a smaller aperture facing south which is visible only at first-floor level within the tower because its outer face is obscured by the internal wall of the later aisle extension. Of these two, the west window is faced with dressed stone externally and is round-headed internally, though its brick arch at the inner wall face probably replaces an original hardwood lintel of the same kind as the one still in place at the quatrefoil window above it. The south aperture is very narrow and seems to have had a horizontal head, only taking a triangular shape near the inner wall face. Although recognized as a feature characteristic of Saxon style, triangular-shaped window-heads are not exclusive to pre-Conquest times; they are also found over small windows in later towers. These two openings, one with stone dressings externally and an uncertain type of original head internally, and the other with a virtually flat head are therefore dubious grounds for a Saxon attribution for the tower, particularly in view of all the evidence for a later date.

The main evidence that the octagonal belfry is contemporary with the circular stage is that the flintwork is similar in both stages and that since the circular stage has no evidence inside or outside of any earlier belfry openings, it was never intended to be a finished tower; the present belfry, with shafted Y-tracery openings, is unlikely to be later than the pointed tower arch, which, as shown, must have been built with the circular stage, and so the circular stage and the octagonal belfry must be contemporary. The shafted mullions of the belfry openings can be understood as coeval with the circular arcade columns.

85. The springing of the tower arch at Sedgeford, showing the discontinuity between the later inner order and the original double-chamfered arch.

Built from the outset with aisles, this was apparently an important church and since it seems improbable that an aisled church of the thirteenth century would have been built without a bell tower, that supposition supports the architectural evidence for the tower being contemporary with the nave.

Shimpling

The tower has an octagonal belfry stage with two-light belfry openings in the cardinal faces and flushwork replicas in the diagonals. There is a large Perpendicular ground floor west window and a small one above it. A newel stair of about 2'6" radius, with access from the south reveal of the tower arch, is incorporated within the tower wall and nave west wall and circles one-and-a-half turns between ground and first floor level (86). It has a brick newel, brick risers and a brick arch where it enters the first floor. Externally, it shows as a thickening of the tower south wall, filling the re-entrant angle between tower and nave west wall (87).

The tower's circular stage is faced externally with coursed rubble flint incorporating quite a lot of medieval brick, and the octagon material is similar with perhaps relatively more brick, and medieval brick quoins. Similar brick 'quoining' is also used at the shallow angles of the wall enclosing the stair, whose flintwork is similar to the tower walling and bonds and courses with it. An unusual feature is the incorporation within the circular stage fabric of vertical bands of medieval brick headers; these comprise single header bricks one above the other in unbroken lengths of six feet or more, irregularly spaced around the tower at about six to eight feet apart. There is one series near the top and another lower down. Within the tower at first floor stage, there are similar bands in

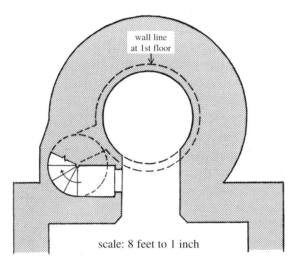

86. Shimpling. Plan of tower showing off-centre tower arch and stair accommodated within the wall thickness.

the internal wall, three about five feet high from floor level and above these, seven about seven feet high. There are no indications in the flintwork of the circular stage, externally or internally, of any former blocked belfry or other openings.

At ground level the internal diameter of the tower is 7'8" and the walls are 4'7" thick, but at first floor level the diameter is nine feet, with correspondingly thinner walls. The pointed tower arch is five feet wide in reveal and about twenty feet tall, with a plain plaster finish and ten-inch chamfers towards the nave; measured at the apex of the arch, the wall is five feet thick. Although the tower itself is central relative to the nave, the tower arch is off-centre within the tower by a few inches to the north.

The circular stage of the tower has no visible evidence of Saxon or Norman work but several indications that it was added to an existing twelfth- or thirteenth-century church during the second half of the fourteenth century, and that the circular stage and octagon are contemporary.

If it could be shown that the tower stair was built with the tower rather than as a later insertion into the wall of an earlier tower, then this would establish the tower's date as being no earlier than the date of the medieval bricks used in the stair construction. There is a wealth of evidence to show that tower and stair construction were contemporary:

1. There is no indication in the external fabric of any discontinuity that might suggest that a

complete breach about five feet wide in the tower south wall adjacent to the nave west wall had been made, as would have been necessary if a stair of this type had been constructed within the wall of an existing tower.

2. At 4'7" thick, the ground floor walls of the tower are considerably thicker than most round tower walls; a likely reason for that could be that they were designed for the incorporation of a stair within their thickness.

3. The position of the tower relative to the nave is such that the combined thickness of the tower east wall and the nave west wall measured at the tower arch apex is five feet. This is more than the tower wall thickness and considerably thicker than the equivalent measurement on most other added towers. The reason for this was probably to maximise the wall area on plan within which an integral stair could be formed.

4. As a result of positioning the tower arch off-centre northwards relative to the tower axis, the wall area on plan behind the south reveal of the tower arch is further increased to allow space in which the stair could be formed.

5. At first floor level, i.e. the level at which the stair terminates, the tower wall thickness is reduced by about eight inches. Above this level there is no need for a wall of sufficient thickness to accommodate a stair.

6. The external flintwork of the south wall enclosing the stair is similar to that on the tower; it courses with the tower flintwork and there is no discontinuity where the stair 'bulge' merges with the circular tower wall. This indicates that the tower wall and stair wall were of one build.

7. There is no evidence of a blocked upper door in the east wall of the tower internally which might be expected if the tower had originally been without an integral stair.

87. The stair turret at Shimpling integrally built with the tower as part of its original construction.

The pointed shape of the tower arch, which has no evidence of alteration, persuasively dates it and the tower as post-Norman, and medieval bricks at random in the tower fabric and in the vertical bands of headers inside and out provide further evidence in support of a date for the circular stage suggested by the stair brickwork. The way that the bricks in the bands course with the flintwork and the uniformity of their mortar setting with that of adjacent flintwork (particularly inside where the walls have not been repointed) seem to show that they are part of the original construction and not later insertions or repairs.

Given that brickmaking is not thought to have revived in East Anglia until the late thirteenth century, and that provision of tower stairways seems to have been a later feature of round towers, the circular stage is considered unlikely to be earlier than fourteenth century.

The tracery of the belfry openings is of the type having two ogee trefoiled lights with a central reticulation unit above, a pattern typical of the 'Reticulated' phase of the Decorated style mainly prevalent during the middle two quarters of the fourteenth century and sometimes later as well. It is possible that the building of this tower and belfry was the building work towards which the Rector left the sum of one mark in 1386.

The absence of any evidence of former belfry openings in the circular stage means either that the present octagonal belfry replaces an earlier one (which, of course, could not have been earlier than the circular stage) or that it is contemporary with the circular stage. In the light of the apparent closeness of the judged dates of the two stages, the greater likelihood is that they are contemporary.

Rockland St Peter

The church has no evidence to suggest that it is earlier than the fourteenth century and the same can be said of its round tower and octagonal belfry. The tower and its integral stair turret were almost certainly built together and at the same time as the church, and there is also convincing evidence to show that the tower's circular and octagonal stages are contemporary.

The tower has two circular stages surmounted by an octagonal belfry stage. The lower circular stage is about twice the height of the upper one and rises from a flint plinth weathered with dressed Barnack stone. The three stages are separated by dressed stone string courses and have similar fabric comprising closely-packed rubble flint more noticeably coursed in some areas than others, with a few long stone ties in the south face of the upper circular stage. Within this stage there are three rectangular stone windows at first-floor level, and in the octagonal belfry stage two-light Decorated belfry openings in the cardinal faces alternate with stone blank windows of similar proportions in the diagonal facets, and indicate a fourteenth-century date.

The main evidence that the tower and church are contemporary is found within the tower at first-floor level. Whereas on the ground floor the tower east wall is flat at the tower arch position, at first-floor level the floor plan shape is fully circular, and in the east wall the splayed

reveals of a recess that penetrates the full thickness of the wall show the wall to be monolithic, thus proving that the nave west wall and tower were a single build. Since the tower was furnished with a stair from the outset, the recess would never have been an upper door, and this is confirmed by its splayed reveals; at the nave wall face, it has two small openings – to the nave and to the roof-space. Further evidence of unitary construction of church and tower is provided by the small trefoil window in the nave west wall that lights the tower stair.

The integral stair turret on the south-east face of the tower (88) rises through the two circular stages, with the tower's plinth and string course details continued in its structure. The turret flintwork is similar to that on the tower and, particularly on the east, merges and courses undeviatingly with the tower wall; the turret though, contains many more stone ties, probably because its walls are thinner than the tower walls. The plinth weathering in particular provides

88 The tower at Rockland St Peter is another in which an integral stair turret was incorporated.

confirmation of the unity of construction of tower and turret because not only are the weathering stones identical in both, but the re-entrant angle between them where the turret wall meets the tower is formed by a single mitred stone. Between the nave wall and the tower on the north side, a flat fillet, rather wider than normal, fills the re-entrant angle; it too has a similar stone-weathered plinth.

There is little doubt that the octagonal belfry is contemporary with the circular stages, which, apart from the three rectangular windows at first-floor level, have no other windows, nor do their walls have any signs of former blocked openings inside or out. The stone-dressed entry to the tower stair at ground-floor level has a shouldered lintel, and repetition of this detail at the stair entries to the first floor and to the bellchamber supports a common date for the three stages of the tower and the stair. But the most significant evidence is the fact that the octagonal belfry is circular internally with the same diameter as the externally-circular first floor below, and at the cill level of the belfry openings, i.e. the level at which the outside change of shape occurs, which is about five feet above the bellchamber floor, there is no variation of the internal fabric of the wall between the belfry openings, above and below this level.

CHAPTER 19

TOWERS IN WHICH CIRCULAR AND OCTAGONAL STAGES MERGE WITHOUT A STRING COURSE

Round towers with an octagonal belfry usually have a stone string course between the two stages, but on some, like those at Wramplingham, Horsey, Edingthorpe, Ilketshall St Andrew (89), Rushall, and Burgh St Mary, the circular shape merges into the octagon above without a string course separating them. Similar flintwork in both stages suggests that they are contemporary where this method is used. An exception, though, occurs at Mutford; there, the octagon is later than the tower, but it was probably built at the same time as the upper storey of the circular stage, which is a different build from the tower's lower part, perhaps replacing an earlier belfry,

Wramplingham

In addition to the merged junction of the octagonal belfry to the circular stage at Wramplingham, the main corroborative evidence for the two stages being contemporary is the similarity of their flintwork and the extent to which medieval bricks are used in both stages. They occur in putlog holes, inside and out, and in the first- and second-floor windows of the circular stage, and they form the external angles of the octagon as well as appearing in the belfry windows inside. The absence of any evidence of former belfry openings in the circular stage provides further grounds for considering that the circular stage and octagon are contemporary.

As one of a few added towers that is almost tangential to the nave west wall rather than being partially built on it, its east wall is over three feet thick where it meets the west face of the 2' 6" thick nave wall. Possibly a west entrance to the formerly towerless church, the opening through the nave wall is a plain straight-sided, round-headed arch; within it, a smaller pointed arch facing the nave has been inserted, but the original profile is still visible behind. Behind that, starting from the semi-circular arch shape at the nave wall face, the opening progressively splays, heightens and alters shape until at the tower's inner circumference it is wider, higher and pointed. This transformation within the thickness of the tower's east wall is clearly an original constructional artifice, and together with the medieval bricks in the features and fabric of the circular stage, puts a post-Norman date for the whole tower and its fillets beyond doubt.

Ilketshall St Andrew

The nave has Norman north and south doorways and Caen stone quoins of typical Norman pattern at the south-west and north-west corners. The nave walls, except the later upper part, are uncoursed flint rubble containing no brick.

The tower is circular for about half its height with 4'4" thick walls and has a two-stage octagonal upper part. The tower fabric is the same in the circular part as in the two octagonal stages and, by contrast with the nave, consists of well-coursed flint rubble incorporating a few medieval bricks, possibly rather more in the upper octagonal stage, and the walls contain well-marked putlog holes formed with medieval bricks. Apart from a later west window on the ground floor, there is one other window in the circular part, near the top on the south side – a pointed lancet framed with medieval bricks and with a brick hoodmould.

The junction of the octagon to the circular part is made without a string course but the two-stage octagon has stone quoins and stone string courses between its two stages and the flushwork parapet (89). The belfry openings in the cardinal faces of the upper octagonal stage have lost their tracery but flushwork replicas in the diagonals are of a two-light Decorated style.

Internally, the tower east wall is curved but the tower arch is formed as two distinct openings, of the same width but of different heights. Both have pointed heads. The lower arch facing the nave is the thickness of the nave west wall, and as the arch within the tower is 1'9" higher, the flat west face of the nave wall is visible above the apex of the nave-side arch. This configuration, indicative of separate arches formed in the nave west wall and in the tower wall, is strong evidence that the tower is an addition to the church, and confirmation of this is provided by the fabric difference of nave and tower.

Above first floor level internally the tower is circular for its full height and shows no significant change of material or workmanship at the level of the external transition from circle to octagon. This suggests continuity of construction where the exterior shape changes without the use of an external string course. At all levels the internal walls contain medieval brick putlog holes and occasional similar bricks randomly in the fabric. The south window embrasure is splayed with well-formed jambs in alternating medieval bricks and flint with a pointed head of brick, and there is nothing to suggest it has been altered or inserted. There are no signs of any blocked openings in the circular stage or of an upper doorway; nor is there any evidence of major restoration work to the walls following a fire said to have occurred in the nineteenth century. The belfry openings in the octagon are framed internally in the same manner as the south window in the circular stage, a further indication of coeval workmanship of the circular and octagonal stages.

The medieval bricks and putlog holes

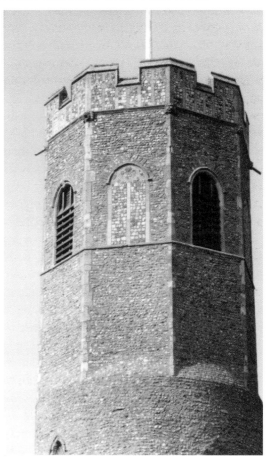

89. At Ilketshall St Andrew the junction between the contemporary circular and octagonal stages is made without a string course.

in the tower fabric inside and out, the pointed south window framed with brick externally and brick and flint internally, the pointed tower arches, all of which appear to be original unaltered features, and the lack of any earlier evidence in the tower strongly point to a post-Norman date for the circular stage. Since medieval bricks are also used internally, there is no reason to suppose that a re-facing might account for the presence of the bricks externally, or that all these features could be later insertions, alterations or repairs. Nor is it a likely possibility that the tower bricks are reused Roman material because there are none in the older nave fabric.

In the light of present knowledge of the date of the revival of brickmaking in East Anglia, it is unlikely that the tower can be earlier than late thirteenth century. The Decorated style of the flushwork feigned windows is probably of the second quarter of the fourteenth century, a date compatible with the bricks in the circular stage.

Complete replacement of an earlier belfry seems unlikely for the constructional continuity reasons mentioned and so all the evidence points to the whole tower being a single build. It was probably built in the second quarter of the fourteenth century but there may have been a short pause between the two octagonal stages, arising perhaps from the Black Death, which could account for the small difference in their fabric.

Rushall

The tower, with an internal diameter of 7'5", is circular for about two-thirds of its height and has an octagonal belfry stage. The four-foot-thick walls of the circular stage are faced with even-sized rubble flints and non-flint erratics laid uncoursed, and at roughly halfway up there is a set-back of a few inches in the external profile. Facing west in the lower part, there is a cinquefoiled lancet window and higher up, a circular feature that has been the reason for a belief that the tower might be Saxon.

The fabric of the octagonal belfry contains random medieval bricks but is otherwise similar to the circular stages; two-light belfry openings in the cardinal faces of the octagon have a simple fourteenth-century tracery pattern that is typical of the transition period between the Decorated and Perpendicular styles.

At first floor level in the tower east wall there is a blocked upper doorway, not now visible from the nave but showing in the tower. At this opening, it can be clearly seen that the tower is structurally separate from the nave west wall. There is a vertical straight joint between the nave wall and a 10" thickness of flintwork covering it that forms the tower's inner curved wall at this point. The opening through the original nave west wall, blocked at the nave face, has a pointed arch with plastered reveals splayed towards the nave that clearly witness that this opening was originally a window in the west wall of a formerly towerless church. Around the edges of this opening, at what would have been the outside face of the nave west wall, ragged flintwork suggests that stone dressings have been removed. This altered window is irrefutable evidence that the tower has been added to a pre-existing church, and as it was a pointed one, the tower must be post-Norman. This is corroborated by the depressed pointed tower arch. If the window was thirteenth-century, and assuming that there would have been a reasonable lapse of time between its date and the subsequent obscuring of it by the building of the tower, the tower is unlikely to be earlier than the fourteenth-century. The style of the tower's ground floor west window is not inconsistent with this date and it wouldn't be too fanciful to imagine that its jambstones could originally have come from the nave west window that was converted into the upper door.

At the base of the belfry octagon, the transition from circular to octagonal shape is made without a string course or other separating feature. Each of the octagon's angles starts with three dressed limestone quoins, but above them, the angles are formed with medieval bricks. Although externally the octagonal shape starts at the bottom of the dressed stone quoins, internally the circular shape is maintained up to the level of the top of them, i.e. about 2'3" higher, without any break or variation in the internal flintwork at the level of the external change of shape, indicating that the base of the octagon formed with dressed stones at the angles was part of the circular stage build. This, and the absence of any external or internal evidence of former belfry openings below the octagon suggest that the circular stage on its own had never been intended to stand as a finished church tower, but that an octagonal belfry on a circular lower stage had been a predetermined design feature of this tower from the outset. Above the level of the top of the stone quoins, the internal shape is octagonal.

However, the amount of brick in the belfry walls and its brick quoins, in contrast to the virtually brick-free fabric of the circular stage and the stone angles at the octagon base, suggest that the belfry is a different build from the circular stage. If so, this would mean either that the present brick-quoined belfry replaces an earlier octagonal one with stone quoins built with the circular stage (the lower quoins of which remain), or that building ceased when the level of the top of the the external stone quoins (the top of the circular stage internally) had been reached, to be continued under different circumstances after a gap of some years. The first alternative seems unlikely because of the apparent short time interval between a conjectured earlier stone-quoined belfry and the present one that that would be imply, and so a temporary suspension of construction seems more probable. It is suggested that the tower was being built during the 14th century and work was abruptly halted by the Black Death in 1348 and not resumed until later in the 14th century. A break in construction would account for the change from stone quoins to brick and the different belfry fabric which start at the level where the internal shape changes from circular to octagonal.

The circular feature in the west wall of the tower (XIX) is formed with concentric rings of medieval and later bricks – the outer ring is of medieval bricks with remnants of a ray-type medieval brick arch above it, and the inner ring is of thicker bricks which could be seventeenth- or eighteenth-century; the external wall flints adjacent to the outer ring of bricks are not laid radially as a window surround as in early circular windows like those at Gissing or Forncett St Peter. Directly behind this feature at first floor level within the tower, there is a pointed window embrasure with brick jambs and a medieval brick arch going through the full thickness of the wall (XX). It is almost certainly contemporary with the building of the wall in which it occurs and supports a fourteenth-century date for the circular stage. There is no evidence that it has been altered from an original Saxon circular window, nor is there any plausible constructional or aesthetic reason why it should have been. Neither has it been inserted later, because a brick arch of this kind could not have been formed through the full thickness of a four-foot thick wall without access from above, and there is no indication in the external or internal flintwork above the arch of reinstatement of a hole of such size as would have been necessary to enable a man to reach the centre of the wall to build the arch and to "pin up" from it to support the walling above.

It is suggested that this was an original pointed window that had external jambs of medieval bricks and a brick arch whose remnants are still visible, and that subsequently the bricks from the exterior jambs of the opening were removed and re-set at the outside face of the wall in the circular pattern we now see, *as the surround for a clock*. The later bricks of the inner circle may have been introduced as part of the modification of the window for the clock or used for reinstatement after its later removal. Close examination, inside and out, reveals that the circular feature is the result of alteration to, not from, a circular shape.

In the nave west wall, in the south-west corner of the church, is the blocked doorway to a former tower stair, and at first floor level in the south-east quadrant of the tower internally, the blocked opening at the top of the former stairway is visible; it has a roughly semi-circular head and has been just cut through the wall without an arch or dressings to the jambs. In the light of the tower's date established by the evidence described, it is tempting to think that the stair was built at the same time but this is improbable because if it had been, there would have been no need for an upper door and the old nave west window would have been totally lost, disappearing behind the tower wall's inner facing. Also, it is unlikely that the stair opening into the tower at first floor level would have been formed without a proper brick arch and jambs like those of the first-floor west window behind the circular feature; the contrast between that brick-dressed opening and the rough flint jambs and head of the blocked tower stairway highlights the difference between an opening clearly built with the wall and one cut through a wall later. So, the stair came later; was this when the building of the belfry was resumed or later still? There seems no way of being certain.

The position of the former stair entry in the south-west corner of the nave west wall, now blocked and used as a cupboard, is such that it cannot have given access directly into the tower wall, and so there must have been an external stair turret in the re-entrant angle between the tower and the nave west wall. The external flintwork of the walls of nave and tower in this area can be seen to be different, showing where they have been reinstated after removal of the stair turret.

A dating for the tower might therefore be:

Mid-14th century: First phase of tower built against existing church, up to and including the stone belfry quoins, with a stone-framed ground floor west window and a brick-framed first floor west window. Pointed west window in nave converted into an upper door and its facing stones possibly reused in the tower ground floor west window.

Late 14th century: Second phase of tower built, comprising octagonal belfry stage with medieval brick quoins.

? 15th century: External stair turret between the nave and tower built on south side, with a doorway in the south-west corner of nave and an opening through the tower wall emerging in the south-east quadrant of the tower at first floor level.

17th or 18th century: Pointed first floor west window altered externally for installation of a clock, subsequently removed.

? 19th century: Tower stair turret removed and affected nave and tower walls reinstated externally. Stairway entry into tower at first-floor level blocked.

Edingthorpe

The tower is circular for about two-thirds of its height, above which the belfry is octagonal and at the transition from circular to octagonal, simple cambers in the flintwork merge the two shapes without any form of stringcourse.

The fabric of the circular stage is a mixture of coursed cobbles and knapped flints. Some of the knapped flints appear in rough bands approximately 18" high; these occur at about 12 feet and 20 feet above the ground on the south side and there are suggestions of two more bands lower down on the north. There are some medieval brick putlog holes in the lower half and a few bricks in the fabric. The upper half of the circular stage contains more knapped flint – about 75% of the facing material – by comparison with about 25 to 30% in the lower half.

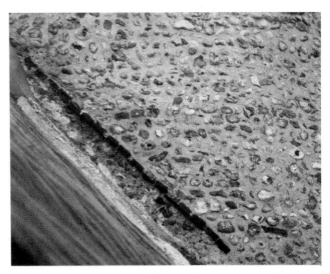

90. Weathercourse of medieval bricks in the east wall of Edingthorpe tower.

A small Perpendicular window facing west in the ground floor with a square head and a hoodmould can be seen internally to be a later insertion into a larger embrasure framed and arched in medieval brick.

The tower has an internal diameter of about eleven feet and a wall thickness of 4'6". A small pointed doorway between nave and tower is an insertion within a larger brick-framed tower arch opening that has a depressed pointed head of medieval brick and splays to a width of about five feet in the tower. The overall wall thickness at the apex is a little under four feet.

At about eight feet below the base of the octagon, a pointed south-facing slit window framed with medieval bricks lights the first floor; internally, it has splayed reveals, medieval brick in the jambs and a brick arch that goes through the full thickness of the wall. There is no evidence in the surrounding flintwork inside or outside of the window having been inserted, or of it having been reduced from a larger opening like the ground-floor window. Internally, in the west wall at the same level, there is a blocked recess of similar size and construction to the south window embrasure. There are no other window openings in the circular stage of the tower, or any evidence inside and out of the blocking of former ones.

The earliest dateable feature of the church is probably a pointed door in the nave north wall that Pevsner calls Transitional of circa. 1190. This wall is of ferricrete and cobbles, and evidence that the tower is later is provided by its materials – knapped flints and medieval bricks. The amount and quality of knapped flint in the fabric of the circular stage and the extent to which medieval brick has been used in the formation of the tower arch, in the circular stage windows and upper door and in a weathercourse in the east wall (90) are proof that its date is unlikely to be earlier than the fourteenth century, and consequently it must be an addition to an originally towerless church. None of these brick features show any evidence of insertion or of earlier construction that has subsequently been modified with inserted bricks; thus, being part of the original construction of the circular stage, the brick features establish the earliest date that it could have been built.

At first floor level, an upper door opening about seven feet high by 1'10" wide in the east wall has been blocked, leaving a recess about 2'4" deep. It has straight reveals with jambs of medieval brick and flint, and although the head has been repaired at the face, the original pointed arch, built in the same manner as the brick arches in the south and west window embrasures, can still be seen behind the repair and is clearly part of the tower build, whereas the brickwork of a separate, narrower arch seen at the back of the recess is, no doubt, the dressing to the opening cut through the nave gable when the tower was added to the church.

As can be seen on the tower outside, the change of shape from circular to octagonal starts about five feet below the belfry openings, but inside, the tower continues as circular up to about fifteen inches below this level, and there is no variation in the internal flintwork that might suggest a different building phase at the level where the change of shape occurs externally. This is compelling evidence for the conclusion that the circular stage and octagonal belfry are contemporary. Furthermore, the absence of any evidence inside or out of former belfry openings in the circular stage implies that the circular stage had never been intended to stand on its own as a finished church tower and that the octagon had been envisaged as a feature of the tower design from the outset. A suggestion that the south window is an original belfry window made smaller can be dismissed for four reasons: there is no evidence of its reduction; there were only two such windows; they were too low, and they were at the same level as the upper door and it is most unlikely that an upper door would have opened directly into a bell-chamber. All these considerations point decisively to a circular tower with a contemporary octagonal belfry.

The octagon is faced with knapped flints with a few cobbles amongst them and has medieval brick quoins. It has two-light belfry windows in the cardinal faces, all of which have suffered drastic repairs involving unsympathetic use of incompatible brick. The two facing north and east have pointed arches but a few jamb stones and the stone hoodmould are all that remain of the original eastern one; the north one still has its outer stonework and hoodmould and remnants of stone tracery, with brick repairs below. The two facing south and west have square-headed Perpendicular stone windows with panel tracery but their mullions have been replaced with brick. Internally, the octagonal belfry walls are mostly rebuilt modern work.

On the premise that the circular and octagonal stages were of one build, dating of the octagon can provide a date for the whole tower. The remnant of stone tracery in the apex of the pointed north belfry opening is probably original and can be identified as a straight-sided reticulation unit, attributable as Late Decorated or Early Perpendicular. It suggests a date in the second half of the fourteenth century, making this one of the later medieval round towers.

The square-headed belfry openings facing south and west seem to have been altered in the fifteenth or sixteenth century. The style of the small ground-floor west window suggests it may have been inserted at the same time, and judging from the size of the original embrasure internally, it would probably have replaced a stone lancet of similar size to those at Rushall and Thorpe Abbotts.

CHAPTER 20

ADDED OCTAGONAL BELFRIES ON ROUND TOWERS

ecause of uncertainty as to whether the octagonal belfries of a few towers are contemporary with their circular stages or later additions, it is not feasible to establish a precise number of towers with added octagonal belfries, but there are probably about thirty. The octagonal stages at Clippesby, Roydon and probably Brome are Victorian, but of the medieval ones, except for a few with lancet openings such as Raveningham, or with Y or cusped Y-tracery – Great Ryburgh, South Pickenham and Great Shefford (XXII) for example – the majority have later styles of window tracery or flushwork implying fifteenth-century or later dates. By comparison, most of the octagonal belfries that are contemporary with the circular stage are no later than the fourteenth century. This seems to show that the architectural trend of an octagonal belfry on a circular lower stage first found expression in towers built to that design from the outset, to be followed in due course by the addition of octagons to existing towers, surmounting or replacing existing belfries. When this was done, an intervening string course at the junction between the new and the old would probably have been regarded as essential both aesthetically and constructionally and this practice became the norm in those circumstances.

Later octagonal belfries built on top of existing ones are easily recognised where the former belfry openings are unambiguously identifiable below, and in those cases the height of the circular stage above the nave roof is sufficient to accommodate east-facing openings. At Beachamwell and Bexwell there is no mistaking the earlier belfry openings in the circular stage beneath the octagons – of Saxon-style at the former and Norman at the latter. At Needham and Surlingham, pointed openings at the four cardinal orientations near the top of the circular stage – those at Surlingham blocked – clearly proclaim themselves as former belfry openings thereby attesting post-Norman dates for the towers; likewise there is no doubt about the original function of the eight lancets in the octagon below the later knapped flint belfry at Topcroft. Less obvious though, because of skilful external blocking, are the four former belfry openings just below the two-stage octagon at Woodton that have round-headed flint arches internally, and the pointed ones below the octagons at Fritton St Catherine and Rickinghall Inferior. As described in Chapter 12, the blocked belfries at the latter two towers were themselves apparently replacements of Norman ones.

There are, it hardly needs to be said, no Norman or earlier octagonal belfries, but in order that it can be established with certainty that an octagonal belfry is a later addition to a tower and not part of its original construction, it is necessary that the circular stage below has clear evidence that it is earlier than the octagon. In addition to those with earlier belfry openings that obviously meet this requirement, the most convincing indication that the circular stage is earlier than the octagon is a round-headed tower arch between nave and tower, and this is a feature of many, for example Bedingham or Quidenham. Post-Norman circular stages such as Needham, Surlingham, Topcroft or Old Catton, of course, have pointed tower arches, and at Woodton the tower arch has apparently been altered to a pointed shape since remnants of stone imposts of an earlier arch are visible. Pointed tower arches with more elaborate profiles like those at South Pickenham, Roydon, Mutford or St Etheldreda, Norwich for example may be later alterations to the arches of earlier circular stages.

Other features of circular stages that are clearly earlier than the octagons include a round-headed tower west window at Taverham, round-headed stone windows at South Pickenham, Stanford and Gisleham, and Norman stone quoins at the west end of naves that are likely to be contemporary with their towers as at Breckles, Fritton St Catherine or Quidenham.

Brampton

The octagonal belfry at Brampton (91) is unique in two respects. Firstly, whereas several octagonal belfries have brick window dressings or quoins, this is the only one in which the belfry walls themselves are built of brick; and secondly, the dressed stone quoins at the angles, unlike those of all other medieval octagonal belfries on round towers, are of equal height and regular size. The rhythmic alternation of these uniform quoins and the arresting visual contrast they make with the red brick walls demonstrate an almost classical architectural effect of a kind not seen in any round tower octagons of the fourteenth and fifteenth centuries. This suggests that the belfry is unlikely to be earlier than the sixteenth

91. Stone weathercourse in the east wall of Brampton tower. The lower length was probably built with the tower wall, the upper length being inserted when the higher ridge of the widened nave roof no longer met the tower centrally.

century, and it could be as late as the early seventeenth. Parallels in Norfolk for quoining of this kind are found at Blickling and Felbrigg Halls but these are both of circa 1620. Earlier precedents can be seen further afield: in Cambridge the early sixteenth-century Gatehouse of Jesus College must be one of the earliest examples, and from a little later the gatehouse turrets of St John's and Trinity Colleges bear a striking resemblance to the Brampton belfry although their ashlar quoin stones are not precisely equal. The two-light belfry window pattern at Brampton – simple Y-tracery under a four-centred arch – is typical sixteenth-century late Gothic.

The brick construction and style of the belfry clearly differentiates it as a later addition to the flint circular stage. Below the belfry, three lancet windows at first-floor level are too low and too small to have been former belfry openings, and as there is no evidence of others, the present octagonal belfry is probably a replacement of an earlier one because the circular stage as now seen is unlikely to have stood without a belfry. Medieval bricks below the cills and brickwork in the internal jambs of the three stone lancet tower windows suggest that they may have been inserted into earlier openings. A stone weathercourse built into the tower east wall is an indication that the circular stage is likely to be of post-Conquest date and, if the lancets were later insertions, probably Norman.

This is one of those round towers that poses the question as to why the tower arch is not central within the tower. The pointed arch, 5'8" wide, is offset to the south to the extent that its south reveal is virtually tangential to the inner circumference of the tower. The horseshoe plan shape seen beneath the first floor and the flat east wall at that level, show that the tower was probably added to a towerless nave. The flat part of the east wall is central relative to the tower and about four feet wide, its northern margin aligning with the north reveal of the tower arch opening. It seems that an original central tower arch, four feet wide, was widened southwards by about 1'8", the north jamb remaining in its original position. To understand why this was done, it is necessary to try to elucidate the history of the church's considerable alterations.

Reused Roman materials in the quoins at the north-west corner suggest an eleventh-century date for the nave, but despite the common alignment of the north walls of the nave and the chancel, they are probably not contemporary because there is a marked difference in the exterior flintwork of the two walls and the thickness of the chancel wall is about six inches less than the nave wall. A buttress now conceals the constructional detail where they meet.

The east-west axis of the tower lies about 6'9" from the inner face of the nave north wall, and assuming that the tower was built centrally to the nave, the original nave width would have been about 13'6". The chancel, though, measured at the chancel arch is nearly two feet wider than that, and so not in line with the tower. This, its different fabric and its thinner walls seem to show that the present chancel is not the original one; it must have been completely rebuilt, and its windows suggest that that would have been in the fourteenth century.

It appears that the rebuilding of the chancel was part of a major reconstruction scheme in which three new contemporary interdependent elements were built – the wider chancel, a southward widening of the nave, and a south-east chapel, now demolished, in the re-entrant angle between the enlarged nave and the wider chancel. Arches in the chancel south wall and in the nave east wall, both now blocked, that linked these three spaces are evidence that they were likely to have been built at the same time. Judging from the built-in stone weathercourse in the nave east gable, the south-east chapel was in effect an eastward continuation of the nave extension – not a transept. It is probable that it was also at this stage that the tower arch was widened southwards in order to bring it into better alignment with the wider chancel.

Prior to this reconstruction, there had probably been no chancel arch in the original narrow church, and so a major part of the reconstruction was the building of a nave east wall containing the chancel arch and the arch to the south-east chapel. The chancel arch was positioned appreciably off-centre southwards in the chancel, no doubt to relate better to the widened nave. This wall was carried up as the east gable of a new roof spanning the full width of the wider nave, with a corresponding half-gable wall at the west end.

The new, wider chancel and the south-east chapel would have had separate gable roofs; the outer slopes of these roofs would probably have been continuous with the slopes of the new nave roof, with the inner slopes abutting the new nave east gable. Dressed stone weathercourses for the inner slopes, still visible, were incorporated in the gable, proving that it must have been contemporary with the widened chancel and the chapel. The positions of the two weathercourses show that there must have been a lead gutter between the chancel and chapel roofs on the line of the new chancel's south wall. The weathercourse defining the chapel roofline has since been chopped back flush with the wall flintwork, presumably when the chapel was demolished.

As the southward enlargement of the nave and the building of the chapel necessitated contemporary construction of the larger roof, an arcade would not have been formed in the original south wall which would have been demolished when the nave was widened.

The width of the widened nave is such that its centre-line, and consequently the roof apex falls about two feet to the south of the tower, allowing sufficient space clear of the tower wall to form a thatch ridge. If it had been less, that could not have been achieved satisfactorily.

When the original nave roof was replaced by the higher one spanning the full width of the widened church, it appears that the north limb of the weathercourse that had been incorporated in the tower's east wall during its construction was extended upwards in the tower wall (91). Compared with the evenness of the original lower length, the poorer standard of setting and alignment of this later upper length reflects the difficulties of inserting sloping stonework into an existing curved rubble flint wall. It is possible that under the rendering on the tower east wall below the weathercourse, remnants of its original south limb may still be in place.

On the basis of the evidence described, a dating for the church might be:

Eleventh century: Original towerless church built, with nave and chancel probably same width.

Twelfth century: Round tower added with a central tower arch axial to the church.

Thirteenth century: First-floor stone lancet windows inserted into earlier openings in tower.

Fourteenth century: Chancel rebuilt wider, with arch to south-east chapel; Nave south wall demolished; New south and west walls for nave widened southwards; Nave east gable wall built with chancel arch and arch to south-east chapel; South-east chapel built; Larger nave roof and gable roofs to chancel and chapel; Nave north windows inserted; Existing stone weathercourse in tower east wall extended upwards to suit taller nave roof; Tower arch widened; Porch built.

Sixteenth century: Original belfry replaced by octagonal brick belfry.

Probably pre-nineteenth century: Chapel demolished and arches to nave and chancel blocked.

Nineteenth century: South vestry built.

Heckingham

The octagonal stage of the tower, which has brick quoins and stone-framed lancet belfry openings, is about twice the height of the circular stage. Its flintwork looks different from the circular stage although this may be due to its flushed pointing. At first sight it certainly appears that the octagon could be a later build on a low circular stage, but there are grounds for belief that not only the octagon, but all except the lowest four or five feet of the circular stage have been added to an earlier base, and that the upper part of the circular stage and the octagon are contemporary.

The main evidence for this is that at about four feet above the ground, there are several pieces of limestone in the fabric of the circular stage, including at least four short lengths of Norman billet moulding that have been used to form putlog holes (92). The pieces of limestone appear to have been squared dressings and some have mortices in them.

It is suggested that these stones are probably remnants robbed from the outer order of the Norman north doorway when it was removed from the original 2' 10" thick north wall of the church for resetting in the 2' 4" thick north aisle wall. If this is so, it dates that part of the circular stage in which they occur as contemporary with the formation of the north aisle, which on the evidence of its Y-traceried east and west windows, is probably early fourteenth-century. This accords with the lancet belfry openings in the octagon and the early brickwork at the angles. (The brick quoins in the lower half of the octagon, however, seem to be later renewals, probably of the same date as the brick facings of the west window in this stage, and may represent the work to which bequests of 1486 and 1507 refer).

The close-packed, largely uncoursed flintwork above the level of the billet-mould putlog holes is typical of the thirteenth and fourteenth centuries, and it seems that the tower was rebuilt from that level, or at least its outside face was. It is unlikely that the octagon represents another building phase later than the upper part of the circular stage because of the proximity of dates implied by the belfry openings and the reused Norman stones derived from the aisle construction phase.

Evidence for the existence of an earlier tower comes from the tower arch (37). It is a simple Norman round-headed arch 3'10" wide x 11'5" high to the crown, with limestone dressings at nave and tower wall faces that can be seen by the shuttering impressions on the arch soffit to be part of

92. Norman billet moulding reused as framing and bridging to a putlog hole in the wall of the circular stage of Heckingham tower.

the arch's original construction; the board-marks are contiguous with the back edges of the stone voussoirs. The arch is set back an inch or two from the reveals and springs from chamfered stone imposts with short returns on the tower wall but not on the nave face.

The style of the tower arch implies that the original tower of which perhaps only four or five feet remain externally, would have been Norman and this would be consistent with a similar attribution for the church, built with the original tower.

Limestone amongst the rubble flint of the nave west wall tends to confirm a post-Conquest date for this wall, and more limestone in the fillets between tower and nave than might reasonably be attributable to repairs, suggests that the fillets are at the earliest, Norman in their lower parts.

Mutford

Mutford church has one of the tallest of all round towers and it is circular for about three-quarters of its total height, with fillets between the tower and nave west wall on both sides of the tower. A later octagonal belfry, which joins the circular stage without a string course, has stone corners and although the belfry windows in the cardinal faces, originally two-light, have lost their mullions and tracery, flushwork replicas in the diagonals have a fourteenth-century pattern with cinquefoil ogee lights and a reticulation unit in the apex. The belfry is crowned with a fine flushwork parapet.

Below the octagon, the tower's circular stage has windows at three levels. In the ground stage, there seem originally to have been three narrow flint-framed loops. Two, facing north and south, have been blocked and no evidence of them is visible internally because the ground-stage walls are plastered. The western one has been replaced by a taller, wider stone-framed lancet.

At first-floor level, there were three more windows facing south, west and north. Those facing north and south now show externally as blocked flint-framed loops, apparently similar to the ones below, but the one facing west has had a modern narrow wooden lancet inserted; internally, its deeply-recessed embrasure (93) has a round arch with flint voussoirs and rubble flint reveals that run straight for about two feet and then splay inwards towards the aperture.

The arch shows shuttering board-marks in the mortar on its unsplayed soffit, and this mortar appears to be continuous with that on the splayed parts of the reveals. The overall size of the opening measured at the internal wall face is four feet wide by about eight feet high. Although blocked flush with the wall, the north and south-facing windows still show round flint arches of about four feet span.

These first-floor windows present a particular problem: their design internally is so unusual that it is difficult to be certain to what extent, if any, they have been altered. Their size and straight jambs suggest that they could have been belfry windows, but on the other hand, as they are below the nave ridge and as the upper door gives access to the chamber in which they are situated, that seems unlikely. Slight indications in the external flintwork that the openings might have been reduced are inconclusive.

The external fabric of the tower is well-coursed flintwork up to a level of about $2^1/2$ feet

93. Interior of first-floor west window in the tower at Mutford.

above the heads of the first-floor windows, i.e. roughly the level of the nave roof ridge, and on the north side of the tower the flintwork in the west and north walls of the nave is similar. Caen stone quoins of typical Norman proportions at the north-west corner show no evidence of later insertion – in fact mortar in the weathered joints between the stones can be seen to be continuous with that in the adjacent wall flintwork – and suggest a Norman date for the nave and hence the tower also.

However, fillets between tower and nave, flint-framed windows in the tower, and an upper door with a triangular-head are features that have been identified as being characteristic of Saxon workmanship and so could suggest a pre-Conquest date for the tower. All such features though, have also been found in post-Conquest buildings (see Chapter 5) and are not therefore proof of Saxon date. In any event, if the first-floor flint windows were originally larger round-headed openings subsequently reduced, their exterior flint frames must have been post-Conquest.

Above the nave roof ridge level, the flints look smaller, their coursing discipline is less marked and occasional medieval bricks are to be seen in the fabric. These are quite distinct from the obvious brick repairs at the top. A corresponding change can be detected at the same level internally and supports the probability that the tower's upper circular part is later. It is suggested that the tower, built in the twelfth century, originally had a contemporary belfry but during the fourteenth century that belfry was replaced by the present upper circular stage with its small stone lancet facing south-west, and the present octagonal belfry. The absence of a string course between the upper circular part and the octagon suggests that they were of the same build.

The nave north wall is about three feet thick and has two two-light Perpendicular windows; internally, below the eastern one, a Norman arch with chevron decoration spans a recess – probably a wall tomb. The arch voussoirs were no doubt salvaged from elsewhere in the church and reset in this position, and measurement shows that the span of the arch from which they came would have been about 7'9".

The pointed tower arch is tall, about eleven feet to springing level, and spans 10'6". Facing the nave the jambs of the opening have 45-degree splays 2'2" wide, but as the opening is the same width as the tower's north-south diameter, the reveals of the opening within the tower are continuous with the tower walls, being tangential to the inside curvature. Above the tower arch and at first-floor level the internal tower plan shape is circular.

Since the tower east wall internally is curved and the wall thickness above the tower arch is not greater than the nave west wall by at least the thickness of a layer of flints (it is in fact slightly less than the nave west wall), the tower and the nave wall must have been built together at the same date, as corroborated by the similarity of the flintwork of the nave north and west walls to the lower walls of the tower.

If the tower is Norman, the tower arch has obviously been altered; its four-times-chamfered pointed arch suggests a fourteenth-century date, contemporary perhaps with the upper circular stage. It would have replaced an original Norman arch, and that arch could have been the source for the Norman voussoirs of the arch over the wall tomb in the nave north wall. Its span (7'9") is not incompatible with the width of a Norman tower arch, as for example the one at Wissett.

Because of the apparent conflict between the nave's Norman evidence and tower features referred to that could suggest a pre-Conquest date, it is difficult to be certain about the tower's age; the relative strength of the conflicting evidence therefore has to be weighed. On balance, since the nave stone quoins seem to be an original part of the structure with no indications that they might be later insertions, and in view of the possiblity that the arch-voussoirs of the wall-tomb could be from a Norman tower arch, a Norman date for the tower seems most likely.

Mutford round tower is the only one to which a galilee porch has been added. Its walls of uncoursed flint are quite different from the lower tower walls and are simply butted up against the tower west wall without any bonding. Despite its round shape, the Gothic details of the entrance arch, the trefoiled windows in the side walls and the pointed west doorway into the tower all suggest a fourteenth-century date. The church apparently underwent a major reconstruction at that time because the chancel, south aisle and the tower alterations all seem to be from that same period.

St Etheldreda, Norwich

This is another round tower in which not only the octagonal stage but the upper part of the circular stage is also an addition to the original tower. Only about 14 feet (measured at the tower-to-nave junction on the north side) of the original tower structure remains; above this level, up to the corbelled base of the octagon, the tower walling contains much knapped flint and vertical brick bands at about six-foot intervals. These bricks seem to be post-medieval, like those in the corbelled base of the octagon and in its quoins.

There is little positive evidence in the lower part of the circular stage itself on which to judge its date except that the similarity of the flintwork in the wall and fillets to that in the nave west wall suggests that the original church and tower could be the same age; if so, positive Norman evidence in the church walls, described below, would also establish the tower as Norman, and the pointed tower arch with stone dressings between nave and tower would seem to be a later insertion. Alternatively, the lower part of the tower might be post-Norman, contemporary with the tower arch.

In the context of the debate on the origins of round towered churches – whether they are pre- or post-Conquest – St Etheldreda is archeologically one of the most important because it is the only one in which the nave walls themselves, rather than doorways or windows in them, can be positively dated as post-Conquest, thus establishing that other characteristics of the church could not be earlier.

The main evidence for this is a Norman moulded string course of Caen stone, and an early shallow buttress in the south wall which probably defined the western end of the original chancel. Supporting evidence is provided by the western nave quoins of Caen stone and the Norman south doorway.

Remnants of the string course moulding which is interrupted by later windows, run the full length of the nave on both sides of the church with, on the south, a short length at a lower

94. Part of the chevron-moulded Norman string course of Caen stone in the nave wall of St Etheldreda's church, Norwich. The curved section is in the north wall, above a later doorway.

level east of the early buttress. The moulding is about 4" high and projects about 3" from the wall face and is decorated with the typical Norman zig-zag motif. At the west end on the north side, it rises to form a small semi-circle as if it might have been a window hoodmould (94); below it, there is a wider door with a four-centred arch.

The case for a Norman attribution for the nave walls and hence probably also the tower and fillets, rests principally on the premise that the moulded string course of Caen stone, a material unavailable before the Conquest and probably not obtainable before the Cathedral was begun in 1096, was incorporated in the walls as they were being built and that the dressed stone quoins of the early buttress are also part of the original wall fabric.

Whereas doorways, windows or quoins have sometimes been inserted into earlier walls without showing any tell-tale evidence, it is not credible on grounds of reasonable constructional practicability that a stone string course could be a later insertion into an existing wall of uncoursed flint rubble, and there is no evidence here to suggest that it has been. Insertion of this stonework would have entailed cutting a deep chase into irregular flintwork for the full length of the nave wall both sides and apparently the chancel also, and then bedding and wedging the stones into the chase to an even level and line, in slow-setting mortar; it is highly unlikely that such an extensive, troublesome and almost impracticable venture would have been undertaken for such a minor, unfunctional decoration. The even setting and jointing of the string course stones and the precision with which those in the small arch on the north side have been laid could probably only have been achieved if the stonework had been set as the wall was being built.

At the south-west and north-west corners of the nave, the string course bonds neatly into Caen stone quoins of typical Norman size and proportions, showing that quoins, string course and wall were almost certainly built concurrently.

The early buttress on the south wall is built of flint with dressed stone corners; it is about 2' 8" wide with a projection of about six inches. This type of buttress (it is not a pilaster), is a characteristic Norman element and there is no reason or evidence to support speculation that its stone corners are later embellishments of a Saxon flint pilaster rather than original parts of the buttress. It has an exact parallel in the similar feature on the Lazar chapel in Norwich, founded in the time of Bishop de Losinga, (1090-1119).

The nave west quoins and Norman south door, the stone-quoined shallow buttress, and above all, the moulded Norman string course provide compelling visible evidence that the nave walls are post-Conquest. There are no Saxon features, but a pre-Conquest dating has been proposed, depending entirely on unsubstantiated criteria of wall thickness and nave width and that all the Norman stone features are later insertions. This church's archaeological importance lies in the fact that, contrary to the theory that Norman walls were never less than three feet thick and Norman naves never less than 20 feet wide, it proves beyond any reasonable doubt that flint church walls as thin as 2'4" and naves narrower than 20 feet were built by the Normans.

CHAPTER 21

ROUND TOWERS WITH SOUTH DOORS

The three churches of Sustead, Gresham and Aylmerton are close neighbours within two miles of each other as the crow flies, and all have round towers. One cannot fail to be struck by the similarity of these three towers to each other. All are circular to the top and are about the same height with an internal diameter of less than eight feet and comparable wall thicknesses; all have belfry openings with Y-tracery and have no evidence outside or inside of former belfry openings below the present ones, or of an upper door. More significantly though, although several round towers have external doorways or evidence of blocked ones in their west walls, each of these three towers has or had in their south wall a doorway with a pointed arch.

Although the three towers have Y-tracery belfry openings, there may be doubts as to whether this was the original pattern. At Sustead, much of the external stonework of the openings has been renewed and even the older stone in the north and east openings could be later than the date suggested by the tracery style. A drawing of 1823 by Ladbrooke appears to show a quatrefoil above the mullion, which could suggest either a c.14 style or earlier plate tracery, or it may be an error. Internally, in the sections of wall between the belfry openings, medieval bricks incorporated in the structure indicate a post-Norman date, while the rough rendered jambs of the openings and their pointed heads without voussoired arches give the impression of having been altered, perhaps from lancets.

At Gresham, since the whole of the tower's top half has been rebuilt from about the level of the modern round-headed west window, the question arises as to whether the present belfry openings, with cusped Y-tracery in the south window and plain Y in the others, faithfully represent those that they have replaced. Ladbrooke's drawing of 1824 shows them as two-light with rather indeterminate tracery, possibly of a fourteenth-century pattern. The lower part of the tower, however, is original, and comparison of its fabric with the nave west wall clearly shows the tower to be an addition to an earlier church: it has relatively small rough-coursed rubble flintwork with occasional lumps of ferricrete whereas the nave west wall contains a lot of ferricrete and larger flints (VII).

At Aylmerton, a difference is noticeable in the external flintwork of the tower upwards from the belfry cill level, a consequence, no doubt, of the considerable reconstruction of the belfry carried out in about 1912, further evidence of which is seen internally in the renewed flintwork and modern brick arches of the four openings. Although, like at Sustead, much of the stone dressings and tracery have been renewed, enough of the original stonework has been reset to establish Y-tracery as the original pattern. This is corroborated by Ladbrooke's drawing and a statement in the church guide that the 1912 belfry reconstruction followed the old design, re-using the old stone and flints.

It is suggested that all three towers were built at about the same time, as additions to previously towerless churches, perhaps late in the thirteenth century or in the first quarter of the fourteenth. The tower doorways and the ground-floor lancet window at Aylmerton would be consistent with those dates. Since none of the three towers has any evidence inside or out of former belfry openings below the present belfries, the belfry stages, even if modified later, were seemingly part of the original construction and not later increases of height.

The south door into the tower at Sustead has simple once-chamfered dressed stone jambs and arch externally; internally it has a rough, plastered pointed arch about a foot higher than the outside stonework, a straight west reveal with a stone interior jamb, and a splayed east reveal containing a wall recess. Since the ground stage of the tower has no windows, this recess may have been for standing a lamp.

Internally at ground floor level in the south wall of Gresham tower, there is a blocked and plastered recess with a pointed arch, about three feet wide by eight feet high, and confirmation that this was a doorway is provided by the external flintwork at this position which, on careful examination can be seen to be different from the surrounding fabric.

The position of the tower door at Aylmerton (95), being off-centre in the tower south wall and tucked in close to the nave west wall, pointedly suggests that this was a door of minor importance, and unlikely ever to have been the main entrance to the church. Externally, its jambs are formed with flints, and it has an arched head comprising two large stones with curved soffits, propped against each other, springing from stone imposts, features which have been the cause for a belief that the opening, and thus the tower, is pre-Conquest. There are however reasons for regarding these as

95. The south door into the tower at Aylmerton has flint jambs and Barnack stone imposts and arch.

dubious grounds for a Saxon attribution and there is also convincing evidence for a later date. The Saxon attribution rests principally on two pretexts: firstly, that the stone arch is not built with voussoirs, but 'in the Saxon fashion' with two long stones claimed to be a large erratic split in two forming a triangular head, and secondly, that flint jambs would never be built when dressed stone was available. On the first of these points, the two long stones are, in fact, not erratics but Barnack stone, the same stone as was used for the tower's ground-floor lancet window, and their under-edges are dressed to a curve following the arch soffit behind them. This shows that the head of the arch was not formed as a triangular shape with the stones being shaped later as has been proposed, but that the opening was built to a curved pointed profile with compatible arch stonework. The method of forming small arches with two propped stones, though rare, is not alien to

Gothic practice and several other examples have been noticed, for example the tower south door at Stiffkey, the priest's door at Syderstone and the belfry windows at Hardley. On the second point, the dressed Barnack stone used for this arch and its imposts shows that flint jambs were indeed built when dressed stone was available.

In addition to the arch shape and the use of Barnack stone in its construction, further evidence which corroborates a post-Norman attribution for this doorway is the design of the internal rere-arch. It has rebated reveals and its depressed pointed head, though 'triangular' rather than curved, is about eighteen inches or so above the apex of the external arch – a form of construction typical of doorways from Early English times onwards, but not of pre-Conquest ones which usually had round-headed rere-arches and straight reveals. Since there is no reason to suppose that the exterior pointed arch or the internal rere-arch have been altered, the evidence for a Gothic attribution for this doorway seems to outweigh the grounds for supposing it to be Saxon, having in mind that external angles formed with flints can be shown not to be exclusive to pre-Conquest work.

Sustead has no tower arch between nave and tower, nor is there any evidence in the tower's east wall internally of a former blocked one. There seems no reason why an existing tower arch would have been blocked, but had there been one here, it is to be expected that any blocking of it would show in the tower as a recess within the profile of that arch because it is unlikely that the blocking would have been made the full thickness of the wall between tower and nave or that it would have reinstated the tower's internal curvature without trace. But here, the tower's east wall maintains its internal circular shape without interruption. It seems then, that there never was a tower arch and that the tower must have been added to an existing church purely as a bell tower, without other liturgical or functional purpose; a squint in the tower giving a view of the altar tends to confirm this. An external doorway would have been the simplest and cheapest means of access to such a tower, without the disturbance to the church that a tower arch to the nave would have necessitated.

It is understandable that, in the absence of a tower arch, an external door to the Sustead tower was necessary, but why was there need for one at Gresham and Aylmerton both of which have a tower arch? The answer is probably that when those two towers were originally added to an existing church they were built without the formation of a tower arch, in the same way as was apparently done at Sustead. It is difficult to envisage why a side door into a tower would have been required if there had already been an opening in the nave west wall when the tower was built, or if one had been formed then, and so it was probably not until much later that the tower arches at Gresham and Aylmerton were cut through and the evidence at both is consistent with this idea.

The tower arch at Gresham, almost the full width of the tower, is about seven feet wide and about 13 feet high; it is embellished on the nave side with an archway of two orders, having a four-centered head springing from demi-octagonal capitals on shafts with moulded bases. Its Perpendicular style shows that it was probably not formed until one-and-a-half or two centuries after the tower with its south door were built (as dated by the Y-tracery of the belfry openings). That, no doubt, would have been when the south door was blocked.

At Aylmerton, the opening between tower and nave is a simple pointed arch, 4'7" wide x 10'5" high to the apex, with a plaster finish and without imposts or mouldings.

Stripping of the plaster from the nave wall face around the arch to alleviate salt problems has revealed that no stone dressings were used in its construction and the absence of any kind of arch voussoirs, whether flint, brick or stone in the head indicates that this arch was broken out through an existing nave west wall and not constructed with it. It may have been cut through when the nave was widened in perhaps the late fourteenth century. The church guide records that the tower south door was re-opened in 1912 after having been blocked for centuries; as at Gresham, it would presumably have been blocked after becoming redundant when access to the tower was provided by formation of the tower arch.

It is clear from the lack of access between tower and nave at Sustead and the probability that the tower arches at Gresham and Aylmerton were not original features of the nave west wall, that the south doors of these three towers were never entrances to the churches. This is borne out by their awkward position relative to the conventional tower arch position, which would have been very inconvenient for ceremonial. They must therefore simply have been to give access to the tower, and this would account for their modesty and thus for the unpretentious flint jambs at Aylmerton.

High up in the west gable of the nave internally at Aylmerton, a shallow recess which has the appearance of the upper part only of a blocked former opening has been the cause of speculation as to its purpose. It is about three feet wide and has a somewhat distorted pointed shape at its head[1]; the whole feature is plastered in with the wall and has rounded edges. Below its apex, the wall is recessed about five inches or so, but downwards from there, the depth of the recess gradually diminishes until its outline disappears about three feet lower, fading flush into the wall plaster at the bottom.

This feature seems too high in the wall to have been an upper door to a tower chamber and there is no evidence of it in the tower. Alternatively, it might have been a high-level window in the nave of an originally towerless church. If so, and if the distorted pointed shape at the top can be relied on as the original shape of the window head, that would indicate a post-Norman date for the supposed window and would therefore obviously date the tower as post-Norman in confirmation of the tower's own evidence. As the window would obviously have been below the roof, it would also establish that the original nave roof ridge level must have been at aproximately its present level, though presumably it would have had a steeper pitch.

A suggestion in the church guide that the feature might have been an earlier belfry window above a lower nave roof is unconvincing for several reasons: firstly, since the apex of the feature is at about the same level as the ridge of the chancel roof (probably rebuilt in the third quarter of the fourteenth century), the nave ridge, assuming that a belfry window might have been about five feet high, would have needed to have been at least that amount lower than the chancel ridge, and that seems unlikely because an original nave roof of the same pitch as the chancel roof but five feet lower would have resulted in improbably low nave walls; secondly, the deduced height of a tower suggested by belfry openings at this level would have been very low for a tower of the thirteenth-century date implied by the apparent lancet form of this conjectured belfry opening, and thirdly, there is no sign of a window within the tower at this level or of any evidence of corresponding blocked openings at south, west or north. Although the church guide says that reconstruction of the upper part of the tower in 1912 obliterated all traces of other windows, it seems from examination of the tower's flintwork externally and internally that the reconstruction was only upwards from about the present belfry cill level; hence, the tower fabric below this level would have been unaffected and if it had contained any earlier belfry windows below the present belfry level, it is to be expected that there would still be some evidence of them, but there is none.

There is, however, another possible explanation for this feature in the nave west wall. It may not be a blocked opening at all. Assuming that the tower stood at its present height or thereabouts when the nave was widened in the late fourteenth century (which the evidence suggests it did, see next para.), if the widened sections of the west wall each side of the tower had been built plumb and the upper part of the tower walls had a slight batter, it would mean that at the positions where the plumb end walls met the curve of the battered tower wall on each side, shallow, tapering, vertical returns starting at nothing and gradually increasing in depth, would develop as the new walls' height was built upwards. At the level at which these returns attained the depth of a layer of flints, dependant on the degree of batter of the tower wall, the plumb nave-face flintwork of the walls from each side could be arched over to meet in the same plane, completely covering the tower wall from there upwards. When plastered with rounded edges to the returns and arch, this would show in the nave as a gradually deepening recess starting from nothing at the bottom, with a simple arch at the level where the recess attained a depth equivalent to a layer of flints. This is the impression given by the nave west wall feature, and in the absence of any evidence of a blocked opening in the tower behind it, or of any evidence of the 1912 belfry restoration extending down to its level, perhaps the most probable explanation.

The church guide states that the belfry had to be raised to clear the new nave roof when the nave was rebuilt wider and higher (after the chancel had been rebuilt in the second half of the fourteenth century), but as mentioned above, the existing belfry openings, although much restored, contain some apparently original Y-tracery stonework datable to about a century earlier. This suggests that when the nave was enlarged, the tower already stood at its present height or thereabouts; furthermore, if the belfry had been built when the nave was enlarged, it would be expected to have had late Decorated or Perpendicular belfry openings, not Y-tracery. The reported heightening of the nave when it was widened may therefore have been accomplished simply by means of taller side walls, made possible by a new roof of lower pitch but with a ridge level not significantly different from its original, and present, level.

Thwaite

Barely two-and-a-half miles south of Sustead stands All Saints church, Thwaite. Like its three near neighbours described above, its round tower is circular to the top, has Y-tracery belfry openings and has no evidence of an upper door or former belfry openings below the present ones. It too has a blocked south door, but whereas at Sustead there is no tower arch, and arguably that was originally also the case at Gresham and Aylmerton, at Thwaite a round-headed arch between nave and tower apparently pre-dates the tower.

The ferricrete quoins at the west corners of the nave and the amount of ferricrete in the nave west wall could imply an eleventh-century date for the nave and that would be compatible with the unembellished tower arch without imposts. By contrast, there is no ferricrete visible in the tower walls either externally or internally, though considerable areas of the external fabric may have been refaced; they comprise irregularly sized and coursed flint cobbles – quite different from the nave west wall. Internally, although some areas above first-floor level have been renewed, much of the first-floor walls and those in the belfry appear to be original medieval cobble flintwork.

Inside the tower at ground-floor level in the south wall a blocked doorway with straight reveals is 3'2" wide x 7'3" high to the apex of its arch which is of roughly Tudor-style shape and formed with medieval bricks; externally, the opening is blocked with cobble flints and has a round arch of elongated cobble voussoirs above a concentric sub-arch of medieval brick headers. Facing west at first-floor level, a single lancet window has stone dressings externally, and internally its splayed reveals with flint dressings show no evidence of later insertion, and its arched head of Tudor shape is formed with medieval bricks.

Although the Y-traceried belfry openings and, indeed, the whole of the belfry stage externally, give the impression of having been restored, Ladbrooke's drawing of 1822 shows Y-traceried belfry openings and a shallow parapet like the present one. Internally the belfry walls are well-preserved in apparently their original medieval state, including flint jambs to the belfry openings with pointed arches of medieval brick in good condition.

The tower arch is 4'9" wide x 12'9" tall to the crown, and above it the tower east wall is curved; the wall at the arch apex is about a foot thicker than the nave west wall outside the tower, established by comparing the external and internal measurements to the north door. This difference in thickness is compatible with the tower having been added to an existing church.

The similarity of the internal cobble flintwork at first-floor level and in the belfry seems to show that the tower was of a single build and this is confirmed by the medieval bricks in the internal arches of the blocked south door, the first-floor lancet and the belfry openings. In the absence of any Norman or earlier evidence in the tower, a post-Norman date of about the same as the other three towers seems likely, but the round-headed tower arch suggests that there would have been an earlier tower than the present one. It is suggested that an original tower with thicker walls, probably contemporary with the nave, perished, to be replaced by the present one built on the original foundations; corroboration for this idea is provided by the wider plinth around the base of the present tower, probably the base of the original one.

The question remains as to why a south door was provided in the 'new' tower when a tower arch already existed. The answer lies, perhaps, in the influence on this tower's design of the other three nearby towers built apparently at about the same time or maybe just before. It was built to the same general design as the others and it may simply have been considered an additional convenience to incorporate a south door as seemed to be a current local practice at that time. It certainly seems more than a coincidence that four round towers of the same general design, seemingly of about the same date and situated so close to each other, all incorporated a south door – a feature thought to be unique to these four.

---

[1] Since this feature was observed, replastering has tidied its outline to symmetrical shape.

CHAPTER 22

ROUND TOWERS OUTSIDE EAST ANGLIA

All the three round church towers of Sussex, Lewes St Michael, Southease and Piddinghoe, lie within five miles of each other, on or near the river Ouse. Their walls are circular to the top, none have fillets of the East Anglian pattern in the re-entrant angles between tower and nave and all are roofed with shingled spires, a feature common to many Sussex church towers. To the extent that they share this basic form and that their belfry openings are not major features of their design, they could be considered as expressions of a style rather different from the East Anglian towers; nevertheless, because of the sea link between their location and the East Anglian ports, there remains the possibility that the inspiration for the circular plan derives from their eastern counterparts. Since the concept of the circular tower plan did not spread in the southern flint areas, it is easier to see these three isolated towers as a parochial manifestation of an external influence rather than an indigenous invention born out of local geological constraints. A lack of suitable stone for quoins is hardly a convincing explanation for flint construction and circular shape here, in view of the availability in Sussex of Cretaceous sandstones such as Wealden and Reigate. Being, therefore, not a functionally-inspired form in this area, these three round towers were probably an aesthetic choice based on emulation, and as such are unlikely to be pre-Conquest.

The earliest of the three towers is probably Southease (XXI), and a reported[1] flat east wall within the tower suggests that it was added to an existing church. The nave contains two stone round-headed windows, to the west of the porch and high up in the north wall, and a little to the east of this a remnant of a stone internal cornice. The nave retains dressed stone quoins at the north-west and north-east corners and some of these appear to be of Caen stone.

The tower itself has a rather forbidding appearance since only two openings remain in its uncoursed rubble flint walls neither of which is visible as one approaches the church; one is a small ground-floor west window framed externally in eighteenth-century brick with splayed jambs and head internally, and the other, facing slightly east of north at belfry level, is a stone-framed lancet with a pointed head. About five feet above the west window, the remnants of another window comprising a stone cill and three left-hand jambstones can be seen but they give no indication of its head shape; otherwise the walls have no convincing evidence of other blocked openings.

Despite a low, pointed tower arch, the round-headed and internally-splayed west window suggests a twelfth-century date for the tower.

Attached to a church that has a Norman north arcade and an early thirteenth-century south one, the circular tower at Piddinghoe is probably also Norman. Its flintwork is a mixture of flint rubble and knapped, or rather, cleft flints, the latter making up about a third of the total. In East Anglia, work of this kind would suggest a date no earlier than the late thirteenth century but, as with the use of dressed stone, there is no certainty that those guides to dating are applicable to the south coast area.

Two single-light windows in the tower face west – at ground-floor and first-floor levels; both are framed with dressed stone externally with a small chamfer to their inner edges and have semi-circular heads formed with two stones jointed at the apex. The belfry openings are narrow single-light slits, six in number and also faced with dressed stone, but with arch-lintel heads cut from a single stone. The two facing south-east and north-east are blocked, being partially covered by the nave roof whose ridge is now at the level of the eaves of the tower's shingled octagonal spire.

St Michael's, Lewes stands on the north side of High Street, the south wall of its south aisle being built right up to the footpath; with the round tower at the west end of the nave, a small forecourt allows entry to the church at the west end of the aisle. The church itself was extensively rebuilt in the mid-eighteenth century and further alterations made in the last quarter of the nineteenth. The round tower and part of the west wall to which it is attached are all that remain of the original church. The tower arch is pointed.

Externally, the tower is pebble-dashed and has no visible features earlier than the thirteenth century. A large lancet window at ground-floor level facing west is stone-framed but its head has been restored; a little below the eaves of the shingle-covered roof spire, two circular quatrefoiled bell openings face west and just east of south. The little of the east wall of the tower that can be seen externally above the nave roof is flat, and above the nave roof ridge there are indications of a former, steeper roofline whose apex is at the tower roof eaves level; to the outside of these indications, and aligned more or less parallel to them, a series of dark brown 'quoin' stones mark the junction of the tower's curved walls to its flat east wall and their positioning suggests that the tower would originally have been higher before it received its present roof, and may have been contemporary with the original church. Its date is judged to be thirteenth-century – apparently later than Southease and Piddinghoe.

A fibreglass sculpture of St Michael the Archangel by Harry Phillips, mounted on the tower south wall was completed in 1976 and is reminiscent of Epstein's bronze on Coventry Cathedral.

The variations of roof shapes of these three towers make interesting comparisons. Piddinghoe has a plain tapered octagon, octagonal from eaves level; Southease is almost conical but just below the top its pitch steepens and it almost develops into polygonal shape; at Lewes the lower few feet are circular but the conical shape soon changes to a steeper pitch and develops into a slender octagonal spire.

The two round tower churches of Berkshire, at Welford and Great Shefford, both lie on the river Lambourn with little more than two miles separating them. Their proximity, and the fact that they are the only examples of circular towers in Berkshire and neighbouring counties, is surely more than coincidence, suggesting cross-influence between the two one way or the other, though the reason for this isolated occurrence of the circular tower plan is obscure. Both are built of flint but if that only had been the reason for the shape, its wider adoption in the region would be expected. It is suggested as a possibility that these two instances could have arisen from links to an East Anglian round tower church or churches through a common patronage in early times.

Before it was rebuilt in 1852, the tower at Welford (96) was probably the older of the two, with Norman lower stages and an Early English belfry and spire. The church guide leaflet records that during the rebuilding all the tower stonework was carefully marked and then re-erected to its former place, and the present appearance of tower conforms accurately with a sketch dated 1802 reproduced in the leaflet. The flintwork of the tower is at least seventy-five percent cleft or knapped material and recognisably Victorian rather than medieval, and details such as voussoirs formed with erratics above the stonework of all the round-headed openings in the tower walls clearly point to nineteenth-century rather than Norman practice.

96. The church and round tower at Welford, Berkshire, rebuilt in the nineteenth century. This is the only round tower with a stone steeple, the original medieval stonework being reused.

The four stages of the tower, separated by stone string courses, are surmounted by a stone spire rising from a machicolated base. The lower stage has a north door and west window of Norman style, and the second stage has single-light round-headed stone windows facing north and south. The third stage contains the belfry openings at the cardinal positions extending into the top stage; they comprise paired lancets with a plate-tracery quatrefoil above. The top stage is octagonal with stone shafts at the angles.

Unique in round towers, the octagonal spire is stone, with two-light dormer lucarnes in each face of similar design to the belfry openings, and much of their stonework can be seen to be re-set weathered material from the medieval predecessor.

At ground-floor level, the tower walls are over five feet thick and the wall thickness at the tower arch is a massive seven feet. The round-headed ashlar tower arch, described by Pevsner as elephantine, is a pseudo-Saxon parody of a true Saxon arch such as the chancel arch at Wittering, and is unlikely to be a faithful reproduction of the original!

ROUND TOWERS OUTSIDE EAST ANGLIA

The general appearance of the round tower at Great Shefford (XXII) is similar to many in East Anglia. It has three stages separated by stone string courses, the belfry stage being octagonal. Uncoursed rubble flint walls rise from a single course of squared stone on a chamfered stone base course, and at the re-entrant angles where the tower joins the nave west wall, there are flat fillets at right-angles to the nave wall.

In the west wall, the lower stage has a large stone-framed lancet window that could be original although the stonework of its pointed arch is probably restored. With their cill level on the string course that separates the lower and middle stages, three single-light windows at first-floor level facing south, west and north have stone frames, the north and south ones with pointed heads and the west one with a round arch; internally, these three windows all have dressed stone jambs and pointed arches. In the east wall of the chamber in which they are located, and visible also from the nave, an upper door has stone dressings to its jambs and to its pointed arch.

Externally, the level of the nave roof ridge coincides with the string course that forms the base of the octagonal belfry. Its two-light belfry openings with cusped Y-tracery under two-centred arches imply a fourteenth-century date, but the style and finish of the battlemented parapet suggest that the parapet could be a fifteenth-century Perpendicular addition.

Inside the tower, the west face of the wide, pointed tower arch is flat, but above its springing level a transition from flat to the circular shape above is achieved by means of squinch arches formed with dressed stonework – probably a unique use of this technique in round towers. Where similar situations arise in stoneless East Anglia,, e.g. at Sedgeford, the transition is made by progressively oversailing the flintwork in the spandrel areas of the tower arch. The squinch stonework, like the dressed stonework in tower and nave of the three-times chamfered tower arch itself, appears to be integrally constructed with the tower, the tower arch and the nave west wall, thus probably establishing the nave and the lower stages of the tower as contemporary – perhaps early thirteenth-century.

Several features of the nave could be dated to the Norman/Early English Transitional period, in particular the south door with a pointed arch that yet retains Norman chevron ornament and shafts with beast-head capitals, and so a date of circa. 1200 would be appropriate for the nave and the tower's lower stages.

As the middle stage of the tower is no higher than the nave roof, and the upper door gives access to the first-floor chamber within that stage, it is improbable that it was a former belfry. Unless therefore, the original tower stood unfinished for a hundred years or more, the cusped Y-tracery style of the present belfry openings of at least a century later than the original building implies that the present belfry must have replaced an earlier one.

There is no evidence that any of the five round towers situated outside East Anglia is pre-Conquest and except for the rebuilt one at Welford none of them seems to be later than the early thirteenth century.

[1] Goode, *Op.Cit, 1994, p.201*

APPENDIX A

SCHEDULE OF ROUND TOWERS AND AUTHOR'S ATTRIBUTIONS

In the schedule below, all the round towers are alphabetically listed, county by county, except that those at Belton, Bradwell, Burgh Castle and Fritton near Yarmouth, now in Norfolk since the local government reorganisation of 1974, appear under their former county, Suffolk, in order to harmonise with other books that have followed this practice.

The author's attributions of architectural periods are applicable to the towers only, (excluding parapets, some of which post-date their belfries) and are shown by means of letter symbols. These attempt to differentiate separate building phases where evidence shows that there has been more than one. In these symbols, the letter on the left indicates the lowest stage of the tower, those to the right representing subsequent stages. A single letter indicates an attribution for the whole tower including its belfry. The symbol + denotes the base of an added belfry, but where also marked *, the belfry is apparently the same date as a rebuilt part of the circular stage immediately below. Letter symbols used have the following meanings:

S = Probably Saxon.
O = Saxo-Norman Overlap.
N = Norman.
P = Post-Norman medieval.
R = Post-Reformation.
L = Late, i.e. c.19 and c.20.
U = Uncertain, i.e. inadequate grounds for reasoned conclusions.
C.Oct. = Octagonal stage(s) contemporary with circular stage.
A.Oct. = Octagonal stage(s) a later addition to the circular stage.

As mentioned in Chapter 9 and shown in Chapter 5, since all features considered as characteristic of Saxon technique have also been found in post-Conquest buildings, few, if any, towers can be attributed with absolute certainty as pre-Conquest. For this reason, all Saxon attributions (letter symbol S) should be regarded as being qualified by the word 'probably'.

Round Tower	*Attribution*	*Remarks*
Norfolk		
Acle	P	C.Oct.
Appleton	S	Ruinous. Carstone.
Ashmanhaugh	L	1849
Aslacton	S	
Aylmerton	P	
Barmer	PL	an 1831 drawing shows a taller tower.

Bawburgh	P	
Beachamwell	O+P	A.Oct.
Bedingham	SP +P*	A.Oct.
Beeston St Lawrence	S+P	
Bessingham	S	Carstone
Bexwell	SN+P	A.Oct. Carstone.
Brampton	N+P	A.Oct.
Brandiston	L	Rebuilt with octagonal top in 1890.
Breckles	N+P	A.Oct.
Brooke	U+P	
Burgh St Mary	P	Ruinous. C.Oct.
Burlingham St Peter	P	Ruinous.
Burnham Deepdale	U	
Burnham Norton	O	
Bylaugh	P	C.Oct.
Clippesby	N+L	A.Oct. Major c.19 restoration.
Cockley Cley	P	Tower partially collapsed.
Colney	S	Belfry possibly later.
Cranwich	S	
Croxton	P	C.Oct.
Denton	PR	Major post-medieval construction.
Dilham	L	Remnant of a rebuilt tower of 1835.
East Lexham	O	
East Walton	P	
Eccles	P	
Edingthorpe	P	C.Oct.
Feltwell	N	Truncated remnant.
Fishley	N+P	
Forncett St Peter	S	
Framingham Earl	N	Probably heavily restored.
Freethorpe	P+L	Major post-medieval restoration.
Fritton, St Catherine	NP+P	A.Oct.
Gayton Thorpe	O	
Geldeston	P+L	Major post-medieval restoration.
Gissing	O	
Great Hautbois	S	
Great Ryburgh	N+P	A.Oct. Carstone.
Gresham	P+L	Major post-medieval restoration.
Haddiscoe	O	
Hales	SN+P	
Hardley	O	
Hardwick	S	Truncated remnant.
Hassingham	P	C.Oct.
Haveringland	S	
Heckingham	NP+P*	Part circular stage and octagon added.
Hellington	N	
Hemblington	P	

Horsey	P	C.Oct.
Howe	SL	Upper part rebuilt. No belfry.
Ingworth	N	Truncated remnant.
Intwood	S+P	A.Oct.
Keswick	P	
Kilverstone	N	
Kirby Bedon St Mary	P+P	Ruinous.
Kirby Cane	SP	
Letheringsett	S	
Little Plumstead	OP	
Little Snoring	SP	Detached tower.
Long Stratton	N+P	
Matlaske	U+P	A.Oct.
Mautby	P	C.Oct., probably.
Merton	N	
Morningthorpe	NP	Extensive medieval reconstruction.
Morton on the Hill	P	Truncated remnant. Had oct. belfry.
Moulton	P	No belfry stage.
Needham	P+P	A.Oct.
Norton Subcourse	P+L	Belfry stage rebuilt in c.19.
Norwich, St Benedict	P	C.Oct. Tower only. Church bombed.
Norwich St Etheldreda	NR +R*	Part circular stage and octagon added.
Norwich St Julian	S	Truncated remnant.
Norwich St Mary, Coslany	S	
Old Catton	P+P	A.Oct.
Poringland	P	C.Oct.
Potter Heigham	P	C.Oct.
Quidenham	N+P	A.Oct.
Raveningham	N+P	A.Oct.
Repps	P	C.Oct.
Ringstead St Peter	U	Ruinous tower only. Detached.
Rockland St Peter	P	C.Oct. Integral stair turret.
Rollesby	P	C.Oct.
Roughton	S	Partially ferricrete.
Roydon	P+L	A.Oct. Major c.19 restoration.
Runhall	P	
Rushall	P	C.Oct.
Sedgeford	P	C.Oct.
Seething	N+P*	
Shereford	N	
Shimpling	P	C.Oct. Integral stair turret.
Sidestrand	L	New 1881 with C.Oct.
South Pickenham	N+P	A.Oct.
Stanford	N+P	A.Oct.
Stockton	P	
Stody	P	
Surlingham	P+P	A.Oct.

Sustead	P	No tower arch.
Swainsthorpe	U+P	A.Oct.
Syderstone	P	
Tasburgh	S+P	
Taverham	O+P	A.Oct.
Thorpe Abbotts	P	C.Oct.
Thorpe next Haddiscoe	O	
Threxton	P	
Thwaite	P	
Titchwell	SN	
Topcroft	P+P	C.Oct. and A.Oct. belfry.
Tuttington	P	
Wacton	P	
Watton	N+P	A.Oct.
Weeting	L	Rebuilt 1868
Welborne	P	
West Dereham	N+R	Ferricrete. A.Oct.
West Lexham	P	
West Somerton	P	C.Oct.
Wickmere	SP	Lower parts ferricrete.
Witton	U	
Wolterton	P	Ruinous. Detached. C.Oct.
Woodton	S+P	A.Oct.
Worthing	PR	
Wramplingham	P	C.Oct.
Yaxham	N P	

Suffolk

Aldham	PR+L	
Ashby	P	C.Oct.
Barsham	P+P	
Belton	L	Rebuilt 1849
Beyton	P+R	A.Oct.
Blundeston	N+P	
Bradwell	P	
Bramfield	P	Detached tower.
Brome	U+L	Major c.19 restoration. A.Oct.
Bruisyard	UP	
Bungay	S	
Burgh Castle	P	
Fritton, St Edmund	P+R*	Major post-medieval restoration.
Frostenden	P	
Gisleham	N+P	A.Oct.
Gunton	N+P	
Hasketon	P	C.Oct.
Hengrave	N	
Herringfleet	O	

Higham	L	New church and tower built in 1861.
Holton St Peter	N+P	
Ilketshall St Andrew	P	C.Oct.
Ilketshall St Margaret	S+P	
Little Bradley	P	C.Oct.
Little Saxham	N	
Lound	P R	
Mettingham	P	
Mutford	NP +P*	A.Oct.
Onehouse	P	Largely recently rebuilt.
Ramsholt	P	Largely septaria.
Rickinghall Inferior	NP+P	A.Oct.
Risby	N	
Rushmere	NP+P	
South Elmham All Saints	N+L	Major post-medieval restoration.
Spexhall	L	Rebuilt 1910.
Stuston	P	C.Oct.
Syleham	P	
Theberton	P	C.Oct.
Thorington	N	
Weybread	P	
Wissett	O	
Wortham	N	Tower partially collapsed.

Essex

Bardfield Saling	P	Contemporary stair turret.
Broomfield	N	
Great Leighs	NP	
Lamarsh	N	Parts of tower wall rebuilt in stud.
Pentlow	P	
South Ockenden	P+L	

Cambridgeshire

Bartlow	P	
Snailwell	N	

Berkshire

Great Shefford	P+P	A.Oct.
Welford	L	Rebuilt 1852

Sussex

Lewes	P	
Piddinghoe	N	
Southease	N	

SUMMARY

The following table shows the numbers of round towers of each attribution in each county. The attributions relate to the earliest parts of the towers.

Attributions	S	O	N	P	L	U
Norfolk	25	10	25	54	5	7
Suffolk	2	2	13	20	3	2
Essex			3	3		
Cambridgeshire			1	1		
Berkshire				1	1	
Sussex			2	1		
Total	27	12	44	80	9	9

APPENDIX B

MODERN ROUND TOWERS BUILT IN THE 19th AND EARLY 20th CENTURIES

Norfolk   Ashmanhaugh
              Brandiston
              Sidestrand
              Weeting

Suffolk   Belton
              Higham
              Spexhall

Berkshire   Welford

APPENDIX C

ROUND TOWERS WITH MAJOR POST-REFORMATION RESTORATIONS

Norfolk   Clippesby
              Denton
              Freethorpe
              Gresham
              Roydon

Suffolk   Brome
              Onehouse
              South Elmham All Saints

Essex   South Ockenden

APPENDIX D

REMNANTS OF ROUND TOWERS ATTACHED TO CHURCHES FIT FOR USE

Norfolk	Cockley Cley
	Dilham
	Feltwell
	Hardwick
	Ingworth
	Morton on the Hill
	Norwich, St Julian
Suffolk	Wortham

APPENDIX E

RUINOUS ROUND TOWERS

Norfolk	Appleton
	Burgh St Mary
	Burlingham St Peter
	Kirby Bedon St Mary
	Ringstead St Peter
	Wolterton

GLOSSARY

ABACUS The top element of a capital.

ARCADE A series of arches supported by columns or piers.

ASHLAR Squared freestone masonry.

BARNACK STONE A shelly freestone from Barnack quarries near Stamford. It was worked out by the late 15th century.

BILLET MOULDING A Norman ornament of small half-cylindrical blocks.

BLANK or BLIND ARCADING Arcading as a decorative theme applied to a wall surface.

BROACH A two-facetted tapered feature used as a chamfer-stop where a chamfered corner meets a square one.

BUTTRESS A vertical projection from a wall to provide lateral stability.

CAEN STONE A fine-grained freestone from Caen, Normandy, imported after the Norman Conquest.

CANT BRICKS Bricks with a chamfer on one corner.

CAPITAL The crowning element of a column or pier.

CARSTONE A brown sandstone used for building that outcrops in West Norfolk.

CHAMFER The splayed face produced by cutting the angle off a square corner.

CHEVRON A Norman moulding comprising repeated V-shapes forming a zigzag pattern.

CINQUEFOIL See TREFOIL.

CLEFT FLINT Flints that have been severed to provide a roughly flat face.

COLONETTE A small shaft.

CONGLOMERATE See FERRICRETE.

CONQUEST The Norman Conquest, AD 1066.

COURSE A continuous horizontal layer of bricks, stones, or flints etc, in a wall.

CUSHION CAPITAL A cubical capital whose lower part is worked to a hemi-spherical shape to meet the circular shaft on which the capital rests.

CUSP The point between adjacent lobes of Gothic foliated tracery.

DECORATED A stylistic division of Gothic architecture in Britain covering mainly the last years of the 13th century and more than half of the 14th. Characterised by ogee curves.

DENTILLED A linear decoration of small projecting square blocks.

DOUBLE-SPLAYED Of a window, a type in which the aperture is located at about the centre of the wall and the inner and outer reveals and arches are splayed to a greater width than the aperture.

DRESSED STONE Ashlar stonework that has been worked to form fair faces to angles, openings or other features.

EARLY ENGLISH A stylistic division of Gothic architecture in Britain covering the 13th century, characterised by lancet windows.

EMBRASURE An internally splayed window recess.

ERRATICS Boulders or fragments of flints or stones of any kind that have been displaced from their source, typically by glacial action.

FERRICRETE Coarse dark brown ferruginous stone containing small pebbles or flint fragments in a finer-grained matrix. Also called CONGLOMERATE or PUDDINGSTONE.

FERRUGINOUS Rust-coloured, impregnated with iron oxides.

FILLET In the context of round towers, the vertical filling of the re-entrant angle between a round tower and the nave west wall.

FINIAL The topmost terminal feature of a pinnacle, spire or gable etc.

FLINT RUBBLE Flintwork comprising unsorted 'as-found' flints and broken pieces.

FLUSHWORK The use of freestone in combination with knapped flints to create flush patterns on a wall surface. In BRICK FLUSHWORK, bricks fulfil the role of the stone.

FREESTONE Any even-grained type of stone that can be freely cut and worked in all directions.

GALLETING The decorative practice of inserting small pebbles or chips of flint, stone or brick into the exposed mortar joints of a wall.

GEOMETRIC STYLE A style of stone window tracery of the second half of the 13th century using plain or foliated circle motifs.

GOTHIC Descriptive of the 'pointed' architectural style, embracing Early English, Decorated and Perpendicular styles in Britain, from the 13th to the 16th centuries.

HEADER BRICKS The short end of bricks seen in the face of a wall.

HOODMOULD A projecting moulding in stone or bricks above an opening whose purpose is to throw off water. When horizontal, also called a LABEL.

IMPOST A horizontal moulding at the springing of an arch.

JAMB The straight side of a doorway or window opening.

KNAPPED FLINT Flints that have been cut or split to present a flat surface of the core material, and those trimmed to regular shapes.

KNOPPED Having a projecting concentric ring on a shaft, usually about half-way up.

LABEL See HOODMOULD.

LANCET A slender single-light pointed window.

LESENE A narrow vertical strip of masonry having a small projection from a wall surface, also called STRIPWORK or a PILASTER STRIP.

LIMESTONE Sedimentary stones of calcium carbonate extensively used in English churches, of which Barnack and Caen stones are examples.

LINTEL A horizontal beam over a doorway or window opening.

LONG-AND-SHORT WORK Quoins comprising alternately upright and flat stones.

LOOP A small slit window.

LUCARNE A small gabled opening in a spire.

MACHICOLATIONS Decorative corbelling with mini-arches between the corbels, below a projecting parapet.

MOUCHETTE A curved variation of the Gothic dagger tracery motif.

NEEDLE AND PROP To support temporarily the walling above an opening formed in an existing wall.

NORMAN STYLE The post-Conquest English Romanesque architectural style of the late 11th and the 12th centuries, characterised by round-headed arches.

OGEE Double curvature in the shape of arches and in tracery, comprising a concave and a convex curve, prevalent from the early 14th century.

OVERSAILING Building outwards to project beyond the vertical face of the wall below.

PANEL TRACERY A style of Perpendicular tracery sub-divided into straight-sided panels.

PIER A large masonry or brick support usually for an arch or the arches of an arcade.

PILASTER The representation of a column or pier in shallow relief on a wall surface, as for example, in blind arcading.

PILASTER STRIP See LESENE.

PINNING UP The operation of building up from an arch or lintel inserted into an existing wall to 'pick up' and support the walling above.

PLINTH Projecting base course to a wall, buttress or pier.

POINTING Renewing mortar jointing at a wall face.

PUDDINGSTONE See FERRICRETE.

PUTLOG HOLES Recesses, about six inches square more or less, left in the face of masonry walls during construction to support horizontal members of the scaffolding (putlogs).

QUOINS Corner stones, bricks or flints that form the external angles of a building.

QUATREFOIL See TREFOIL.

REBATE A rectangular set-back at the edges of an opening to receive a door or window frame.

RE-ENTRANT ANGLE The internal angle formed at the junction of two walls in different planes.

REFORMATION The religious revolution in 16th-century England, as Protestantism succeeded Catholicism following the Dissolution of the Monasteries, circa 1538.

RENDERING A cement or plaster coating to the surface of a wall.

RERE-ARCH, or REAR-ARCH The arch over a doorway or window on a wall's inner face.

RESPOND Half-pier, half-column or the end of a length of wall from which an arch emanates.

REVEAL The return face of the masonry , splayed or at right-angles to the wall, at the sides of door and window openings.

SALIENT ANGLE The external angle formed where two walls join at a corner.

SAXON The period in England preceding the Conquest, or its architectural style.

SAXO-NORMAN The post-Conquest period of the late 11th century and early 12th during which Saxon architectural features continued to occur in buildings.

SEPTARIA A light to medium-brown clayey limestone of coarse texture that outcrops near the Stour, Orwell and Deben estuaries, found in buildings in those areas.

SHUTTERING Temporary support for arches or laterally for walls during construction.

SOFFIT The under surface of an arch or lintel.

SPANDREL The roughly triangular area of wall to the side of the curve of an arch or between adjacent arches.

SPRINGING The level at which the curve of an arch rises from its supporting wall, pier or column.

SQUINCH A small arch spanning diagonally across the re-entrant angle at a corner.

SQUINT A small hole through a church wall that allows a view of the altar.

STAGE A visual subdivision of the height of a building, wall or feature into distinctive separate parts.

STRATIFICATION Horizontal banding in rubble flintwork where the flints are levelled at 'lifts' of about a foot, probably representing the extent of construction between the intervals allowed for the mortar to attain adequate strength to support succeeding work.

STRING COURSE   A projecting course or moulding of stone or brick running horizontally along the face of a wall.

STRIPWORK See LESENE.

THROUGH-STONE A long horizontal stone passing through the thickness of a wall, supported centrally on a mid-wall shaft, providing the central bearing for the two small arches of a two-light Saxon belfry opening.

TOWER ARCH The archway between a church tower and the nave.

TRACERY Ornamental stone ribwork in the upper part of Gothic windows and other openwork features.

TREDINGTON FASHION Non-radial arrangement of the stones, flints bricks etc. that form the voussoirs of an arch.

TREFOIL A motif of three lobes with cusps between them. The lobes may be round or pointed or both. Universal in Gothic tracery. QUATREFOIL, CINQUEFOIL, as for TREFOIL but with four or five lobes respectively.

TYMPANUM The surface between the lintel over an opening and an arch above it.

VOUSSOIRS The wedge-shaped blocks forming an arch. The term also covers bricks, stones or other materials forming an arch though not wedge-shaped.

WEATHERCOURSE A projecting moulding of stone or brick built into a wall where it is abutted by a lower roof, to provide a weathering at the roof-to-wall junction.

Y – TRACERY A common pattern for a two-light window in which the mullion branches into a Y shape. In windows of more than two lights, it is known as Intersecting Tracery. Typical of circa.1300 but often used later.

BIBLIOGRAPHY

Baldwin Brown G. *The Arts in Early England; Vol.II, Anglo-Saxon Architecture.* John Murray 1925.

Batcock N. *The Ruined and Disused Churches of Norfolk.* East Anglian Archaeology Report No.51, 1991.

Bryant T.H. *County Churches, Suffolk.* George Allen, London, 1912.

Cautley M. *Suffolk Churches.* Boydell, Ipswich, 1937, 4th revision 1975.

Cautley M. *Norfolk Churches.* Adlard, Ipswich, 1949.

Clapham A. *English Romanesque Architecture, Vol.I Before the Conquest,* 1930, *Vol.II After the Conquest.* 1934, Oxford.

Cox J.C. *County Churches, Norfolk.* George Allen, London, 1910.

Fernie E. *Architecture of the Anglo-Saxons.* Batsford, 1983.

Gage J. *Archaeologia, Vol.XXIII.* Society of Antiquaries, London, 1831.

Goode W.J. *East Anglian Round Towers and their Churches.* Friends of the Round Tower Churches Society, 1982.

Goode W.J. *Round Tower Churches of South-East England.* Round Tower Churches Society, 1994.

Harris A.P. *Late 11th- and 12th-century Church Architecture of the Lower Yare Valley, Norfolk.* Unpub. Thesis, University of East Anglia, 1989.

Hart S. *Flint Architecture of East Anglia.* Giles de la Mare, London, 2000.

Hart S. *Cockley Cley Church Tower – A Constructional Analysis.* Norfolk Archaeology. Vol.XLII Part II Norfolk & Norwich Archaeological Society 1995

Heywood S.R. *Minor Church Building in East Anglia during the Eleventh and Early Twelfth Centuries.* Unpub. Thesis, University of East Anglia. 1977.

Heywood S.R. *The Round Towers of East Anglia Chapter XII in Minsters and Parish Churches. The Local Church in Transition 950-1200.* Ed. J Blair. Oxford University Committee for .Archaeology, Monograph no. 17, 1988.

Heywood S.R. *Round Towered Churches.* Chap.23 in *An Historical Atlas of Norfolk.* Ed. Wade-Martins. P. Norfolk Museums Service.

Heywood S.R. *The Round towered churches of Norfolk and Northern Europe.* Norfolk Churches Trust Annual Report, 1999/2000

Ladbrooke R. *Views of the Churches in Norfolk Illustrative of Blomefield's History of that County, from Original Drawings.* J.B.Ladbrooke, Norwich 1823, and other collections of prints from drawings by R and J.B.Ladbrooke and J.Sillett.

Messent C. *The Round Towers to English Parish Churches.* Fletcher, Norwich. 1958.

Pevsner N. and others *The Buildings of England; Suffolk, North-East Norfolk and Norwich.* 1962, and *North-West and South Norfolk.* 1962, Penguin.

Rodwell W. *Anglo-Saxon Church Building: Design and Construction.* in Butler L.A.S. and Morris R.K. (Eds). Council for British Archaeology Research Report No. 60, 1986.

Shreeve D. *The Round Tower Churches of Norfolk.* 124 line sketches, with descriptive text by Stilgoe E.M. Canterbury Press, Norwich 2001.

Taylor H.M. and Taylor J. *Anglo-Saxon Architecture, Vols. I & II.* 1965, *Vol.III.* 1978, Cambridge University Press.

INDEX AND LOCATIONS OF ROUND TOWERS

B = Berkshire, C = Cambridgeshire, E = Essex, N = Norfolk, S = Suffolk, SX = Sussex
Figures in brackets indicate illustration numbers.

Herringfleet S	TM 477978	10, 17, 18, 20, 22, 32, 42, 43, 44, 64, 66-67, 77, 78, 79, 112, 168, (47)
Higham S	TL 747656	22, 30, 170, (24)
Holton St Peter S	TM 403779	22, 32, 34, 48, 50, 53, 78, 96, 111, 112-114, 170, (77)
Horsey N	TG 458231	25, 27, 118, 125, 140, 168
Howe N	TM 275000	7, 8, 9, 10, 24, 61, 62, 87, 168, (IX)
Ilketshall St Andrew	TM 379873	27, 29, 45, 51, 60, 129, 140-142, 170, (89)
Ilketshall St Margaret	TM 350853	19, 62, 170, (10)
Ingworth N	TG 193297	29, 168
Intwood N	TG 196042	62, 168
Keswick N	TG 214047	6, 25, 42, 118, 168
Kilverstone N	TL 894840	7, 17, 21, 77, 78, 168, (9), (56)
Kirby Bedon St Mary N	TM 279054	22, 29, 96, 168
Kirby Cane N	TM 373941	20, 22, 62, 70, 71, 73, 88, 168, (49), (63)
Lamarsh E	TL 890361	29, 170
Letheringsett N	TG 061389	50, 62, 168
Lewes SX	TQ 409100	24, 162, 163, 170
Little Bradley S	TL 682521	2, 48, 105-107, 129, 170, (72)
Little Plumstead N	TG 307109	169
Little Saxham S	TL 799638	11, 17, 22, 44, 45, 47, 75, 77, 78, 79, 112, 170, (55), (X)
Little Snoring N	TF 953326	1, 24, 87, 168, (16)
Long Stratton N	TM 197923	29, 88, 168
Lound S	TM 505990	25, 29, 32, 34, 118, 170
Matlaske N	TG 151349	29, 168
Mautby N	TG 481124	27, 28, 126, 168
Merton N	TL 912980	17, 34, 36, 78, 168, (29), (58)
Mettingham S	TM 363899	7, 170
Morningthorpe N	TM 218925	32, 88, 168
Morton on the Hill N	TG 126159	29, 129, 168
Moulton N	TG 402067	24, 60, 168
Mutford S	TM 486886	7, 140, 147, 151-153, 170, (93)
Needham N	TM 231819	24, 25, 28, 29, 50, 147, 168, (22), (32)
Norton Subcourse N	TM 407987	4, 23, 34, 88, 168
Norwich, St Benedict	TG 226088	1, 6, 27, 129, 168, (21)
Norwich St Etheldreda	TG 235078	147, 154-155, 168, (94)
Norwich St Julian	TG 233080	3, 10, 20, 24, 62, 168
Norwich St Mary, Coslany	TG 228092	61, 168
Old Catton N	TG 231123	22, 25, 45, 51, 60, 118, 122-124, 147, 168, (80)
Onehouse S	TM 017594	24, 50, 170
Pentlow E	TL 812461	6, 42, 51, 54, 57, 170
Piddinghoe SX	TQ 435031	78, 162, 163, 170
Poringland N	TG 271017	3, 129, 168
Potter Heigham N	TG 419199	2, 25, 28, 37, 55, 60, 118, 121-122, 129, 168, (XVI)

Quidenham N	TM 028877	26, 28, 42, 44, 54, 76, 147, 148, 168, (33)
Ramsholt S	TM 307421	22, 34, 37, 51, 55, 102-105, 170, (38), (XIII)
Raveningham N	TM 398964	28, 147, 168
Repps N	TG 422169	101-102, 129, 168, (71)
Rickinghall Inferior S	TM 039751	2, 21, 23, 26, 34, 76, 88-91, 147, 170, (64)
Ringstead St Peter N	TF 702403	1, 168
Risby S	TL 802664	54, 170
Rockland St Peter N	TL 990970	22, 29, 33, 43, 129, 131, 138-139, 168, (88)
Rollesby N	TG 446158	27, 29, 139, 168
Roughton N	TG 220366	17, 21, 35, 50, 61, 86, 168, (41), (42)
Roydon N	TM 096804	29, 147, 168
Runhall N	TG 058069	32, 45, 47, 51, 52, 168, (34)
Rushall N	TM 198827	7, 27, 46, 50, 51, 140, 142-144, 146, 168, (XIX), (XX)
Rushmere S	TM 495880	21, 23, 24, 32, 35, 44, 76, 93-95, 96, 170, (65), (66)
Sedgeford N	TF 707365	27, 32, 55, 129, 132-135, 165, 168, (83), (84), (85)
Seething N	TM 320980	32, 36, 77, 78, 79, 81-83, 88, 168, (57), (60)
Shereford N	TF 887297	23, 168
Shimpling N	TM 156827	29, 47, 50, 56, 129, 135-138, 168, (86), (87)
Sidestrand N	TG 260398	30, 168
Snailwell C	TL 642676	17, 53, 78, 170
Southease SX	TQ 423053	162, 163, 170, (XXI)
South Elmham All Saints S	TM 330828	7, 29, 53, 112, 170, (75), (76)
South Ockenden E	TQ 595829	29, 111, 170
South Pickenham N	TF 857041	28, 147, 148, 168
Spexhall S	TM 378802	30, 101, 170
Stanford N	TL 857947	148, 168
Stockton N	TM 388941	24, 168
Stody N	TG 056351	29, 50, 168
Stuston S	TM 134778	24, 34, 129, 170, (18)
Surlingham N	TG 306065	2, 37, 55, 118, 147, 168
Sustead N	TG 183370	6, 156-160, 169
Swainsthorpe N	TG 219009	55, 169
Syderstone N	TF 833327	23, 26, 36, 169, (15), (30)
Syleham S	TM 204790	4, 5, 24, 25, 41, 50, 112, 170, (19)
Tasburgh N	TM 201959	5, 8, 19, 23, 47, 54, 62, 70, 71, 72, 73, 169, (51)
Taverham N	TG 161138	61, 62, 148, 169
Theberton S	TM 437659	129, 170
Thorington S	TM 423741	5, 17, 32, 39, 53, 70, 71, 72, 73-75, 78, 170, (52)
Thorpe Abbotts N	TM 188789	4, 25, 27, 29, 44, 59, 129-131, 146, 169, (XVII)
Thorpe next Haddiscoe N	TM 436981	5, 17, 20, 32, 33, 42, 47, 70, 71-73, 75, 78, 112, 169, (50)